# STRIVING TOWARDS WHOLENESS

# STRIVING TOWARDS WHOLENESS

*by Barbara Hannah*

London · George Allen & Unwin Ltd
*Ruskin House Museum Street*

First published in Great Britain in 1972



ISBN 0 04 150041 5

This book was originally published in the USA and American spelling and usage have been retained.



Printed in Great Britain
by Redwood Press Limited
Trowbridge, Wiltshire

# ACKNOWLEDGMENTS

PASSAGES in this volume from *The Collected Works of C. G. Jung*, Bollingen Series XX, ed. G. Adler, M. Fordham, H. Read, trans. by R. F. C. Hull, vol. 7, *Two Essays on Analytical Psychology* (copyright (c) 1953 & 1966 by Princeton University Press), vol. 9ii, *Aion* (copyright (c) 1959 & 1968 by Princeton University Press), vol. 10, *Civilization in Transition* (copyright (c) 1964 by Princeton University Press), vol. 11, *Psychology and Religion* (copyright (c) 1958 & 1969 by Princeton University Press), vol. 12, *Psychology and Alchemy* (copyright (c) 1953 & 1968 by Princeton University Press), and vol. 14, *Mysterium Coniunctionis* (copyright (c) 1963 by Princeton University Press) are reprinted by permission of Princeton University Press.

Acknowledgment is also due the following publishers for their kind permission to quote from copyrighted material in these pages:

Columbia University Press for passages from F. E. Ratchford's *Brontë's Webb of Childhood*;

Faber & Faber, Ltd. for the material from *Voyage to Windward* by J. C. Furnas;

Pantheon Press for the quoted passages from C. G. Jung's *Memories, Dreams, Reflections*;

And Princeton University Press for selections from *Aurora Consurgens*, ed. by Marie-Louise von Franz, trans. by R. F. C. Hull and A. S. B. Glover, Bollingen Series LXXVII.

B. H.

# CONTENTS

# AUTHOR'S NOTE

It is now nearly forty years since I gave my first lecture on "The Writings of the Brontë Sisters (An Early Victorian Manifestation of the Problem of Modern Woman)" at the Psychological Club, Zurich. The late Toni Wolff (President of the Club at that time) pointed out to me that as the individuation process evidently appeared in an unusually clear form in the writings of the Brontës, it probably was also equally visible in their lives; and if so this would undoubtedly be a rich field for research, though perhaps too difficult. She followed this suggestion by instigating longer seminars on the subject at the C. G. Jung Institute, and I soon extended the research to several other writers.

The results struck me as very worthwhile, and I was often asked to give the lectures a more durable form. It was by no means my wish, however, to write a book only for readers who were already acquainted with Jungian psychology; yet I knew it was difficult to make the importance of the individuation process and of wholeness intelligible to the general reader in these days of one-sided specialization and collective ideals. Then one day the image of the Garden of Eden presented itself, so to speak, as the connecting thread. I am glad to say that I was still able to discuss using this image with Professor Jung. Most of the book was written after his death, but his warm approval of the general idea was often a great support and help to me in completing my task.

My best thanks are due to Marie-Louise von Franz for her

patience in discussing my difficulties, for reading the manuscript and for offering many valuable suggestions; to Vernon Brooks of the C. G. Jung Foundation for what I can only call his genius in editing the book; and to the late Joanna Hogg for her eagerness in typing the manuscript.

*Barbara Hannah*
Küsnacht-Zurich
March 1971

# STRIVING TOWARDS WHOLENESS

# 1 INTRODUCTION

IN EARLIER DAYS it was self-evident that every living creature was striving to complete the pattern of its existence as fully as possible. In our rational times, however, with their ever-increasing demand for specialization, this fact seems to be almost forgotten, although in the unconscious the urge towards wholeness appears to have become all the stronger for being repressed and forgotten. It has become very difficult to express what one means by "wholeness" in terms that are likely to convey something intelligible to the present-day reader, yet most people still feel an immense satisfaction when they see a tree or a plant, for instance, that has fulfilled the pattern of its being to the greatest possible extent.

While the human body necessarily follows the life pattern of every other animal, increasing in strength till the middle of life and then slowly decreasing towards inevitable death, our spirit seems to be far more aptly symbolized by the image of the tree that goes on developing, becoming stronger and more whole, until the forester decides it is ripe for a change, fells it and it is later converted into another form. So our spiritual, psychic life can go on developing until the blow of the forester—when the body dies—converts it into another (unknown) form.

One of the principal reasons the urge towards wholeness has been forgotten today is that the Christian religion has been urging man, during the last two thousand years, to strive for perfection. But perfection is necessarily one-sided, it attempts to develop the light side of man exclusively, to dismiss the dark side as sin which must be resisted at all costs, whereas everything that exists consists of both light *and* dark. The Swiss psychologist, C. G. Jung, had already recognized in boyhood that life is no longer satisfied with Western man's one-sided traditional attempt to strive after perfection in all the Christian virtues, but is now demanding the recognition of certain thoughts which definitely come from the other, the dark side of man.[1] Further experience and his analytical practice strengthened this early conviction. The impossibility of fulfilling the Christian ideal led and leads increasingly to dangerous feelings of inferiority and to neurosis. Indeed, St. Paul himself complained of this weakness in the Christian program: "For the good that I would, I do not; but the evil which I would not, that I do" (Romans 6:19). How much more problematic this has become in our complicated, over-populated, modern world where the dark side of man seems to be flourishing as never before! Jung became more and more convinced that a satisfactory solution to the contradictions inherent in this one-sidedness could only be found by giving up the hopeless search for perfection and replacing it with a quest for wholeness.

As he studied the human psyche in its endless variety, Jung found that the empirical data revealed that the psyche's central core has a fourfold structure. It is difficult perhaps for the general reader to realize the vital importance of the number four in the realm of the psyche, but from the beginning mankind has unconsciously produced this number in every area of the world. Pythagoras (c. 582-507 B.C.) was probably the first to realize *consciously* that four is the number of totality and to draw attention to this vital fact. The earliest Eastern *mandalas* (to use a Sanskrit word for the sacred image of fourfoldness) were all built upon the square or circle which is generally divided into four or a multiple of four. We find the same image in the Mayan culture and in fact everywhere in man's earliest attempts to produce an abstract image for the deity or for the innermost center of the soul.

[1] Cf. *Memories, Dreams, Reflections*, pp. 36ff.

Although historians have a passion for searching for outer connections between images and ideas, these basic structural images are far too universal to be pinned down in this way. One might as well try to show that patterns of behavior in animals and insects are passed on *outwardly* from one generation to the next or from one place to another. But it is a proved fact, for instance, that the Yucca moth is dead long before its eggs are hatched, yet the little caterpillars know exactly what to do and this is only one of countless examples.

No naturalist and hardly any layman now doubt that most of the "wonders of nature" in the animal world are produced by innate patterns of behavior, faithfully and instinctively carried out by the young living creatures. Yet when it comes to man, the idea that we also may have innate patterns of behavior is very seldom taken into consideration, in fact often passionately denied. Therefore the historian—with a praiseworthy diligence—will go to great trouble to attempt to prove outer connections in every instance, because he is convinced that these *must* exist. (Naturally, in many places historical connections do exist and are very interesting. But apart from this, there are independent *basic human patterns* of behavior such as the production of the square and the circle built up on the number four.)

It is true that, as consciousness developed, the possibility of deviating from these innate patterns developed also. The development of the intellect and reason and an arbitrary use of the will have become the goals of the human being, and it is difficult to reconcile such goals with obedience to our instinctive patterns. To take a banal analogy: Balance in bicycling is an instinctive matter; once we have learned to ride a bicycle we do so quite unconsciously. If, however, we begin to think about where we should place our weight, the chances are that we will lose our instinctive balance at once. It could be done, no doubt, by a careful and long synchronization of balance and thought, but very few people would be willing to make the effort.

This inadequate example gives some idea of the difficulty of keeping to our instinctive patterns of behavior once we have begun to think and reason about them. We are far too prone to deny our instincts, to repress them, and thus to reach that one-sided condition in which we overestimate reason, will and rational arguments and which has consequently led to so many of our problems today. Not that I wish in any way to depreciate intellect, reason, the human will, or, above all, consciousness. They represent a kind of Promethean fire, won from the gods, an achievement of which man is justly proud and which all of us are bound to defend with all our might. To lose what we have gained on this side would be disastrous beyond measure.

With the catastrophic threats that hang over our heads today—atom warfare, starvation from over-population, and so on—we are obviously in the utmost danger of losing these values, to say nothing of most of our other values. As an example of a world that has lost its orientation to these human Promethean gains, I need only point to the world predicted by Aldous Huxley in *Ape and Essence*, a world which is the result of atomic war. Over-valuation of either side—human reason or natural instinct—can hardly fail to lead to such a disaster. Only the middle way, with its respect for the *totality* of human nature, presents a ray of hope: that we can do something about it in ourselves.

But it is no part of my intention to speculate about future events on our planet. I am trying to make clear the enormous importance of the natural totality, for a realization of this is our best hope of uniting our developing consciousness with its eternal basic roots. When I stress the dangers that threaten us in the loss of the rational side or of the irrational, instinctive images and patterns from which we have now moved too far, I am trying to show that such a split separates us from our totality and from the four-square image that represents it.

Yet in every living creature the urge for its own totality

is perhaps the strongest and most fundamental of all urges. Once one has realized this *through experience*, it is so self-evident that it is difficult to realize that it is probably by no means self-evident to a great many people these days. One-sided—one might say one-pointed—knowledge and direction have become almost essential for survival. We have largely forgotten that our first obligation, after all, is to be a simple human being, and the simple human being always has a certain quality of wholeness. He has a certain wholeness because nothing in him is over-developed *at the cost of the rest*. One can see this natural wholeness in primitive people, undisturbed by civilization, in peasants living in natural, ancestral conditions, in children and in animals. Directly this natural, instinctive wholeness is disturbed by the excessive over-development of a *part*, a certain loss of equilibrium is inevitable, because, in order to have enough energy to develop one part to an unusual degree, it is necessary to appropriate it from some other part of the totality.

Let us return to our *point de depart:* the strong urge for wholeness in every living being. When we consider that we have all descended from ancestors who possessed a natural wholeness and—at least equally important—have ourselves gone through such a stage in childhood, it should be clear that somewhere—whether we are aware of it or not—we are suffering from homesickness for a more balanced natural condition. It is absolutely necessary for physical and psychic well-being to feel at home in our own skins.

Now the form of natural wholeness that I have referred to is the "condition of the beginning," so to speak. One can consciously recapture it sometimes in places where nature is especially undisturbed or where it has a special quality for us. A feeling of extraordinary harmony pervades us, strain, tension, worry and all deficiencies are mercifully suspended for the time. This is originally, of course, a completely unconscious condition in which there is not as yet any deviation from the will of God, to use the Eden story from Genesis as an image of this state of natural wholeness. The four rivers of the Garden of Eden are one of numberless symbols of the fourfold, natural division of the original totality which we must always leave behind, just as our original parents did, for, as Wordsworth describes so well in his "Intimations of Immortality," adult life calls us inexorably away from the paradise of childhood where we are still at one with our original wholeness. There would be no human consciousness without this separation.

So we find ourselves sooner or later outside the walls of our unconscious, early paradise; we are unable for many, many years, if not for all our lives, to re-enter it, as the angel with the flaming sword so aptly symbolizes. Then—to continue with the imagery of the Garden of Eden—as Adam and Eve were unable to return, I have always imagined Eden as a walled garden with four gates to match the four rivers. If we picture it in this way, we would then be obliged to go out by one of these gates and to follow one of the rivers out into the world, or at all events to choose a direction in which to move. We have now turned our backs on the totality and, whether we will or not, it is our destiny to leave it behind. Perhaps our path follows only one of these rivers, or perhaps we may extend our knowledge of the countryside until it reaches the river on the right or the left of us, or even possibly on both. But it is practically impossible, in any human life, not to ignore and eventually to forget entirely the gate and the river behind us, the river that took the opposite direction to the one we chose to follow.

We cannot push such images too far, and they must not be taken too literally; yet they are a certain help in expressing the essentially inexpressible. From the rational point of view, one has to make one's way in the direction one has chosen, to give one's whole attention to it, and any dim homesickness for that early totality must be dismissed as wanting the penny and the cake. There is a great deal to be said for this point of view, particularly in the first half of life when, in general, we rightly consolidate our position in the outer world. The angel with the flaming sword guards the gates of paradise at God's behest, and this is a symbol we cannot possibly ignore.

But the essence of the totality is the paradox, and we can never escape this fact, either outside or within Eden. And though it is right that we are locked out of the paradise of our totality, yet we carry with us an inner image of it as a kind of "pattern" that is very hard to reconcile with our necessarily one-sided adaptation to the outer world. How much we are aware of this inner image is a very individual matter. Some people seem to forget it altogether; in these days, it seems as if the great majority has quite forgotten it. Others are constantly aware of something which makes them feel that outer life is unsatisfying and that starts a quest in them to find something less one-sided somewhere, somehow. Others—although less today than in other centuries—carry this inner totality over into some form of organized religion and feel contained and satisfied there.

All the great religions are based on this idea of totality, a totality which includes human and divine nature, time and eternity, and—to a greater or lesser degree—all the other opposites as well.[2] To speak but briefly of the symbols of totality in the Christian religion, I would remind the reader that in addition to the four rivers of paradise there are also four evangelists, frequently pictured with Christ as the

[2] In his Introduction to *Psychology and Alchemy*, Jung goes very deeply into the enormous importance of the paradox and the disrepute into which it has fallen in our modern world. He says:

> Has it not yet been observed that all religious statements contain logical contradictions and assertions that are impossible in principle, that this is in fact the very essence of religious assertion? As witness to this we have Tertullian's avowal: "And the Son of God is dead, which is worthy of belief because it is absurd. And when buried He rose again, which is certain because it is impossible." If Christianity demands faith in such contradictions it does not seem to me that it can very well condemn those who assert a few paradoxes more.

*quinta essentia* in the center, and a four-square element in all the sacred buildings, most evident in the cloisters of monasteries and cathedrals. Yet the basic dogmas of the Christian religion are built up on the number three, on the Trinity, that is; for it is inevitable—as I have tried to show in the simile of the departure from Eden—that the individual turn his back on the fourth as he walks out into the world. This applies to everyone, even to the Fathers of the Church. Then the forgotten fourth which has been left behind must to some extent be repressed; consequently it falls into disrepute. Thus the fourth place in the Godhead has fallen into disrepute, for it is mainly occupied by Christ's great adversary Satan, who as Lucifer was seen to fall from Heaven by Christ who had also descended from Heaven to earth though in a more reputable manner.

The late Pope Pius XII showed a most unusual psychological insight when he realized, consciously or unconsciously,

---

Not everyone possesses the spiritual strength of a Tertullian. It is evident not only that he had the strength to sustain paradoxes but that they actually afforded him the highest degree of religious certainty. The inordinate number of spiritual weaklings makes paradoxes dangerous. So long as the paradox remains unexamined and is taken for granted as a customary part of life, it is harmless enough. But when it occurs to an insufficiently cultivated mind (always, as we know, the more sure of itself) to make the paradoxical nature of some tenet of faith the object of its lucubrations, as earnest as they are impotent, it is not long before such a one will break out into iconoclastic and scornful laughter, pointing to the manifest absurdity of the mystery. Things have gone rapidly downhill since the Age of Enlightenment, for, once this petty reasoning mind, which cannot endure any paradoxes, is awakened, no sermon on earth can keep it down. A new task then arises: to lift this still undeveloped mind step by step to a higher level and to increase the number of persons who have at least some inkling of the scope of paradoxical truth. If this is not possible, then it must be admitted that the spiritual approaches to Christianity are as good as blocked. We simply do not understand any more what is meant by the paradoxes contained in dogma; and the more external our understanding of them becomes the more we are affronted by their irrationality, until finally they become completely obsolete, curious relics of the past.—Pars. 18-19.

that some recognition must be accorded the fourth. Listening to the visions of simple people he established the dogma of the assumption of the Virgin (the *Assumption Mariae*).[3] Mary is not made an equal figure with the Trinity, but she has been placed beside them and there is now—for the discerning Catholic, at any rate—a *fourth figure in Heaven.* But Lucifer, that earlier prince of Heaven, is still on earth and, though world events show only too clearly that he *must* now be reckoned with, is still denied; for the primal pair of opposites that the Christian Church has torn apart and not yet reconciled is what we call good and evil.

The re-establishment of the quaternity necessarily includes the problem of the opposites. We find this clearly indicated in the story of the Garden of Eden where the tree of the knowledge of good and evil grew. When the fruit of this tree was eaten by our first parents, they were able to discriminate between good and evil, i.e., between the opposites. Wholeness consists of pairs of opposites (four can also be understood as two pairs of opposites, each opposite to be reconciled with the other, and each pair with the other pair), and we can never refind our lost wholeness until we have granted both opposites their full and equal rights.[4] This is perhaps the most burning and urgent problem of our age, for darkness and evil have broken loose from their bonds and are threatening to destroy the whole world. The solution which was valid 2000 years ago, when it was necessary to differentiate the light opposite at all costs, no longer works today. Apuleius' *Golden Ass* gives a vivid picture of the unconscious, pervading darkness, full of black magic and witchcraft, from which Christianity was born. Mankind had to differentiate and develop the Christian virtues in order to have any chance for survival and progress. But nothing can be repressed forever; the longer anything is caged, the more savage it becomes,

[3] Cf. Jung, "Answer to Job," in *Psychology and Religion*, pars. 553-758.
[4] Cf. the closing paragraphs of the definition of "Symbol" in Jung's *Psychological Types*, pars. 824-829.

as our age is teaching us daily. So we are now confronted with a new task: to have it out with the dark opposite, not to repress it again, for that is impossible and at best only a temporary solution, but somehow to give it its just due and to reconcile it with the light opposite, without losing everything we have gained in the last 2000 years. As Jung has pointed out again and again, the only place where this is possible is in the individual, and we shall see in the examples of the writers given in later chapters that the problem of the opposites was in the foreground with each of them.

If we try to continue with the Garden of Eden image we might say that when the early Church Fathers, in the normal course of human fate, were forced to leave the eternal symbol in its totality and establish whatever they remembered of it in the temporal world, like everyone else they had to choose a direction by which to get out into the world. Since they moved towards the light, and since the sun was one of their favorite images for Christ,[5] we may assume that they left by the south gate, towards the maximum light, the sun at midday. But they certainly included the territory to the east of Eden, looking to the rising sun, and to the west, to the setting sun, as soon as possible, thus establishing themselves on the widest basis possible to them, that is, they included the whole territory adjacent to three rivers. There they built their Church, that mighty ship which brought numberless souls safely through almost twenty centuries. Many of their symbols had a four-square basis, but their main symbol was trinitarian; the fourth, in this case the

[5] Many examples may be found in von Franz, *Aurora Consurgens*, for instance, p. 250: "The new birth is called 'the sun of Justice,' an image from Malachi 4:2, which the Church has always referred to Christ." And on p. 238: ". . . Ecclesia Luna, who represents a 'composition of souls fully initiated into the mysteries,' in her final glorification becomes the sun, the image of Christ, whose light calls forth the wonder of man." Further, on p. 206f: "A liturgical commentary says: 'The dawn shining in the heaven of redemption and grace, from whose womb the sun rises outshining her a thousandfold, is Mary.'"

north, thus remained behind their backs, as a vaguely, sometimes very clearly, felt enemy; in fact, the north was early identified with the abode of the Devil.[6] I need only remind the reader of the Inquisition, with its persecutions of all heresy and of witches, and indeed of a certain narrowness in the whole Christian doctrine which has been inclined to condemn anything outside its own doctrine as being without doubt of the Devil.

The point I want to make is that even a world-wide, highly intelligent, indubitably well-meaning institution like the Christian Church has that fourth river, gate or territory, *at its back*. It is not included in the conscious outlook. Yet the many quaternity symbols also show that the lost paradise is still functioning there as an archetypal image or pattern, forever trying to realize itself. Like Goethe in *Faust*, the Church found a solution by removing the possible achievement of totality from the present world into the world beyond the grave, as is shown, for instance, by the conception of the Heavenly Jerusalem of the Revelation, which is based on four or a multiple of four. In this way it was not necessary to decide what to do about the dark and doubtful fourth; it could thus still be condemned or ignored, that is, left to God to decide.

To return to the individual life. If the first half of life

[6] Cf. Jung, in *Aion*, where he writes: "Nostradamus, the learned physician and astrologer, would certainly have been familiar with the idea of the North as the region of the devil, unbelievers, and all things evil. The idea, as St. Eucherius of Lyons (d. 450) remarks, goes back to Jeremiah 1:14: 'From the north shall an evil wind break forth upon all the inhabitants of the land,' and other passages such as Isaiah 14:12f: 'How art thou fallen from heaven, O Lucifer, son of the morning; how art thou cut down to the ground, which didst weaken the nations! For thou hast said in thine heart, I will ascend into heaven, I will exalt my throne above the stars of God, I will sit on the mount of assembly in the far north.' The Benedictine monk Rhabanus Maurus (d. 856) says that 'the north wind is the harshness of persecution' and 'a figure of the old enemy.' The north wind, he adds, signifies the devil, as is evident from Job 26:7. . . . St. Augustine says: 'Who is that north wind, save him who said: I will set up my seat in the north?' "—Par. 157.

is to be lived fully, it must lead, on a broader or a narrower basis, *away* from the original totality, away from Eden. But in many people, consciously or unconsciously, a certain sense of dissatisfaction or incompleteness makes itself felt about the middle of life. The things which once seemed wholly desirable no longer exercise their former fascination. This is a time when the image of totality makes itself felt again and leads to all kinds of efforts to find something to fit the bill. If we consider it in terms of the quaternity, the left-behind fourth is vaguely missed for the first time.

If we want to do something about this, the way necessarily leads through the most inferior and neglected parts of our personality. We have to leave the countryside that has become wholly familiar to us, where roads have been laid down and everything is civilized and well known, and go into the unknown country that has always lain behind us, for the most part unguessed at or suspected of being dangerous, even evil. It almost seems as if the only way we can re-enter Eden, the original wholeness, in our lifetime is through the gate directly opposite and behind the gate by which we left. We have to make do with small paths in place of highways, so to speak; indeed the way often leads where there are no paths at all, through impenetrable places where we may get lost, even fall into despair.

The foregoing is meant only as a rough indication of the way a searching spirit would be able to find the way to the lost Eden. It would be the same Eden, yet not the same, for it would no longer represent an unconscious condition but one in which the old is totally new because it is seen *consciously* for the first time. Goethe's *Faust* presents such a picture and Goethe, in his own life, approached such a development. His dying cry for more light could be understood in this way.

Not everyone, by any means, sets out on the pilgrimage of life and lives it out in a similar way. Many people, especially in our days, begin their lives in a normal way but never seem to feel dissatisfied with their limited view or they diligently repress any such dissatisfaction. Our age is a materialistic one, and materialism's opposite—the spirit—has never before been denied in such a wholesale way as it is today. Unless the opposite, in whatever form, is sincerely sought, there can be no return to the fourth and no lasting realization, in this life at any rate, of the lost totality.

There are many other people who never really succeed in leaving the vicinity of Eden at all. They are driven out like everyone else, of course, but they camp around its walls, unable to tear themselves away. They do not forget it, as the majority of people do, and are therefore unable to find satisfaction in the one-, two- and three-sided pleasures and businesses of the world; they are always tortured by a feeling of incompleteness and disappointment in connection with everything they try to do. It is as if the turning point, which should normally begin to set in about the middle of life, was there for this minority from the beginning.

Obviously this attitude is a terrible hindrance in outer life. We see it all too often these days in the *puer aeternus* and *puella aeterna*—the eternal boy and girl—who will not grow up and assume responsibility for their lives. Such people are all too common today and are largely responsible for the totalitarian state and for dictators; a flock of eternal children is obviously an overwhelming temptation to those who love power. But the really negative characteristic in such people is usually laziness. They do not want to make the effort either to turn their backs on the paradise of childhood and leave it by an effort of will, or to realize and accept their limitations and do something creative with them.

The acceptance of limitations is not only possible but can be exceedingly rewarding, as the lives of many creative people illustrate. A great number of poets, painters, sculptors, musicians show us what a short distance they were able to venture out on to the path of life and how near to the walls of Eden they settled down. There they began their task of reproducing as completely as they could the lost totality which attracted them at all times like a powerful magnet and against whose pull they could make little or no progress out into the world.

There are exceptions, of course. There are artists, in the broadest sense of the word, who live very complete lives in the outer world, dealing all the time with the powerful inner image that is claiming expression. But I should say they are exceedingly rare. Goethe was such an exception, and Shakespeare, little though one knows of his life, was probably another. But most "artists" either content themselves with an art that *only* depicts the surface of their limited outer world or the inner image inhibits them in some way from venturing very far into the outer world. The fact that artists are often inefficient at making money or are unable to deal satisfactorily with their sex lives is too well known to require any further comment.

Nevertheless, as Jung once remarked in a private conversation, it is the creative artist, in the widest sense of the words, who has the best chance of bringing the two opposites together, for he is far less one-sided than the rationalist or the intellectual. For this reason I shall draw my examples mainly from literature, for the creators of literary works offer the best material I know to illustrate the images of the lost Eden and their effect on human lives. I am well aware that the image of a lost Eden is too rational (and is itself one- to three-sided) for it to be able to give any real idea of the four-dimensional archetype of totality. It may nevertheless serve, like Ariadne's thread, to guide us through the labyrinth of the unknown.

# 2 ❧ CONSCIOUS AND UNCONSCIOUS

THE TOTALITY of the psyche obviously extends far beyond our comprehension and, as Jung has pointed out again and again, we cannot possibly know or define it.[1] Nevertheless, the concepts of Jungian psychology give us an empirical basis on which we can try out our material. It is my wish and intention in this book to avoid psychological terminology as far as possible, so as to make the material more accessible to the general reader.[2] But since my own standpoint owes everything to C. G. Jung, inevitably I see my material from the Jungian point of view, and I am aware that in places I shall not be able to explain myself without using this or that Jungian term. This chapter, therefore, aims at as simple an explanation as I can achieve of all those terms that I shall be likely to use.

It has been said by critics, who usually have little or no empirical knowledge of the subject, that it is easy, even cheap, to "explain" any material with Jungian psychology. One can only reply, "*Hic Rhodos, hic salta!*"—in other words, please try to apply it to some given material yourself and you will soon see how subtle and difficult this task is. Jung's enormous knowledge of the human psyche—derived from an overflowing practice of over fifty years and confirmed by

[1] For example, cf. *Psychology and Alchemy,* par. 327.

[2] Moreover the less that psychology relies on specialized terminology the better. Jung himself says in more than one place that he sets little store by "concepts" and that if they "provisionally serve to put the empirical material in order, they will have fulfilled their purpose."—*Mysterium Coniunctionis,* par. 129, note 66.

his unique studies of Eastern and Western religions, of Gnosticism, of alchemy of all ages in East and West, to mention only a fraction of his researches—has produced a basic, empirical foundation for his scientific statements upon which all false conclusions and illusory ideas are smashed to pieces. If I try to put over anything which is not basic, the discerning reader, with some knowledge of the subject, will be able to detect it at once.

Misunderstandings often arise from the fact that Jungian psychology is a science and not a philosophy, and that many people find this difficult to grasp. If one has had no experience of the objective psyche, he naturally cannot understand how inner, invisible factors can be *real*, how they can behave autonomously or how they can possess qualities of their own which have to be respected like all other objects of science. Until convinced by experience, such skepticism is very understandable. Jung himself found it impossible to *believe* anything he did not *know*. Some misunderstandings, therefore, are probably inevitable. It is only when criticism or rejection becomes over-emotional or even spiteful that one cannot help wondering whether the critic has not himself had some such experience which he does not want to, or is afraid to, take seriously.

The quaternary structure, which had already revealed itself to Jung in his early researches into the human psyche, seems to have a basic connection with what he called the four functions of consciousness. It soon became clear to him that whereas some people *think*, well or badly, but always think—that is, try to express themselves in terms of meaning—others are wholly concerned with *feeling*, that is, they orient themselves by the values of liking or disliking, accepting or rejecting; others again have a strong sense of reality, that is, they rely on their *sensation*, whereas others are not impressed by reality at all, or rather are not even aware of it, and draw their orientation from *intuition*, hunches, totally irrational convictions.

I need not elaborate on the function types here or on the attitude types, *introversion* and *extraversion*, which color them, for they are well known and have in part even entered our common language. Moreover, the literature is easily available.[3] But it is typology, above all, that influences our choice of the gate by which we leave paradise, following the same pattern as I suggested there. One highly developed function may be relied upon, or two or even three; but the fourth, inferior function is always left behind and can only partially be regained or made conscious, as the result of long and sustained effort.

This effort must lead into the unconscious part of the psyche, into everything that has been left behind us in our efforts to adapt to the world. As a rule the first "figure" we encounter there is the so-called *shadow*, which comes from our dark, completely unknown side, and is related to the serpent who first confronted Eve with the problem of evil and thus led to the expulsion from Eden. I use the term "figure" because contents of the unconscious, particularly the shadow, almost always appear personified in dreams, sometimes as people we know, sometimes as unknown figures. The unconscious uses such personifications to convey its message, with an amazing objectivity and intelligence. Jung adopted this language of the unconscious when he was developing the method of *active imagination*,[4] and even said in "The Relations between the Ego and the Unconscious" that questions to the anima (for instance) should be put in a personal way because it "has the great advantage of recognizing the anima as a personality, and of making a relationship possible. The more personally she is taken the better."[5]

The shadow, in its personal aspect, consists of repressed

[3] For example, see Jung, *Psychological Types* and *Two Essays on Analytical Psychology*, pars. 56-96.
[4] See below, pages 27ff.
[5] *Two Essays*, par. 321.

personal material, elements of which we were once conscious but which were inconvenient or painful for us for some reason so that we preferred to forget them. As a result the shadow consists of our inferior and negative qualities which we obviously were ashamed of but which are yet part of human nature and cannot be denied without psychic loss. The shadow, therefore, is usually an inferior personality, containing all of those characteristics we dislike the most in others. Many people even cling firmly to a *bête noire*, someone of the same sex in their environment, who has all the qualities they deny in themselves. Two old great aunts of mine, one the sister of my grandmother, the other of my grandfather, therefore not related to each other, settled down in neighboring streets in Edinburgh and spent most of their time and energy quarreling or bitterly complaining about each other to their common relatives. But when one died, the other pined away within a few months; they had been more indispensable to each other than the greatest friends, because each depended on the other to provide her lost wholeness.

This happens because of what is known as *projection*.[6] The pieces of oneself that have been lost project themselves onto someone who fits their nature, that is, they appear to us to be there, in the other person. We do not recognize them as belonging to us, but since they unconsciously remind us of our lost totality they fascinate and hold us, whether in a negative or a positive manner.

[6] Projection, as the word is used in Jungian psychology, is another term that is often misunderstood. We do not *make* projections, that is, we do not consciously decide to get rid of something we do not like in ourselves by throwing it onto someone else. On the contrary, we often find in someone else characteristics which we have never recognized in ourselves; and in the other person they usually have a peculiarly irritating or fascinating effect on us. A projection only becomes our own responsibility when we have once seen it as such, for if we continue against light and reason, so to speak, we are really unintentionally making a projection.

The shadow is by no means always negative, for curiously enough quite a few people repress their positive qualities. We all know individuals who are living below their own level, or pretending to be much worse than they really are. Jung even said in a seminar once that it was possible to find up to eighty per cent gold in the shadow. These positive qualities are also usually refound in projection, and a great many cases of homosexuality, or other apparently absurd over- or undervaluations of some member of the same sex, are due again to the fascination exerted by these missing pieces of ourselves that remind us unconsciously of our lost wholeness.

But it is not only the lost personal elements in the shadow that fascinate or repel us. Insofar as the shadow is usually the first figure we encounter on the journey back towards our lost totality, it represents, so to speak, the whole unconscious at this stage. Behind the shadow we sense—although they are still unknown and invisible to us—far more than personal repressions. These are the dominants of the collective unconscious, those elements which mankind has revered or feared from time immemorial. Although we are still only on our way to the unknown territory in the realm of the forgotten fourth, from which we hope to find our way back to our lost Eden through the gate behind and opposite to the one we left, we already feel, consciously or unconsciously, something that ameliorates our one-sided frustration, some breath of air from our lost totality.

We need this breath of hope, for to regain the personal elements that have been discarded all our lives is usually very discouraging and painful work. We would not have thrown them away (and subsequently forgotten about them) had we recognized their value; even if they are positive in themselves, we had our reasons for discarding them. Good qualities and talents spell responsibility and hard work and, if we regain them, we shall have to overcome a great deal of laziness and fear.

Before we leave the stage where the entire unconscious is represented by the shadow, I should like to refer to a novel which might almost be called the modern classic of this stage of development in the search for totality: Robert Louis Stevenson's *The Strange Case of Dr. Jekyll and Mr. Hyde.* Stevenson has Dr. Jekyll say, in describing his early work in his laboratory, "I thus drew steadily nearer to that truth, by whose partial discovery I have been doomed to such a dreadful shipwreck: that man is not truly one, but truly two. I say two, because the state of my own knowledge does not pass beyond that point. Others will follow, others will outstrip me on the same lines; and I hazard the guess that man will be ultimately known for a mere polity of multifarious, incongruous and independent denizens." [7] Stevenson's intuition not only provided him with an unsurpassed description—though admittedly highly colored and dramatized—of the encounter with the shadow, but he hazarded a guess as to future knowledge of the psyche which agrees to a great extent with the findings of Jungian psychology some half a century later. He will therefore be taken as our first example from literature (Chapter 3).

Stevenson's realization that man contains many figures within himself [8] will perhaps make it easier for the reader to understand why, in using examples from literature, we see fictional characters as projections of the figures in the author's own unconscious. One of these figures usually very clearly represents the conscious ego, generally with another of the same sex as its shadow. The other figures come from a deeper layer of the unconscious. If the process of individuation is clearly present, four of these figures will be the cornerstones, as it were, around which the others will find their places.

Indeed, the work on the personal shadow, with which an analysis usually begins, is, as Jung has often pointed out, mere child's play compared to the work that awaits us when

[7] Second page of "Henry Jekyll's Full Statement of the Case."

[8] Origen, in the second century, had already drawn the same conclusion.

we go further into the unconscious and arrive at what is really unknown territory. "No one need remain ignorant of the fact that he is striving for power, that he wants to become very rich, that he would be a tyrant if he had the chance, that he is pleasure seeking, envious of other people and so on. Everyone *can* know such things of him or herself, because they are mere ego knowledge." [9]

By ego knowledge Jung means personal knowledge, knowledge belonging to what is generally known about human beings—although we may have failed to see that it could also apply to ourselves. But, he continues, knowledge of the totality is "something completely different, it is learning to know of the things which are unknown." [10]

Although we were in paradise in our early childhood, it is only a vague memory in later life, for we were unconscious as children are of anything but a vague at-oneness and harmony with ourselves. To reconquer Eden means entering the absolutely unknown, risking ourselves in the same sense as the explorer on earth or the explorer in outer space risks himself when he enters unknown territory, although much less well prepared than the latter. I remind the reader of the heroism and endurance required of such men as Christopher Columbus, Vasco da Gama, Nansen and Scott and the astronauts of recent years, to mention only a few among thousands, in their voyages of discovery.

After we have sufficiently explored the probably unpleasant but basically familiar ground of the personal shadow,[11] we then come up against a fact which is partially known but which is always being forgotten, namely that men have a feminine counterpart and women a masculine counterpart within themselves of which they are originally quite unconscious. I say it is partially known because the Church has

[9] E. T. H. Lectures, 1940-1941, p. 71; old edition, p. 83; quoted more extensively below, p. 272.
[10] *Ibid.*
[11] I have not yet taken elements of the collective shadow into account, although these often break through and contaminate the personal aspect of the shadow. See below, p. 25.

long regarded man's soul as feminine, largely drawing this belief from the Scriptures themselves. The Song of Solomon, for instance, is really a love story between man and his soul; and Hugh de St. Victor, a twelfth cenutry learned man and monk, actually wrote a dialogue between himself and a woman whom he addressed as "my soul"—to mention only two examples among a multitude.

The fact that no human being is exclusively male or female is equally well known in biology. Even the layman knows that there are masculine and feminine genes in every foetus and that the sex of the child is determined by the majority, often only a majority of one. Very early in life Jung asked himself what happened to the minority, which were also present in every human being, and this was another path by which he approached the same question.

Jung, who called this feminine counterpart in man the *anima*, made her an object of scientific research for the first time. He was not satisfied with accepting a given fact, as the Church appears to do, or as the poets sing again and again, or to accept it unquestioned as biology seems to do; he ventured to test the hypothesis in the hard school of individual human life where any erroneous theory can have fatal results. Above all he tried it out first in terms of his own psychology—on himself. He accepted the hypothesis, extraordinarily humiliating and disagreeable to any man, that he might not be exclusively masculine, but that there were places in his psychology where he reacted as if he were a woman, even an inferior sort of woman. By submitting his own reactions in daily life to such a scrutiny, he gradually reached a conclusion which is especially clearly expressed in "The Relations between the Ego and the Unconscious." [12]

In this book Jung presents three principal reasons for considering the soul [13] of man to be feminine. From child-

[12] *Two Essays*, pars. 202-406.

[13] The word "soul" is used here in its psychological sense, i.e., as the feminine part of the psyche of man.

hood on, a man's experience of individual women, beginning with his mother, tends to form in him a relatively autonomous image of woman.

> Woman, with her very dissimilar psychology, is and always has been a source of information about things for which a man has no eyes. She can be his inspiration; her intuitive capacity, often superior to man's, can give him timely warning, and her feeling, always directed towards the personal, can show him ways which his own less personally accented feeling would never have discovered. . . .
>
> Here, without a doubt, is one of the main sources for the feminine quality of the soul. But it does not seem to be the only source. No man is so entirely masculine that he has nothing feminine in him. The fact is, rather, that very masculine men have—carefully guarded and hidden—a very soft emotional life . . . which is why a man in his love-choice is strongly tempted to win the woman who best corresponds to his own unconscious femininity—a woman, in short, who can unhesitatingly receive the projection of his soul. . . . This would explain some highly remarkable conjunctions.
>
> It seems to me, therefore, that apart from the influence of woman there is also the man's own femininity to explain the feminine nature of the soul complex.[14]

Jung goes on to point out that that the wide recognition given such books as Rider Haggard's *She* and Benoit's *L'Atlantide* indicates that there must be some supraindividual quality in the inner image of the feminine—i.e., the anima. This quality appeals to all men because it has something typical and racial, the historical aspect so well described in many of Rider Haggard's books.

Jung continues:

> As we know, there is no human experience, nor would experience be possible at all, without the intervention of a

[14] *Two Essays*, pars. 296-298.

> subjective aptitude. What is this subjective aptitude? Ultimately it consists in an innate psychic structure which allows man to have experiences of this kind. Thus the whole nature of man presupposes woman, both physically and spiritually.

Later he writes:

> An inherited collective image of woman exists in a man's unconscious, with the help of which he apprehends the nature of woman. This inherited image is the third important source for the femininity of the soul.[15]

Nearly forty years later Jung summed up these three stages in *Aion* as follows:

> The recognition of anima or animus gives rise, in a man, to a triad, one third of which is transcendent: the masculine subject, the opposing feminine subject, and the transcendent anima. With a woman the situation is reversed.[16]

After the personal shadow has been sufficiently realized to prevent this anima—or, in women, animus—figure from hiding behind it, the *Auseinandersetzung*[17] with the anima or animus can begin, for "she" or "he" now represents the whole unconscious. Here the real difficulties begin because we are no longer dealing with "ego knowledge," with things that once were or could easily become conscious, but with things that are—and to a great extent always have been—*unknown*. On one side the anima or animus are, indeed, quite close to us. They consist of feelings and moods connected with the mother or thoughts and opinions imbibed from the father.

[15] *Ibid.*, pars. 300-301.
[16] *Aion*, par. 42.
[17] This untranslatable German word means "having it out with, discussing, analyzing"—all with a hint of eventually coming to terms.

But on the other side the anima and animus belong to or are connected with the dominants of the collective unconscious, archetypal figures invisible to mankind, yet always the object of man's deepest consideration, which are portrayed in myths and fairy stories all over the world and which have at bottom given rise to all the religions.

Man—that fly which lives for only a day, even in comparison with his own recorded history—has in all things, stages and places been sure that something, he never really knew what, namely the unknown, existed which was eternal and everlasting. He has also felt that, in order to have any continuity or security on this earth, he must have some kind of *Auseinandersetzung* with it. This *Auseinandersetzung* begins when we start the apparently modest task of having it out with our own anima or animus.

It does indeed begin in many cases during the work on the shadow—as we shall see particularly clearly in the case of Stevenson—because, as mentioned, the shadow is the first representative of the totality. Furthermore, before the personal elements are cleared away the archetypes may appear in the shadow figure. The shadow is often contaminated with the Devil, for instance; then the *Auseinandersetzung* can remain a burning problem for years. But the confrontation usually ends in a deadlock, such as we shall see in *Jekyll and Hyde,* unless the figure of the anima or animus is discovered, or reveals itself, in time. It is true that the male-female opposites are much more basic opposites than those represented by two beings of the same sex, much more totally different and therefore in a way wider apart. Yet male presupposes female and female male, and the chances of a creative solution and union between these two opposites are therefore infinitely greater.

The beginning of the work on anima and animus is principally in the personal field. In childhood the images of these two figures are usually identical with the parents. The boy's inner feeling life—his own inner femininity—is very largely determined in later life by his relation to his mother, or to substitute mother figures. His outer life, leading towards his profession and life's work, depends more on the father but he must always reckon, when he begins the work on his own feminine side, on an *Auseinandersetzung* with the mother image in some form or other.

On the other hand a girl, as a rule, first finds her own masculine side projected onto the father, and her first work on the animus usually consists in an *Auseinandersetzung* with everything that she has taken over from him ready-made. Such opinions are apt to have a very didactic character: the small child's "Father said so"—in the sense of "God said so," therefore it is true and cannot be discussed. The woman simply repeats them without even thinking about them or questioning them. And there is a strong tendency in woman to pick up a great many more opinions from her education, her reading and so forth that somehow fit this pattern, till the animus can become as rigid and unyielding as an impregnable fortress! The so-called modern woman has indeed accomplished a heroic task, having cured herself of her traditional dependence on men and, by incredibly hard work and endurance, having succeeded in becoming economically independent. But she has largely paid for it by becoming identical with her masculine side, not in the sense of being a man but in having lost her feminine reactions which normally compensate, reassure and relate to other people, especially to men, and replacing them with pseudo-opinions.[18]

We cannot, therefore, set the clock back. If we want to become whole we will have to face the disagreeable fact that within us there is a counterpart of the opposite sex and, as Jung suggests, have it out with him or her to the best of our ability. This figure, when it is not seen as a part of ourselves, is usually projected onto someone of the opposite

[18] This present-day condition is particularly well described by Jung in "Woman in Europe" in *Civilization in Transition*, pars. 236-275.

sex. It was first projected onto our mother or father, and the normal procedure is for the projection to move, often via the sister or brother, to the loved woman or man. Therefore it is so vitally important to take seriously the fascination emanating from a member of the other sex. If one does not accept the anima or animus in its projected form, it always makes trouble, to say nothing of one's missing a chance for seeing and even integrating a part of oneself.

Dreams prove to be of the greatest possible value here, for the unconscious, even more than the conscious, seems to long for wholeness and unerringly to complement and compensate for our one-sided conscious standpoint in our dreams at night. The more one has to do with dreams, the more respect and admiration one has for the unconscious, for its astonishing objectivity and independence. Dreams have only one drawback and that is that they are very difficult to understand, because their language is always symbolic. It needs a great deal of work to learn to interpret this language, especially in one's own dreams, for dreams always come from the *un*known to us. To assist in this interpretation Jung discovered and developed the technique he called active imagination.

Active imagination is indeed no new method. Its basis is meditation, an integral part of all the great religions. I need only remind the reader of the countless Eastern texts based on meditation,[19] the Spiritual Exercises of St. Ignatius,[20] the books of the Devoti and numerous other Christian examples. Meditation has always served as the royal road towards a realization of the unknown figures of anima and animus and the figures behind them.

Although at first these figures are usually experienced negatively, as unthought-out convictions and opinions in

[19] For example, the *Amitayur-Dhyana-Sutra* (*Sacred Books of the East,* Vol. 49) and the *Shri-Chakra-Sambhara Tantra* (*Tantric Texts,* Vol. 7). Cf. also *Modern Psychology* by Jung, Vol. III.

[20] *Modern Psychology* (E. T. H. Lectures), Vol. IV.

women and as unaccountable moods and emotions in men, this is not always the case, particularly when the man or woman is creative. When we come to the example of Emily Brontë, for instance, we shall see that there was in her a masculine figure that was intensely helpful in her creative work and with whom she had an excellent relation. This is really the deciding point: What is the attitude of the man or woman to his inner counterpart? Jung says of our attitude to the unconscious: "We know that the mask of the unconscious is not rigid—it reflects the face we turn towards it." [21] This applies even more specifically to the representative of the unconscious, be it shadow, anima or animus. Therefore the extraordinary value of conversations with these inner figures, for such conversations give us the opportunity to ascertain their points of view, to explain our own, and eventually to come to terms with them.

The anima and animus are mainly harmful when they press into *outer* life where they do not belong. But again the extent of their influence, harmful or otherwise, really depends on the conscious attitude, for when we are living our outer lives responsibly and as completely as possible, neither anima nor animus need have a disturbing effect.

I will try to make this clearer by an example from a conversation between a woman and her animus. One day, when she was trying to talk to him in active imagination, quite suddenly and unexpectedly she heard him say, "You and I are in a very awkward position, linked together like Siamese twins, and each in a totally different reality." He went on to explain that, just as his reality was invisible and intangible to her, so was hers to him. This woman was trying to distinguish in outer life between what she did and said consciously and what was done and said unconsciously through her by the animus. She had had some bitter experiences when she discovered that she had done and said many things which, far from being what she had intended,

[21] *Psychology and Alchemy*, par. 29.

were exactly the contrary. This hurt her, particularly in her relations with a man who meant a great deal to her. Therefore she said rather bitterly, "If you cannot see my reality, why do you so often interfere in it and do or say what I don't want?" He replied very objectively, "When you leave undone or do not speak when something must be said, you create a vacuum and—whether I like it or not—I am forced to fill it. I quite believe you that I sometimes do it badly, for I am often acting or speaking entirely in the dark."

If the reader can overcome a certain understandable rational skepticism towards the actual psychic reality of these figures, this conversation is extraordinarily enlightening and reveals a great deal about the relation between woman and her animus. She creates the vacuum, and where there is no consciousness the unconscious will obviously flow in, just as when we fail to light a room darkness must flow in. And, like the dark, it may be positive and healing or it may contain lurking dangers, such as burglars. The point is that we cannot see what is there. Nevertheless—to carry this simile a little further—we have a far greater feeling of security in the dark if we have taken all the possibilities into account, locked up the house, seen that the fire is out, and so on. The same applies to the unconscious; the more we try to take the possibilities into account and the more we do what we can to secure our psychic house against them, the greater our feeling of security grows.

We must never forget that the animus is under the masculine principle of Logos, which separates and discriminates and tries to identify and understand everything. In *Mysterium Coniunctionis* Jung points out that the alchemists (among others) used the sun as a symbol of Logos and that the masculine principle accordingly sheds the brightness of sunlight over everything. Everything is visible and clearly *separated* from everything else.

The anima, on the other hand, is under the feminine principle, Eros, which is symbolized by the moon. Jung notes that the " 'mild light' of the moon . . . merges things together rather than separates them. It does not show up objects in all their pitiless discreteness and separateness, like the harsh, flaring light of day, but blends in a deceptive shimmer the near and the far, magically transforming little things into big things, high into low, softening all colour into a bluish haze, and blending the nocturnal landscape into an unsuspected unit." [22]

In dealing, therefore, with animus and anima we must never forget that, by their very nature, they are working from a principle opposite to our own. The woman who had the conversation with her animus was originally a career woman with a correspondingly developed masculinity. She had difficulty with Eros, and when at last she met a man who was her equal and learned how vitally important he was to her she was horrified to find that again and again, when she wanted to do or say something nice, she would do or say something horrid, as if she really wanted to offend him and to keep him away from her. It took her a long time to see that, in giving all of her energy to her career, she had left her whole life as a woman unlived, a vacuum into which, according to the conversation, the animus was forced to flow. He had indeed occupied her Eros side for most of her life, so he had settled down there and now behaved as if he were her rightful lover who must drive all rivals from the field.[23] If she had not neglected her own feminine side, this would never have happened; but the longer the neglect continues the greater the possession by the animus, and the more autonomous, tyrannical, even demonic he becomes. Then it is possible for a real enmity to grow up between them, an enmity that can only be cured by an *Auseinandersetzung* between the two, such as was foreshadowed in the foregoing conversation but which is often initiated from some other cause, such as a dream or an outer event.

[22] *Mysterium*, par. 223.

[23] Cf. for example, "The Relations between the Ego and the Unconscious," in Jung, *Two Essays on Analytical Psychology*, pars. 202-406.

The anima, on the other hand, is more like moonlight in the life of the daylight-loving man. By his own principle—if he lives by it—he will naturally discriminate, separate things from each other and try his best to have a clear picture of the world. An extreme case of the masculine attitude is to be seen in the professor who declared quite seriously that if Rhine's experiments [24] proved undeniably the existence of psycho-kinetic effects he would have no alternative to shooting himself! Jung once said in a seminar that if the matchbox he held in his hand should suddenly free itself from the laws of gravity and float in the air, all of the women in the audience would crowd round joyfully, but the men would deny it or, if that proved impossible, would disappear out the door! The anima represents the exact opposite of the masculine point of view; she has no interest in a clear-cut picture of the world and does her best to relate the man or even to bind him as firmly and invisibly as possible to all the objects in his environment. It is just for this reason that the East has represented the anima as "Maya, who creates illusion by her dancing." [25]

Since we live in a masculine-oriented civilization, it is primarily in the realm of Eros that both animus and anima find the vacuum which they are obliged to fill. The animus can be very helpful in a woman's career, showing his dual nature there as everywhere; but he is usually blindly destructive only in relationships where the woman *should* be functioning herself. The anima can also be very helpful to a man in his relationships if he will accept her challenge to enter this unknown realm. But if he quits the field—and there is little outer encouragement these days for him to remain—like the animus she will become more and more autonomous. If not checked she will then slowly advance from his feminine side into his masculine activities, invade his own principle, after which she can become increasingly demonic and can

[24] Cf. J. B. Rhine, *Extra-Sensory Perception* and *New Frontiers of the Mind.*
[25] Jung, *Aion*, par. 20.

possess the man entirely. Then he—like the woman who is animus-possessed—fails to notice that he has lost his humanity; he is capable of acting in a totally inhuman way and is probably largely unconscious of what he is doing. Unfortunately our age has produced so many examples of this in high places that the reader will be in no need of further illustrations.

But this pattern only occurs to an extreme degree when the conscious is unaware of the existence of its counterpart. Directly the counterpart is *seen*, the situation begins to change. Of course this is a long process. So much of one's life is lived unconsciously and automatically that it is a slow job to become aware of how much is involuntary, that is, how much is lived by one's inner counterpart and not by the conscious personality at all. But once we see and begin to take responsibility of our own outer life, to fill in our own vacuum, the inner counterpart is freed from the necessity of flowing into our outer life and can return to its own place, its own reality.

With this most desirable development, however, the difficulties are by no means at an end, although they will have greatly altered. Theoretically at any rate we have accomplished the Herculean task of cleaning our own Augean Stables of the invasion of inhuman elements, of opinions which are not our own, with which, when we realize them, we often find ourselves in total disagreement, and of feelings and moods which overcome us against our will. This is indeed such a Herculean task that Jung once remarked that the man or woman who had really accomplished the *Auseinandersetzung* with anima or animus could write "Master" after his name.

Theoretically (and I say theoretically because in empirical reality these dynamics always follow an *individual* course that differs in many details from the more general line described above) the individual has now succeeded in regaining, i.e., in making conscious, his human nature and responsibilities.

His Siamese twin has freed himself or been freed from the *outer* world and has returned to his own reality. Now the two have truly become the representatives of conscious and unconscious, two opposites in every sense of the word. If the work has been thorough they will not necessarily be hostile opposites, but each will still have great difficulty in understanding the other's point of view.

Now, as we shall see in *Dr. Jekyll and Mr. Hyde*, the conflict between the ego and the shadow is bound to end in a deadlock if the anima or animus is not discovered or does not reveal itself in time. The opposition between ego and anima or animus is therefore certain to get stuck in either a deadlock or, at best, a partial solution, if the totality is not rediscovered or does not reveal itself in time.

We must now return to the four functions, mentioned briefly above. The work of dealing with anima or animus in daily life has by now led us around Eden to the unknown ground outside the fourth gate, the gate opposite the one by which we left the Garden. For the area in our lives in which we leave the most vacuum is that area in which the fourth, or inferior, function could easily be effective but, since we are unable to use this function, it is almost imposible for us to prevent the vacuum.

A few banal illustrations will make this clearer.

Take a man, for example, who has a really good thinking function, with which he is able and eager to tackle all of the problems he encounters in his profession and who invests practically all of his interest and energy in these concerns. Such a man usually feels completely lost, however, when confronted with a hysterical wife, with problem children or with demanding social obligations. A feeling type, on the other hand, would take these latter problems in his stride, but would feel helpless and hopeless if obliged to solve any of the intellectual problems that are meat and drink to the thinker.

A sensation type, particularly if extraverted, rejoices in

facts. Concrete objects and day-by-day routines are easy for him and he can swing this side of daily life with masterly ease. His belongings, for instance, are always in order and can be found at any moment. But he tends to remain on that daily treadmill until it becomes a terribly lifeless grind; and then he will feel helpless and hopeless, for it is beyond his scope to see a way out. The intuitive, on the other hand, finds his way out of every situation he does not like with masterly ease. New possibilities swarm before his eyes and his only difficulty is in choosing which one to pursue. But to stay with one of these possibilities, to work at it day after day, to keep his possessions in order, his daily objects where he can find them, is agony for him and seems a dreary imprisonment when his wings could so easily carry him on to new possibilities and to change, ever change! The man who wrote the German doggerel:

Schön ist es auch anderswo
Und hier bin ich sowieso.

*What a joy to be elsewhere*
*For I am here anyway.*

was describing the typical intuitive type.

The way to the opposite gate inevitably leads through that part of life we have always shunned because we lack the ability or the necessary tools to deal with the problems we encounter there. By hard and unremitting work we can undoubtedly make a lot of progress in learning to deal with our inferior function, but we shall never really harness it to consciousness, as happens with the superior function which, in spite of its great use as a tool, tends in time to become thin and lifeless, of little more use than cardboard, to be blunt about it. The inferior function, on the other hand, is directly in touch with the unconscious and is largely in the hands of the representative of the latter. Of course it is very often used against us, and negatively, before the *Auseinandersetzung* with shadow or animus has insured a more positive aspect. Yet it can also reveal a wisdom or ability far beyond our conscious powers. We can all remember rare occasions in our lives when our own behavior, or something we said, came as a complete surprise to us. Our reaction may have been positive or it may have been negative, but we had the feeling that someone infinitely beyond us spoke or acted. We often indeed feel that something much greater than the anima or animus has intervened; we could even speak of something divine.

We come now to a term in Jungian psychology that I have so far only alluded to vaguely as the "totality." This is the *Self*,[26] a term which Jung uses in contradistinction to the *ego*[27] to indicate the greater personality which comprises both conscious and unconscious. In terms of our Paradise simile, one could say that while we were still in Eden—while we were still children—we unconsciously lived in harmony with the Self, obedient to it, as Adam and Eve were to God before they ate the apple, but that when we necessarily left that state of innocence behind, we developed an ego, a feeling of being a separate "I."[28] We must develop an ego or we cannot deal with life at all. We must learn that we are separate human beings, that each of us needs to establish himself in the outer world, to the best of his ability, or else we will just camp around the walls of Paradise without ever really being born into the world at all. It is only as an ego that we can follow one, two or three of the rivers into the surrounding countryside. But when the time comes to return to Eden, to find that fourth gate which was behind us all the time, we learn how much too narrow and circumscribed our ego is. Then we rediscover, with relief, that there is something beyond it.

[26] Cf. Jung, *Aion*, pars. 43-67.
[27] *Ibid.*, pars. 1-12.
[28] Cf. Jung, *Memories, Dreams, Reflections*, p. 32*ff*.

Jung has pointed out in many places that the central symbol of each of the great religions has been a symbol of the Self. It is Buddha for the Buddhist, Christ for the Christian, the Tao for the Taoist, and so on. A symbol is the best possible expression for something that lies beyond our comprehension, which cannot possibly be described. So the word "Self" is also a symbol for the unknown and unknowable. We can experience the Self but we cannot define it. It rescues us from our dilemma in dealing with the anima and animus; it knows the way back to the fourth gate; in fact, as far as one can express it, it *is* the fourth gate and the whole lost Paradise as well. It is individual, even unique, in that it is different in every life. All of the experience we had as egos outside the gates turns out to be part of its individuality. And yet it is also universal, for Paradise is no personal concern that we can keep for ourselves. It belongs to all mankind; it belongs to all of life, for animals and primitives, in a way, never leave it and bear its stamp of wholeness from birth to death.

The fact that Jung sees Christ as a symbol of the Self, rather than vice versa, often disturbs theologians and practicing Christians. But their point of view excludes all other symbols of the Self, such as Buddha in the East and the other great founders of religions. I have met with the objection, from Roman Catholics, that Jung has thus put up another great figure, the Self, side by side with Christ. Nothing could be further from the truth. I, for one, never think of the Self as a figure at all, although it is true that it sometimes appears personified in dreams. But such personifications are used by dreams as *images* or *symbols* for a truth that is really entirely beyond our three-dimensional comprehension.

Illustrations of such truths are all necessarily lame and inadequate, but, as I see it, the Self is much more like an invisible root from which great figures from time to time grow. One could liken Christ to a great tree that sprang from that root two thousand years ago. He was a perfect, and at the time complete, expression of that root. All the nations of the West have found shelter under the branches of that tree and have been able to develop their culture there. In the East Buddha was, as it were, a similar tree, protecting the nations of the East in exactly the same way. All the founders of religions, in varying degrees of size and influence, and indeed all the really great men who have had enduring influence on mankind have sprung from the same root.

All of these figures were great individuals in whom, consciously or unconsciously, the process of individuation developed and flourished. This process is really the hallmark of everything that grows from that root. It can also be observed in every human being who is honestly trying to find his lost wholeness; though naturally, instead of being great, visible, world-protecting trees like Christ or Buddha, such individuals are only small, even infinitesimal plants of the same basic structure.

Therefore it seems to me that we have a much better chance of reaching our maximum growth, of becoming the plant that, in the root, we were innately designed to be, if we try to concentrate on keeping our connection to this invisible, underlying root healthy and firm, than if we try to imitate the great tree of Christ, which strikes one as a hopeless task from the beginning. Nevertheless it is clear, of course, that we are still living in a culture that owes its best values to Christianity. As we all know, however, these values have never been in greater danger than they are now; but no outer enemy can destroy, or even see, our connection with the root of the Self. Therefore it would seem that mankind has the best chance for survival, and of retaining its values, if as many individuals as possible turn their attention to this basic root from which alone we can derive the whole individual pattern of our lives.

# 3 ROBERT LOUIS STEVENSON

THE PREVIOUS CHAPTERS have tried to show more or less theoretically that much of our present-day discontent is due to the fact that we have lost touch with the wholeness of our human nature, with its basic four-square roots. In this and the following chapters we will show how this can come about in an individual human life and will also try to point out the opportunities in such a life that could lead back to a *conscious* re-entry into the Garden of Eden.

It must be emphasized once again that the pattern is always individual. Although each pattern is made of the same general ingredients, the combination of ingredients is different, even unique, in every human being. Although in any one pattern we may point out opportunities that have been missed, in order to indicate some of the ways in which our lost wholeness may be looked for, this should not be done in a spirit of criticism, for we cannot judge the pattern of any human life or know how far the individual has fulfilled it. Death is also a goal and presumably a re-entry into Eden, but with death we come to a realm that is beyond our knowledge and comprehension. The Christian Church has always taught that a willingness to accept suffering and to carry one's cross, whatever it may be, is the best preparation for death. Psychology—although it uses different language—is fundamentally of the same opinion.

Robert Louis Stevenson (1850–1894), our first example, illustrates this particularly clearly. Carrying one's cross and carrying one's shadow is only a difference of words—as anyone who has really tried the latter can testify—and Stevenson himself tells us, in *Across the Plains*,[1] how much he suffered from a "strong sense of man's double being which must at times come in upon and overwhelm the mind of every living creature." He puts it more clearly in *The Strange Case of Dr. Jekyll and Mr. Hyde* where he writes that "man is not truly one, but truly two," and that these two are severed into "provinces of good and ill which divide and compound man's dual nature." [2]

It is questionable whether Stevenson realized that this is a problem which can only be solved in one's own individual psyche. He used to say that he had spent a "covenanting childhood," [3] and he was certainly brought up in a strict Presbyterian atmosphere: his father had a "clansman's loyalty to the Church of Scotland," [4] his mother was a minister's daughter and his nurse, in spite of her warm kindness, was by faith a grim Calvinist. Louis broke away from these beliefs when he was a young man and for a time called himself an atheist, but not before a lifelong conflict on the subject of sin and "man's dual nature" had taken possession of him.

Stevension died before modern psychology took up this problem and tried to find a solution for it. Janet, it is true, published his *L'Automatisme psychologique* in 1889, three years after *Dr. Jekyll and Mr. Hyde*, but five years before Stevenson's death. There seems to be no evidence, however, that Stevenson read it. But he had an extraordinary insight into the unconscious—far beyond that of his time—so one cannot doubt that, had he realized how much can be accomplished by analytic work on oneself, he would have been singularly gifted in this respect. As it was, the objective psyche was known to him under another name, although for many years he regarded its as something not identical with him-

[1] Chapter 8, "A Chapter on Dreams," pp. 315*ff*.
[2] The Medallion edition, p. 374.
[3] Balfour, *Life*, Vol. 1, p. 35.
[4] *Ibid.*, p. 22.

self but which could help him in his work. What we call the "unconscious" was "the Brownies" to Stevenson and, unlike most creative artists, he gave them full credit for their contributions to his writings. He even says that his Brownies "do one half my work for me while I am asleep, and in all human likelihood do the rest for me as well, when I am wide awake and fondly suppose I do it for myself." [5] He expresses the same thing differently in a letter to Craibe Angus of Glasgow: "I am still a 'slow study' and sit for a long while silent on my eggs. *Unconscious thought*, there is the only method: macerate your subject, let it boil slow, then take the lid off and look in—and there your stuff is—good or bad." [6]

We see here that Louis realized fully that his conscious side was only a part of him and that he knew the value of unconscious elements. These could have become very negative, as we see clearly in the "Chapter on Dreams" and in his letters; but, to a great extent, he succeeded in transforming the destructive into the creative. The Brownies are a modern version of the Cabiri, those creative dwarf gods of antiquity, which we meet again and again in various forms in mythology. Stevenson—although he admits his debt to them most generously—was inclined to take them much too lightly. One doubts whether he realized their full mythological background or anything like their latent power, when he wrote "A Chapter on Dreams," two years later than *Jekyll and Hyde*.

But before we follow the course of Stevenson's long struggle with the dual nature of man, we should briefly consider the "Eden" from which he eventually, albeit reluctantly, took his way out into the world. He was an only child, dogged by bad health from his second year, yet perhaps, as with the Brontës, too much stress has been laid on his childhood sufferings, for no one who reads *A Child's Garden of Verses*

[5] *Across the Plains*, p. 328.
[6] *The Letters of R. L. Stevenson*, Vol. II, p. 286.

attentively can doubt that childhood was nevertheless the golden age for Louis and that he had the very greatest difficulty in moving out into a one-sided, grown-up world. It is true that he was an only child and he may well have been lonely in Edinburgh, but he had fifty first cousins and he experienced many blissful long holidays with them at Colinton Manse, the house of his maternal grandfather. Most of the poems in *A Child's Garden of Verses* were written when Louis was over thirty, but they are "to all intents and purposes written by a child."[7] They are practically all in the first person and with an unrivaled understanding and love of the wholeness experienced at that age. Louis certainly belonged to the people who never really forget "Eden," though, like everyone else, he was forced to adapt to the far narrower horizon of life outside its walls.

So far we have referred mainly to the positive side of the Garden of Eden. The Garden had its own hair in the soup, however, in the image of the serpent who tempted Eve to disobey God, thereby leading to the expulsion of our "first parents" from Paradise. The Church has, for the most part, completely condemned the serpent and equated him with the Devil. But there have always been voices pointing out that it was the serpent that taught man the knowledge of good and evil; in other words, the serpent led man from a blissful ignorance and unconsciousness onto the paradoxical and difficult path that yet leads to greater consciousness. It has also frequently been pointed out that this was probably God's intention when he created the serpent. Stevenson's consciousness of the "dual nature of man," for example, is a direct result, as it were, of Adam and Eve eating the forbidden fruit of the tree of the knowledge of good and evil which led not only to recognizing the dual nature of man but also the dual nature of God.

After Adam and Eve leave paradise and are prevented from

[7] Browning, Introduction to the 1960 edition of *A Child's Garden of Verses.*

returning by the angel with the flaming sword, all the accounts deal with how they and their descendants fare in the outer world. For the most part they believe, rather against the evidence, in a God who demands only the virtue and innocence that Adam and Eve had before the fall, and thus once again they lose sight of that old serpent who guarded the tree of the knowledge of good *and* evil. So it is not surprising that the fourth gate, by which alone we can re-enter paradise, falls into the serpent's power so to speak, and obviously no one can refind his wholeness without fully realizing the "dual nature of man" and having it out with darkness and evil, which are most commonly symbolized in our Christian world by just the serpent.

This is by no means the case everywhere. I need only remind the reader that the serpent is the symbol of Aesculapius, the Greek god of healing, and that we still find this symbol widely used even in our own rational days. Moreover, in many religions the serpent occupies a most positive place, even representing the highest God, and is a frequent symbol of the union of opposites. Even in Christianity itself, a relatively unknown tradition uses the serpent as a symbol of Christ. And certainly below our Christian and Jewish heritage we come on a most paradoxical serpent which is a very apt symbol for all we have to face before we can refind our lost wholeness.

Louis, from his earliest youth, met the opposites of good and evil torn right apart, as indeed befitted the Victorian age in which he lived, and which is still a part of our Christian heritage. A family of lighthouse engineers, as the Stevensons were, would symbolically be dedicated to spreading the light and abolishing the dark. Robert Stevenson, Louis' grandfather, succeeded in building a lighthouse on the famous Bell Rock, a sandstone reef in the North Sea, which had been a constant menace to navigation on the East coast of Scotland. It was an amazing achievement at that time and we hear from Louis that "perfection was his (grandfather's) design." Perfection was also demanded of his thirteen children, and

Thomas, his youngest son, demanded it also of the delicate, sensitive Louis. Naturally he could not live up to such expectations, which filled him very early with a strong sense of the "dual nature of man."

Although *Jekyll and Hyde* is far the best known of his stories on this subject, it was by no means his first or his last. "Markheim" was one previous attempt and "The Travelling Companions" another. The latter was written some years before *Jekyll* and was refused by a publisher as "a work of genius but indecent." Stevenson burnt it after the publication of *Jekyll*, on the grounds that it had been supplanted by the latter and was just "not a work of genius."

Although *Jekyll and Hyde* brought him instant fame and was a great worldly success, Stevenson continued to be haunted by the subject. *The Master of Ballantrae* has the same theme, for example, in the form of two hostile brothers, the elder surpassing even Mr. Hyde in crime, cruelty and heartlessness. And, as we shall see, it was the same theme—dramatized in the unreconciled Archie Weir and Frank Innes—that brought about the stormy scene between the young lovers, the last words in the unfinished *Weir of Hermiston* that Louis was writing on the morning of his death.

After Stevenson had long been trying to find a "story . . . a body, a vehicle" for his "strong sense of man's double being," he tells us that *Jekyll and Hyde* was suggested by a dream. He "dreamed the scene at the window, and a scene afterwards split into two, in which Hyde, pursued for some crime, took the powder and underwent the change in the presence of his pursuers. All the rest was made awake and consciously, although I think I can trace in much of it the manner of my Brownies." [8]

When our totality is left behind us in the unconscious, it is the conscious ego only that takes this one-sided journey. It is in our dreams that we can look for the elements that compensate and enlarge our too narrow consciousness. This dream of Stevenson's not only gave him the outline of the

[8] *Across the Plains*, p. 330.

story for which he had been searching so long—a point he was swift to seize upon—but it also offered him an extraordinary insight into his own split and suffering psyche, if only he could have seen the connections. But we will first consider the story as Stevenson wrote it, keeping the dream in mind.

The reader will remember that Stevenson used the second part of his dream, the transformation of Mr. Hyde into Dr. Jekyll, as the main theme of his story. He made an exceedingly exciting tale of it, saving the fact that Jekyll and Hyde were one and the same person for the thrilling denouement at the end. But we are not concerned here with the story as a popular thriller but with the *facts* of the case.

The most fatal fact which was added to the dream by Stevenson or his Brownies in the "conscious waking state" is given at the beginning of the final chapter, "Henry Jekyll's Full Statement of the Case." Jekyll tells us there that he found it hard to reconcile "a certain impatient gaiety of disposition" with his "imperious desire to carry (his) head high, and wear a more than commonly grave countenance before the public." Therefore he concealed his pleasures and soon stood "committed to a profound duplicity of life," thus severing "those provinces of good and ill which divide and compound man's dual nature" with an even "deeper trench than in the majority of men." Jekyll says later:

"It was on the moral side, and in my own person, that I learned to recognize the thorough and primitive duality of man." [9]

Since his ambition forbade him even to countenance an "impatient gaiety of disposition"—which he says originally was his worst fault—he naturally soon drove the opposites much further apart than is normally the case. But he still realized that "even if I could rightly be said to be either, it was only because I was radically both." [10]

[9] *Jekyll and Hyde*, pp. 373-374.
[10] *Ibid.*

This is a very psychological statement indeed and Dr. Jekyll was near here to a realization of the paradox in every human life which could have led him (and perhaps thus also Stevenson) back towards his original wholeness. However, such a realization would be exceedingly painful and—this is the fatal point—Jekyll began "to dwell with pleasure, as a beloved daydream," on the possibility of escaping this suffering by separating his two natures into two separate identities. Then, he says, "the unjust might go his way, delivered from the aspirations and remorse of his more upright twin; and the just could walk steadfastly and securely on his upward path, doing the good things in which he found his pleasure, and no longer exposed to disgrace and penitence by the hands of this extraneous evil." [11]

It is quite clear that the fatal end of the story was the direct result of an *unwillingness to suffer*. The value of accepting suffering is one of the great contributions of the Christian religion and Louis certainly threw out the baby with the bathwater when he had Dr. Jekyll repudiate it entirely. Reading his life [12] and his letters,[13] one receives the impression that this was also a mistake of Stevenson himself. His nomadic life was, on one side, a legitimate search for health and, on the other, a constant flight from suffering and himself.

It is true that Jekyll admits he was "made to learn that the doom and burthen of our life is bound forever on man's shoulders, and when the attempt is made to cast it off, it but returns upon us with more unfamiliar and more awful pressure," [14] but unfortunately he learned this far too late to avert the complete catastrophe with which the book ends.

In the meantime, having discovered how to compose a powder that would turn the worthy Dr. Jekyll into the in-

[11] *Jekyll and Hyde*, pp. 374-375.

[12] Balfour, *The Life of R. L. Stevenson*; Furnas, *Voyage to Windward*.

[13] *The Letters of R. L. Stevenson*, edited by Sidney Colvin.

[14] *Jekyll and Hyde*, pp. 375-376.

famous Mr. Hyde, he was able for some time to enjoy the emergence into reality of his "beloved day-dream" and to pursue both his good and evil lives, with each life unchecked and undisturbed by its opposite. When he first looked at Hyde in the mirror, he was "conscious of no repugnance, rather of a leap of welcome. *This, too, was myself*. It seemed natural and human," yet "when I wore the semblance of Edward Hyde, none could come near me at first without a visible misgiving of the flesh. This, as I take it, was because all human beings, as we meet them, are commingled out of good and evil: and Edward Hyde, alone in the ranks of Mankind, was pure evil." [15]

Though exaggerated and dramatized, for reasons we shall consider later, this is perhaps one of the best descriptions in literature of a man meeting his shadow and recognizing him fully as his own: "This, too, was myself." Dr. Jekyll has an unparalleled opportunity here of taking the first step back toward the original wholeness of man. But this involves suffering, agony indeed, and it is the whole purpose of the experiment to escape any such suffering. So when he discovers that the drug will also change Hyde into Jekyll—in his dream this was the change Stevenson had seen—he merely rejoices in what he feels to be his complete security. He says: "I was the first that could thus plod in the public eye with a load of genial respectability, and in a moment, like a schoolboy, strip off these lendings and spring headlong into the sea of liberty. But for me, in my impenetrable mantle, the safety was complete. Think of it—I did not even exist!" When he drinks the draught: "Edward Hyde would pass away like the stain of breath upon a mirror; and there in his stead, quietly at home, trimming the midnight lamp in his study, a man who could afford to laugh at suspicion, would be Henry Jekyll." [16]

His original recognition when he first saw Hyde, "This, too, was myself," very soon begins to fade. As he indulges

[15] *Jekyll and Hyde*, p. 378, italics added.
[16] *Ibid*., p.. 380-81.

his Hyde side, his original "undignified" pleasures become "inherently malign and villainous," Hyde's every act and thought centered on self; drinking pleasure with bestial avidity from any degree of torture to another; relentless like a man of stone." At first Jekyll is somewhat "aghast" but he says that "the situation was apart from ordinary laws, and insidiously relaxed the grasp of conscience. It was Hyde, after all, and Hyde alone, that was guitly." What has become of his realization: "This, too, was myself"?

It is fear, not conscience, that puts an end to this fool's paradise. The change from Jekyll to Hyde, at first so difficult and painful to bring about, begins to happen involuntarily, even in sleep. The first time this happens, it seems like "the Babylonian finger on the wall." The "beloved day dream" is over and Jekyll feels that he must choose between his two personalities. He chooses Jekyll, though he admits with certain reservations that he is keeping Hyde's clothes and his house in Soho.

His search to escape suffering has thus led Jekyll far from his earlier realization "in his own person" of "the thorough and primitive duality of man." How could be believe that it was possible to choose *one* side of his nature and simply ignore the other? But he allows himself this illusion and says: "For two months, I led a life of such severity as I had never before attained to, and enjoyed the compensations of an approving conscience." [17] An approving conscience is the last luxury the harborer of Hyde could afford, and the latter takes his revenge, struggles for his freedom, and once more forces Henry Jekyll to drink the drug. The latter says: "My devil had been long caged, he came out roaring," and the same evening he brutally murders Sir Danvers Crewe for no better reason than impatience with his "civilities." The crime is observed by a maid servant and the murderer identified, so that Jekyll can now only take the form of Hyde at risk of being immediately arrested for murder.

For a moment Henry Jekyll is visited by remorse. He has

[17] *Jekyll and Hyde,* p. 386.

another chance of accepting his suffering but its acuteness is soon succeeded by a sense of joy: There is now no choice! The terrors of the scaffold buttress his resolve to remain Jekyll and once again he believes he can wipe out the past by the brightness of his virtues as the worthy doctor. Before very long he even begins to think that he is, after all, like his neighbors. "I smiled, comparing myself with other men, comparing my active goodwill with the lazy cruelty of their neglect." He thinks this thought while sitting in Regents Park on a sunny winter's day and immediately—without a second's delay—finds himself involuntarily turning into Edward Hyde. A hunted murderer, in the streets of London, he is unable to enter his own house to get the powders, because his "own servants would consign him to the gallows." "Where Jekyll perhaps might have succumbed, Hyde rose to the importance of the moment." He devises an ingenious way of getting his drug, a way which incidentally leads to the indirect murder of one of Dr. Jekyll's best friends, Dr. Lanyon, whose rationality is unable to stand the shock of seeing Hyde turn into Jekyll. From this time on, Jekyll is constantly turning into Hyde and has to live entirely in his laboratory, hidden from everyone. At last his supply of a certain salt gives out, and when finally the door is broken open it is only the self-destroyed body of Hyde that is found.

I have tried to point out those points at which the story might have developed differently and might have led towards wholeness instead of to catastrophe. Experience shows us again and again that the way in which a creative work develops has a strong effect on its creator. One sees this particularly clearly in "active imagination." [18] If someone is able to work out a problem in active imagination, it changes him and makes him more capable of meeting the problems of his

[18] Like active imagination, but with a different goal, creative work can also be related very closely to meditation. The reader will recall that in the quotation from the letter to Craibe Angus (see above, p. 40) Stevenson speaks of "unconscious thought" and describes a "slow study," very similar to meditation.

own individual life. If Jekyll therefore had profited by his extraordinarily deep insights, such as "If I could rightly be said to be either, it was only because I was radically both," it would undoubtedly have changed the whole course of the story and equally its effect on Stevenson himself.

The reader will remember that Jekyll was "made to learn that the doom and burthen of our life is bound forever on man's shoulders, and when the attempt is made to cast it off, it but returns upon us with more unfamiliar and more awful pressure." The same was true to a great extent in Stevenson's own life. We hear that he was never happy after his life at Hyeres, that is, about two years before he wrote *Jekyll and Hyde*. His health improved a lot in the South Seas, nevertheless one does not get an impression of peace or serenity but rather—till toward the end—of a man in tortured flight from himself. This might have been very different if he had treated Jekyll more seriously, and had perhaps found a solution to the problem of the dual nature of man. Once such a problem has been raised—and no one will deny that Stevenson did raise it—the question will automatically go on haunting the one who asks it.

To return to Stevenson's dream: The transformation which he saw and made the theme of his story was Hyde turning into Jekyll after drinking the powder. Now in the story it is Dr. Jekyll who makes and drinks the powders and thus turns into Hyde. At the end the powder will only work that way. What then did Stevenson (or his Brownies) do to this theme, "awake and consciously," as he calls it himself?

If we were to analyze the dream we would consider the facts often referred to in the story, that Hyde was a smaller man than Jekyll and that his principal characteristic was evil; the latter impressed Stevenson in the dream itself. Since the dreamer was no monster of iniquity—as Stevenson most certainly was not—we could safely assume that Jekyll more nearly represented his usual personality, as it appeared to himself and to his friends, and that Hyde represented a repressed and evil shadow that was yet so intimately connected with him that, in extremity, it could assume his shape.

A contemporary dream may make this clearer. A woman who was always overcautious and inclined to be law-abiding, but who had been working very hard for a great many years on the problem of her shadow, had the following dream: A *reckless and lively girl* (whom the dreamer knew well in the dream) *gets into serious trouble with the police*. A *very nice man* (who was engaged to the girl but who was also a great friend of the dreamer) *tells the dreamer that the only thing which can now save this girl is for the dreamer to swallow her! He shows the dreamer how to do this, and the apparently impossible task is accomplished*. The dreamer woke up with a strong feeling of anxiety as to whether or not she could possibly digest the girl. However, she fell asleep again and dreamed the same dream, but this time it continued and, to her surprise, she easily digested the girl without pain or discomfort.

The reckless girl was the polar opposite of the too cautious dreamer and gave her nearly as much trouble as Hyde gave Jekyll. But in contradistinction to the latter, the dreamer had tried for years to remain conscious of the fact that "this too is myself" and was able eventually to swallow—that is, to integrate—her shadow figure and thus to take a valuable step towards wholeness.

Now Stevenson's dream foreshadows a development along the same lines. The dreamer had seen the unruly, even criminal, shadow pursued and had recognized that the only way of escape was for the prototype of the ego—the worthy doctor—to become one with his reckless, even criminal, side. Hyde, "that thing of darkness," had shown Stevenson that he existed and that something must be done, and urgently, to bring together "the thorough and primitive duality of man." It must be Jekyll, the conscious personality, who integrates the shadow figure—as in the dream—and *not* vice versa. Otherwise the conscious becomes the slave of the autonomous shadow, as is so dramatically illustrated at the end of the story. It was probably not possible at that time for Stevenson to realize, as the woman dreamer did, that this was essentially his own problem, but he might have taken the situation very differently in the story he made of it. He took it far too lightly. He saw it merely as an opportunity to write a successful thriller in which he made no serious attempt to find a solution, although one feels he might have. As we shall see, however, before his death he realized his mistake, if not specifically, at least as a generality.

Another point in the dream that he failed to realize was that the transformation took place in public. In the story it is kept a complete secret. This certainly adds to the excitement of the tale but it is disastrous psychologically. The hush-hush politics of the witch is one of his or her most dangerous qualities, and if the secret in *Jekyll and Hyde* had been publicly known the disastrous escape from suffering would not have been possible. Here again Stevenson (or his Brownies) made a dangerous alteration. Yet in another point, Stevenson felt very much bound by his dream. He disliked the use of the powder as too material an agency, but he could not bring himself to change it, for it made such a strong impression on him in the dream. With his pixy-like appearance and his nomadic life, Stevenson was, till almost the end, the typical *puer aeternus* who skimmed the surface of life and hated to be drawn into any real or material situation. Therefore he naturally hated the powder "as too material an agency." But we see that when he was really impressed by a dream motif he was capable of taking it very seriously indeed. In "A Chapter on Dreams" he speaks of the help the Brownies gave in writing *Jekyll and Hyde*: "Will it be thought ungenerous, after I have been so liberally ladling out praise to my unseen collaborators, if I here toss them over, bound hand and foot, into the arena of the critics? For the business of the powders, which so many have censured, is, I am relieved to say, not mine at all but the Brownies." [19]

The tragedy of concealing the transformation is, from the

[19] *Across the Plains.*

psychological point of view, made clearer by another part of his dream, the "Incident at the Window." Mr. Utterson, friend and lawyer of Dr. Jekyll, is out for his usual Sunday walk with Mr. Richard Enfield, his distant kinsman, when the scene occurs. But it should first be pointed out that these two form another pair of opposites in the story, a far more human and less dramatic ego and shadow pair than Jekyll and Hyde, and thus much nearer to the man, Stevenson. Such extremes, as are depicted in Jekyll and Hyde, are entirely beyond our human limitations and enter the archetypal sphere. One could almost say that the infamous Hyde contains all of the qualities that have been left out of our image of God.

The Christian religion, in its conception of the God of Love, has depicted such a summit of the light side that this necessarily casts a correspondingly dark shadow. It may seem blasphemous to speak of Hyde as the image of the archetypal shadow of God in Stevenson's unconscious, yet it is not far from the truth. Nor is this concept very far from the idea of the opposites as they appear in the story of Eden. The serpent, the personification of evil, was even then God's opposite. It "was more subtile than any beast of the field which the Lord God had made" and it at once used that subtility *against* the avowed will of the Lord. And since God had "created man in his own image," Adam and Eve immediately came up against their own dual nature in the shape of the serpent who successfully tempted them to disobey the Lord's command.

Mr. Utterson and Mr. Enfield, however, have nothing archetypal about them. Mr. Utterson is the born observer who takes very little active part in life except through his profession and his friendships. He is "austere with himself" but has an unusual tolerance for everyone else. He used to say: "I let my brother go to the devil in his own way" and thus he was often "the last good influence in the lives of down-going men." Whatever they did "he never marked a shade of change in his demeanour." No one can understand the bond that unites him with Richard Enfield, a "well-known man about town." Their Sunday walks seem to outsiders singularly dull. They say nothing and "would hail with obvious relief the appearance of a friend. For all that, the two men put the greatest store by these excursions, counted them the chief jewel of each week, and not only set aside occasions of pleasure, but even resisted the calls of business, that they might enjoy them uninterrupted." [20] Stevenson, with his extraordinary knowledge of the dual nature of man, has described here two friends, each of whom finds the opposite half of himself in the other in an unsurpassable way.

It is these two men, then, who step into the court of Dr. Jekyll's house one Sunday afternoon and take part in the "incident at the window" which Stevenson dreamed. (It is when Jekyll's sufferings are at their height, when the involuntary change into Hyde can no longer be kept at bay and when he is secluded in his laboratory.) They find Dr. Jekyll sitting by an open window "taking the air with an infinite sadness of mien, like some disconsolate prisoner." Refusing to join their walk, Jekyll nevertheless evinces pleasure at the idea of a talk. "But the words were hardly uttered, before the smile was struck out of his face and succeeded by an expression of such abject terror and despair, as froze the very blood of the two gentlemen below." The window is instantly closed and the two friends leave the court: "They were both pale, and there was an answering horror in their eyes. 'God forgive us, God forgive us,' said Mr. Utterson." [21] And they both relapsed into silence. Stevenson's dream continued with the transformation of Mr. Hyde into Dr. Jekyll, so there is no question that he knew what was happening behind that window. Yet in the conscious waking state, he, or his Brownies, kept Mr. Utterson in ignorance till after

[20] *Jekyll and Hyde,* pp. 307-408.
[21] *Ibid.,* pp. 346-347.

the death of the Hyde-Jekyll figure. If Utterson had known the facts—with his extraordinary toleration for "down-going men"—again Stevenson could have ended his story very differently. Utterson begs Jekyll to tell him his secret on many occasions but is always refused.

The dream of the incident at the window gave Stevenson a glimpse of the original wholeness of man. There are four figures: Utterson and Enfield below, the dual figure of Jekyll-Hyde above. The opposites in the latter pair are larger than human; they are more an archetypal pair of opposites. The change, which the dreamer knew was taking place behind the window, was supernatural, and this characterizes the pair as non-human, archetypal symbols, images which man can apprehend but with which he can never identify without disaster.[22]

In such a dream the dreamer could only afford to recognize the human pair as his own personal responsibility. Interestingly enough, Mr. Enfield—the man about town—is exactly the kind of shadow that Jekyll describes at the beginning of his career. He says: "The worst of my faults was a certain impatient gaiety of disposition, such as has made the happiness of many, but such as I found it hard to reconcile with my imperious desire to carry my head high, and wear a more than commonly grave countenance before the public." [23] Yet Stevenson's dream offers an opportunity for reconciling these two figures, provided that Mr. Utterson, the image of the ego, retains his extraordinary tolerance for others and does not try to reject them for false and ambitious purposes. Yes, the dream even predicts success, for, although the friendship between this pair was incomprehensible to others, their meeting was to them "the chief jewel of each week."

But if we cannot accept the shadow in its human and

[22] Such identification is indeed indulged in far too often; the classical case in our times is that of Adolf Hitler. The illusion breaks up sooner or later and invariably ends in catastrophe.

[23] *Jekyll and Hyde*, p. 373.

bearable form, then we eliminate it and the result is a dangerous vacuum in our immediate neighborhood. If we leave something undone—in this case the attempt to reconcile ego and shadow—we create a vacuum which the unconscious must fill. It is like the pattern of Christ's parable in which the man casts out one devil, presumably his personal shadow with which he ought to come to terms, and then when the house is "swept and garnished"—that is, when a vacuum has been allowed in his most personal sphere—seven devils worse than the first take its place. This is just what happens in *Jekyll and Hyde*. The "impatient gaiety of disposition" is cast out—the house is left swept and garnished—and Mr. Hyde, prototype of the devil himself and quite equal to the seven devils in the parable, takes its place. Interestingly enough, Stevenson tells us himself that, as a boy or youth, he "essayed at divers times to bring up the devil, founding (his) incantations on no more abstruse a guide than Stult's *Juvenile Drama of Der Freischutz.*" [24] This may or may not have had an influence on the much later fact that when he failed to find a vehicle in which the problem "of man's double being" could be tackled, perhaps even solved, in possible human dimensions, the void was immediately filled by the devil himself, against which, constellated as it was, no human agency could possibly prevail.

There is another hole in *Jekyll and Hyde* which very much reduced the chances of a coming to terms between the polar opposites, and that is the absence of any important feminine figure. The struggle between ego and shadow—although it is the first manifestation of the opposites—can seldom or never be solved without the intervention of the following phase, the struggle between the human being and animus or anima, just as the latter can never be solved without the intervention of the Self. There is no anima figure in *Jekyll and Hyde*, except Mr. Hyde's purely negative landlady, "an ivory-faced and silver-haired old woman" with "an evil face" who showed

[24] Furnas, *op. cit.*, p. 32.

"a flash of odious joy" at the prospect of her master being in trouble with the police.[25] It is clear that such an aspect of the anima would be purely destructive and would contribute nothing to the solution of the problem.

*The Master of Ballantrae* was begun two years after the publication of *Jekyll.* I do not know how far Stevenson realized that its theme was again the duality in human nature. This time the conflict is between two brothers, but the theme is essentially the same: the just and unjust struggling for mastery or reconciliation. There are several elements that are more favorable to a solution than in *Jekyll and Hyde.* The brothers have more human dimensions and there is a far more positive anima figure who is equally involved with them both. But again there is no solution; the hatred of the two brothers continues till the grave.

The fact that the opposites fail to unite in Stevenson's many attempts to deal with the dual nature of man plays a comparatively small but fatal role in his last book, the unfinished *Weir of Hermiston,* on which he was still working the morning of his death. Many critics have thought that it would have been Stevenson's masterpiece, a book of another calibre than his earlier work, and he himself commented that it would "either be something different or I have failed."

At all events the book is of the most intense interest in any attempt to show Stevenson's effort to find his way back to the totality of man. Although in no sense an autobiography, Louis wrote that Archie Weir, its hero, was "the same kind of fool as myself." Furnas, in *Voyage to Windward,* maintains that: "Having so often written about himself, he was now writing himself. That is what so sharply distinguishes *Hermiston* from the 'autobiographical novel'—this is a matter not of self-explanation but of self-texture." [26]

As the book is much less well-known than *Jekyll and Hyde*

[25] *Jekyll and Hyde,* pp. 332-333.
[26] Furnas, p. 366.

a short outline will be useful here. Archie Weir is the only child (as was Stevenson himself) of very dissimilar parents. His father, Adam, a famous judge and Lord Advocate of Scotland, is usually known as the "Hanging Judge" and is more or less a self-made man. His wife is the last descendant of the "old riding Rutherfords of Hermiston," a wild Lowland clan, known for their reckless exploits abroad and their white-faced, trembling wives at home. Adam Weir fits well into this pattern, for Jean Rutherford is as "pious, anxious, tender, tearful and incompetent" as her long line of ancestresses, and he—though in a different field—has all the reckless bravery of her male ancestors. With such dissimilar characters, the marriage is not a success, for Jean was even more incompetent as a housekeeper than her ancestresses would have dared to be, and their Edinburgh house suffers from a succession of pious and incompetent cooks. At Hermiston, the elder Kirstie, a distant cousin of Jean but coming of a much more humble line of *bonnet lairds*, takes charge of everything most efficiently, adoring the "effete and tearful lady" and secretly hating Lord Hermiston. Archie is unconsciously but very consistently poisoned against his father by his pious and adoring mother and, by the time she dies—when Archie is about eight years old—she has made him firmly believe that his distinguished father is really "the chief of sinners."

Archie grows up with his father in Edinburgh, a very lonely and withdrawn child, living the usual routine of a boy of his class, first at school, then at college. He voluntarily chooses his father's profession, but "in emulation of Lord Glenalmond and not of Lord Hermiston himself." Lord Glenalmond, a very introverted judge who plays the role of the positive father to the lonely youth, is a friend of the very different Lord Hermiston and skillfully draws Archie's attention to the "sterling industry" and other good qualities of his father. But he does not succeed in dispelling Archie's hatred and distrust which breaks out in a public denunciation of the death penalty and of his father as a murderer after a just but cruel and gloating death sentence which Archie has witnessed in the law courts.

Just after this outburst Archie discovers from the family doctor that his father, in spite of all appearance, is really fond of him. He begins to be ashamed of his tirade. But Lord Hermiston has already heard of it and, in an interview in which Archie learns of his father's objectivity and justice for the first time, shows him that he is not fitted for the bar. Archie begs to be a soldier—a profession Stevenson himself was much drawn to—but they eventually agree that he will go instead to Hermiston, will take charge of the estate and learn to be a working laird. He will run Hermiston as it has never been run before.

Archie goes at once to Hermiston, on the Lowland moors, a place his mother taught him early in life to love. But since he naturally carries his introverted nature with him, he fails to make friends with the neighboring lairds and soon becomes known as "the recluse of Hermiston." In Edinburgh he had only been with men, although he had difficulty there in making friends; shut up alone at Hermiston he is brought in touch with women for the first time since his mother's death, thirteen years before.

His encounter with girls of his own class at a ball is spoiled by his conviction that all girls despise him. But we hear: "If he had but understood the figure he presented, and the impression he made on those tender hearts . . . it may be questioned whether his destiny might not even yet have been modified." Even Lady Flora, the local beauty, makes two shy approaches, but nothing can shake his illusion, even though he feels jealous of those who dance with her. She remains long in his thoughts.

The housekeeper at Hermiston, the older Kirstie, now over fifty but woman all through, rejoices in this opportunity to serve the young laird whom she has not seen since he was eleven. She feels the "loyalty of a clanswoman, the hero worship of a maiden aunt and the idolatry due to a god." She serves him royally and slowly accustoms him to long conversations when she brings in his supper tray. We hear that she has "no hope or thought beyond the present moment" and only longs for things to continue as they are forever. He learns the wild stories of the border clansmen from her, of his ancestors and her own, and she also introduces him to the supernatural that is always so close to the Scots with their "second sight." This contact with an older woman is probably exactly what Archie most needs at the time. Kirstie, in spite of her imperious temper and unforgiving feuds, is a fine woman, still beautiful, generous and able, by her undying devotion, to give him back his shattered belief in himself.

But naturally her hope that this state of things might continue forever is quite unreal and two events happen to change it. For one thing Kirstie's niece, the younger Kirstie, returns from Glasgow and the two young isolated people fall in love at first sight. This natural moorland attraction might well find a reasonable solution were it not for a second event. Two days after the beginning of their acquaintance, Frank Innes appears at Hermiston. Frank was at school and college with Archie; they are not exactly friends but Frank is the only one of Archie's Edinburgh companions who is mentioned at all. Frank is now in difficulties over money so he decides to get free board and lodging with his old companion who is too hospitable to refuse.

The heading of the chapter in which Frank is introduced is in the style of *Jekyll and Hyde:* "Enter Mephistopheles." At first Frank is more an empty-pated, extraverted rattle than in any way the equal of Faust's devil. Archie is an extreme introvert and totally unable either to understand or get on with Frank. The latter, bored with the country, resents Archie's need for solitude and liberty and takes his revenge by libeling his host to other people whenever he has a chance. Unsatisfactory as the relationship is, it would probably have been kept within reasonable bounds had not Frank—nearly a month after his arrival—discovered the younger Kirstie, become attracted by her and determined to do all he can to separate her from Archie.

The latter at first bitterly resents his interference and if he were strong enough he might still keep Frank in bounds. But he is, of course, inwardly very uncertain as to how his father will take such a marriage, for socially the Elliots are "below" the Weirs of Hermiston. So he listens to Frank's warnings and even believes that they are meant well! Unfortunately the older Kirstie, half madly jealous and half really afraid of the inequality of the match, chooses the same evening to warn Archie about his relationship with the girl.

Although Archie's feelings for the younger Kirstie are both genuine and instinctively natural, they are not strong enough to stand this double attack. The next day, on his usual date with the girl, he very unwisely plays the schoolmaster with her and repeats all the warnings he himself has received. He tells her their meetings must be drastically reduced or even stopped altogether. Young Kirstie—though she also fears Lord Hermiston—cannot understand Archie allowing other people to come between them and makes a stormy emotional scene. Archie is swept completely out of his depth and, after foundering in his own moral sermon, is at last moved to cry, "Kirstie! O, Kirstie woman!" "a ring of appeal in his voice, a clang of mere astonishment, that showed the schoolmaster was vanquished." I will quote the last paragraph of the book in full:

"Archie ran to her. He took the poor child in his arms, and she nestled to his breast as to a mother's, and clasped him in hands that were strong like vices. He felt her whole body shaken by the throes of distress, and had pity upon her beyond speech. Pity, and at the same time a bewildered fear of this explosive engine in his arms, whose works he did not understand, and yet had been tampering with. There arose from before him the curtains of boyhood, and he saw for the first time the ambiguous face of woman as she is. In vain he looked back over the interview; he saw not where he had offended. It seemed unprovoked, a wilful convulsion of brute nature . . ."

At this point, on the morning of his death, Stevenson broke off. During the evening of the third of December 1894, in the midst of the usual social family hour at sunset, the "convulsion of brute nature" struck at Louis himself, in the form of a sudden and totally unexpected cerebral hemorrhage. He just put his hands to his head, cried, "What's that? Do I look strange?" and died—without regaining consciousness—a few hours later.

We know from his stepdaughter, Mrs. Strong, how Stevenson consciously intended to finish the novel. Archie persists in his caution and Frank Innes manages to seduce the despairing younger Kirstie. The older Kirstie suspects Archie of being the father of the unborn child and when she reproaches him he learns for the first time what has happened. He assures young Kirstie that *now* he will really find the courage to marry her. Then he and Frank quarrel and the former kills the latter by "The Weaver's Stone." He is arrested and imprisoned, but the older Kirstie at last learns the truth from the younger and incites her nephews, the four famous Elliot Black Brothers, to rescue Archie from jail and to smuggle him to America with their young sister.

In Stevenson's own short "Introductory" there is plenty of evidence that this may indeed have been the plot of the end of the novel as he intended to write it, but we cannot be sure that he would have kept to his program, had he lived to finish it. Of all recent writers, Stevenson was probably the most aware of the unconscious—"his Brownies"—and in the case of one of his books had already had the experience of his characters coming to life, walking off and ending the book in their way, not his. So in attempting to evaluate the book, we shall be wiser in keeping for the most part to the passages written by Stevenson himself.

Although Stevenson's death was entirely unexpected and, thanks to the climate of the South Seas, he was apparently in much better health than for years, there is yet quite a lot of evidence in his letters and talks with his friends that he knew a great change was approaching. Whether or not he associated it with death is uncertain. His tubercular lungs had kept him near to death for many years and he had once told his mother that, after a certain age, it would be touch and go whether "the longevity of the Balfours [her family] or the low viability of the Stevensons would take possession." Only three years before his death, he remarked that he might live forever or "come to pieces like the one-horse shay at a moment's notice." [27]

Like all of us, Louis was probably quite uncertain if the change was to take place in life or death, but certainly he advanced immeasurably in self-knowledge towards the end. He wrote Sidney Colvin only two months before his death that, as a writer, his "was a very little dose of inspiration and a pretty little trick of style, long lost, improved by the most heroic industry . . . I am a fictitious article, and have long known it . . . I cannot take myself seriously as an artist, the limitations are so obvious." [28]

This is nothing less than heroic. Stevenson had become a well-known and popular author, surrounded by praise and flattery, supporting himself at last, at an expensive rate of living. But he was not misled, he faced the truth that his work to date was *not* altogether genuine and, as we have mentioned, he felt that his new book must "either be something different or I have failed." It takes the very greatest courage to face the fact that one was wrong and to start all over again, as Stevenson intended to do here. In my opinion, this marks him as a really great man, far greater than his writings.

In speaking of *Jekyll and Hyde*, I tried to point out that

[27] Furnas, p. 369.
[28] *Ibid*, p. 363f.

Stevenson did not take his characters and their problems seriously enough. We saw, for instance, how he tended to touch only on the superficial side of his dream in order to make it a "thriller," and that this involved a fatal determination *not* to suffer and to keep up the mystery. Although we have no evidence that Stevenson realized anything of this in particular, we do know in general that, two months before his death, he realized he had only "a pretty little trick of style" and that it was just such a trick that made *Jekyll and Hyde,* as it stands, rather a cheap tale. Stevenson was not far from the truth when he said that he had long known he was "a fictitious article." But his remark was redeemed, and indeed was no longer true, when he had the courage to face this realization and to see his own "obvious limitations."

There is a logion in which Christ, speaking of the man working on the Sabbath, said: "Man, if indeed thou knowest what thou doest, thou art blessed; but if thou knowest not, thou art cursed, and a transgressor of the law." [29] It is perhaps difficult for those who have not themselves experienced it to realize how "blessed" it is to face the truth about oneself and what a "cursed" state it is to cherish illusions. Stevenson here, in his own life, repudiated Dr. Jekyll's "cursed" wish to avoid suffering, for, taken seriously—and he certainly took it inexorably seriously—there could be no more painful suffering than is implied in his realization that he was "a fictitious article."

Friends are rare indeed who will help one to maintain such a realization. Most of our friends succumb to cheap consolations—"cheering the poor fellow up" or, worse, assuring him that he is "a great man," with a secret claim of being the "great man's" friend. But I do not think that Stevenson allowed himself to be misled. He showed himself quite determined to face inexorable reality; if he was to face it in life, then in work that would no longer be "fictitious," or,

[29] *The Apocryphal New Testament,* p. 33. (Codex Bezae on Luke VI, 4.)

if in death, then with all the genuine self knowledge he could attain.

Keeping this in mind, let us now examine the evidence provided by the unfinished *Weir of Hermiston.* We know that Stevenson more or less identified with Archie—"He was the same kind of fool"—so that we shall probably not be far wrong if we take Archie as more or less representing the author's *conscious* personality, the ego. The other characters would then personify his unconscious, that part of his psyche that happened to him, the figures that Stevenson himself predicted when he wrote in *Jekyll and Hyde:* ". . . man is not truly one, but truly two. I say two, because the state of my own knowledge does not pass beyond that point. Others will follow, others will outstrip me on the same lines; and I hazard the guess that man will be ultimately known for a mere polity of multifarious, incongruous, and independent denizens." [30] Stevenson stumbled on an important scientific discovery here. One understands that the man who was capable of such insight, years before his time, would feel himself to be "fictitious" when he only used them as the subject of a thriller.

After Archie the next most important figure in the book is his father, Lord Hermiston, the Hanging Judge. He is partly drawn from the famous Lord Braxton, but Furnas has already suggested that symbolically there was a connection between Lord Hermiston and Louis' own father, the very different but also formidable Thomas Stevenson.[31] Taken on Louis' own hypothesis that this figure would represent another denizen of his own psyche, one could suggest an image of the Father archetype which, originally constellated by his own father, was still such a power in Louis' psyche that it paralyzed his action. Although Lord Glenalmond agreeably modifies and mediates between Archie and this overwhelming father figure, he does not play a great enough role to counterbalance the overweight of Lord Hermiston.

[30] *Jekyll and Hyde,* p. 374.
[31] Furnas, *op. cit.,* p. 366.

Archie's mother, on the contrary, plays a very weak role. Except that she unfortunately succeeds in implanting in Archie a deep-seated distrust of his father, she fades away early in the story and is hardly mentioned again. This is in no sense autobiographical, for Louis' own mother outlived him, was indeed living with him in Samoa when he died. But she was a weak figure in comparison with his father, and the great feminine influence and support of Louis' childhood was "Cummie," his beloved nurse Alison Cunningham, who came when he was eighteen months old and looked after him faithfully and devotedly throughout his childhood and youth. He even thought of getting her out to Samoa.

The elder Kirstie is no more a portrait of Cummie than Lord Hermiston is of Thomas Stevenson, but again there is a symbolic connection. It was Cummie's devoted care and service that laid the foundation for the highly positive mother-anima figure of the elder Kirstie. But she has little influence on Lord Hermiston, and though, like Lord Glenalmond, she modifies this figure, there is no background of a related archetypal pair to help Archie in his own attempt to relate to the younger Kirstie.

Frank Innes would represent the personal shadow figure, not only for Archie but to quite an extent for Louis himself. He is almost exactly what Louis was not, extraverted, sociable, rattle-pated and later a disloyal friend and an intriguer. Such unpleasant characteristics are unfortunately also ingredients of the human being and cannot be disregarded or disowned by the whole human being. They belong to the personal realm and to the area where we can have it out with the dual nature of man. In fact Archie Weir and Frank Innes are a far clearer and more detailed example of the "truly two" in human dimensions, where it is still possible to take responsibility for them, than are the brothers in *The Master of Ballantrae*, or even than Utterson and Enfield in *Jekyll and Hyde*.

The Four Black Brothers, the Elliots, nephews of the older and brothers of the younger Kirstie, play a very small role in that part of the story which Stevenson completed. The older Kirstie tells Archie the heroic story of how they all rode out and revenged the murder of their father, and they form a family background for the younger Kirstie. Frank asks Archie whether it would be more possible for him to present the girl to his father "as the future lady of Hermiston" or to face the "Black Brothers" if he has any other intention. Otherwise we know only that Stevenson intended to change their hunt for revenge on Archie into rescue, when they learn that he is not the seducer of their sister and that he has already killed Frank, the real seducer.

Be this last as it may, it is very interesting that this quaternity, this symbol of wholeness, plays a role in the book and that Stevenson was extraordinarily right in his intention of using these four to rescue hero and heroine from the catastrophe which threatens them, for this can only be done by a symbol of the totality. It would amount to an intervention by the Self, an intervention that is possible after Archie has honestly faced the problem with the anima.

We must now turn to the younger Kirstie, the novel's anima figure *par excellence*. She is pretty, fresh, natural and young, genuinely in love with Archie but also very much aware that she has made an important conquest. She longs to marry him and play the role of the lady of the manor, but she would also have given herself to him without marriage rather than betray their love. If the two Kirsties could have understood each other, instead of sacrificing all chance of understanding to an old family quarrel, they might have functioned as an image of the Demeter-Persephone form of the mother-daughter archetype: the old and the young as two aspects of the one eternal feminine. It is the split in the anima, no less than in ego and shadow, that confronted Stevenson in the final episodes in his book. Such a split is over-dramatic and difficult indeed to solve. We know that Stevenson had never worked before at such a high pitch; not only his critics but he himself expressed uncertainty as to whether he could stay the course.

It is interesting that in a great deal of his correspondence, Stevenson tries to justify his intention of having Archie tried for the murder of Frank Innes by his own father and by the latter dying of having to pronounce the death sentence on his own son. He was assured more than once that legally this could not be justified, but he was unwilling to sacrifice the idea. Psychologically it looks as if the father complex in Stevenson was so strong that he could only conceive of Archie's successful break out of prison and his starting a new life with Kirstie in America if the father could die, as it were, in place of the son.

Be this as it may, we still have to consider why Stevenson was struck down just when he had left Archie with the young Kirstie in his arms, feeling as if she were an "explosive engine . . . whose works he did not understand, and yet had been tampering with." He saw "for the first time the ambiguous face of woman as she is," but he could not see where he had offended. "It seemed unprovoked, a wilful convulsion of brute nature."

Beyond quite unsubstantiated rumors, we know nothing of Stevenson's love life, particularly with his contemporaries. He got on very well with older women, had a great friendship with a Mrs. Sitwell, twelve years his senior, and married a woman who was ten years older than he was and already married with three children. As mentioned before, he remained devoted to his old nurse all his life. His marriage is difficult to decipher. His first official biographer, his cousin Graham Balfour, declared: "Of the marriage it need only be said that from the beginning to the end husband and wife were all in all to one another." [32] It should not be forgotten, however, that Stevenson's widow had taken the official biographical rights from Colvin and given them to Balfour and that she was still alive at the time! Many biographers went to the other extreme and portrayed Fannie as what we should call "an animus hound" or a "dread-

[32] *Life*, Vol. 1, p. 175.

naught of a woman." That Fannie had a highly developed animus is more or less proven by the fact that Louis sometimes began his letters: "My dear Dutchman," "My dear fellow" or "My dearest little man," although this does not prove much, as these are more the exceptions than the rule. Moreover he dedicated *Weir of Hermiston* to her, in terms of warmest praise and gratitude.

At all events their relationship had done little to familiarize Louis with the "explosive engine in his arms, whose works he did not understand" or with sheerly passionate "wilful convulsions of nature." All his life Louis had owned that he did not understand women. Now, for some reason which we cannot possibly know, an answer seems to be demanded of him. Apparently it was too much for him, further than he could go. So perhaps the "wilful convulsions of nature" took his life instead.

But looked at from the point of view of the efforts of a lifetime towards returning to the wholeness of man, to Eden, how far Stevenson had progressed since he wrote *Jekyll and Hyde* eight or nine years earlier! In the earlier novel the male opposites held the entire stage, the "explosive engine" —woman or the anima—was practically non-existent, and, from the point of view of returning to wholeness, the problem was handled far too lightly and ended in complete disaster.

But in *Weir*, his last testament so to speak, he has progressed—at all events inwardly—far beyond the "incomplete discoveries" of Dr. Jekyll, who only knew that "man is not truly one, but truly two," and has come to know far more of the "denizens," which even Dr. Jekyll recognized would be discovered later. Unfortunately the "truly two," the "continuously struggling polar twins," although they occupy much less space on stage, are still unreconciled. If we pause for a moment and think how different everything would have been had Archie succeeded in recognizing Frank as himself, we shall see how vital this reconciliation would have been. Archie, struggling to solve his problem with all his might, would have been far more capable of resolving it had he possessed Frank's easy handling of outer realities and his knowledge of women, for Frank, however negatively, did know enough to approach Kirstie successfully. Whenever the natural opposites split into the purely moral opposites, it is very difficult for a highly moral man—the "upright twin," such as Archie and Stevenson himself both were—to see that the "unjust twin" possesses much wisdom that he lacks. Christ knew this when he spoke of the children of darkness being wiser than the children of light, but the Church, on its way out into the world, as we have seen, left the fourth behind and labeled it evil, thus also leaving behind much of the original wholeness of Christ. In the one-sided manner of modern thinking, a man like Archie imagines, no less than Dr. Jekyll imagined so disastrously, that he can choose between the "just" and the "unjust" twins and live only the one he has chosen.

When someone discovers irrefutable evidence that certain qualities, hated and despised in someone else, are undeniably also his own, he usually assumes that this means he *is* just what he hates. If Archie, for instance, had recognized that Frank's ability to go to parties, to flirt with girls and to fritter away hours in doing so was latent in himself, he would probably have tried, with extreme reluctance and most unsuccessfully, to imitate Frank in these ways. But realizing that he has qualities of Frank does not abolish his being Archie, and all he can really do is say: "This, *too*, is myself." He can think of himself as the introverted recluse *and* the latent social extravert. He can "sit for a long while silent on" those "eggs" with the "unconscious thought" that Stevenson prized so highly, and when he takes "off the lid" he will find that the extreme qualities of both Archie and Frank have become relative, that they have approached each other in "simmering and boiling" and that an unexpected middle way between the two is beginning to form. With Archie's and Frank's qualities—good and bad—the problem would also have modified and might not have confronted Stevenson with a situation which seems literally to have killed him.

This unreconciled pair of opposites—ego and shadow, in Jungian psychology—represents the weakness that would probably have prevented Stevenson from finding a total solution, even if he had lived to finish the book. However, the whole cast of characters does come immeasurably nearer to a totality than in any of his earlier books. Above all, Stevenson certainly handles them in the "different" way he knows he must find or risk failure. Each problem is squarely faced in its own right, with the one fatal exception, and nothing is sacrificed, as in *Jekyll and Hyde*, in order to pile on the mystery and produce a thrilling tale. The whole story strikes one as genuine through and through, with no trace of the "fictitious article" which Louis had faced in himself and thus finally overcome. Moreover, in *Weir of Hermiston* Stevenson was confronted with that most difficult task for all men: having it out with the anima. It was extremely difficult for him to face this unknown factor before he had solved the problem of the personal shadow, and yet this problem needs the intervention of the anima if it is not to end in a deadlock between the opposites. We will postpone a further discussion of this difficulty until a later chapter.

I have no doubt that, with the tremendous effort which he made in writing *Weir of Hermiston* and above all with his acceptance of suffering as a result of facing the fact that his previous work had been "fictitious" and full of "obvious limitations," Stevenson penetrated deep into the untracked country which leads back to the fourth gate by which alone paradise can be re-entered. One feels fairly confident that had he lived he would have achieved more "different" genuine books which would slowly have led to a more or less conscious re-entry into his wholeness. But since death called him so early one can only say that apparently he was far better prepared for the great inevitable human change than he had ever been before in his life.

Robert Louis Stevenson is without doubt one of Edinburgh's great sons and has been hailed by posterity as such. But an unusual number of critics have attacked his fame, pointing out that his writings do not support it, though many of them make an exception of the comparatively little-known, unfinished *Weir of Hermiston*. Was it not in himself, in what he made of Robert Louis Stevenson, far more than in his literary production, that he was a genuinely great man?

If we take another simile for a human life and liken it to a voyage between the starting harbor of birth to the goal harbor of death, we have to admit that Stevenson was not given a very seaworthy craft for his voyage. Dogged by bad health from his second year to his last, he never knew when his vessel might founder and go down with all hands. But a good captain, capable of seeing all the weak points of his craft and yet able by sheer skill and endurance to weather every storm, can keep such a craft afloat and reach his goal against all probability. A well-nigh perfect ship, on the contrary, badly handled by its captain can go down on its maiden voyage as, for example, did the Titanic. Stevenson certainly belonged to the first class, and, though his ship went down at last as every human life inexorably does, who shall say that he had not reached his appointed goal?

# 4 ❧ MARY WEBB

MARY WEBB WAS another author who, in her last completed work, made an unmistakable although probably unconscious attempt to return to a condition of psychic totality. She was an exceptionally happy child, living literally in Eden—her beloved Shropshire—with a father whom she was able to deify, and agreeably surrounded by the other members of the family: her mother, and five brothers and sisters much younger than herself. In all of her descriptions of her early life, as well as those of her governess and life-long friend, Miss Lory, one gets a peculiar feeling of the Garden of Eden in the days when God—in Mary's case her adored father—still walked "in the garden in the cool of the day." [1]

Even though common human fate expelled her from her early paradise, Mary was undoubtedly one of those who never venture very far out into the world. "Her god was nature," one of her brothers declared after her death. When her beloved father died, when she was twenty-eight, nature, always vitally important to her, certainly took his place as counsellor and guide. Thomas Moult says: "Mary Webb's great certainty is that if we accept the avenue that takes us back to Nature we shall know 'the lovely ways that lead from our doors into the heart of enchantment' and if we can attain this 'sublime state' there shall be no more sorrow, no more pain and the tears shall be wiped from every eye." [2]

[1] Genesis 3:8.
[2] *Mary Webb*, p. 67.

Although she knew and sometimes expressed the value of suffering, it was her passion for cloudless happiness, it seems to me, that prevented Mary Webb from being able to give birth to an enduring symbol of wholeness, as she so nearly did in *Precious Bane*. Yet it was suffering that made Mary a creative writer. When she was twenty she contracted Graves' disease, that most depressing of all afflictions, from which she never fully recovered and which, complicated by pernicious anemia, brought about her death when she was forty-six. She began writing while she was still at home, as a reaction to the inaction enforced by Graves' disease. She seems to have written almost wholly from the unconscious. Her husband had to have a special fountain pen made for her to keep pace with the rapidity of her creative flow, and we hear that in her most characteristic writing she hardly ever corrected a word afterwards.[3]

Three years after her father's death Mary Meredith married a Mr. Webb, nephew of Matthew Webb, the first man to swim the Channel. The marriage seems to have been a happy one, but it had one great disadvantage for Mary. As her husband admitted after her death, it took her too much from Shropshire, the only soil she could root in. They kept a week-end cottage there, it is true, but neither Weston-super-Mare nor London, nor even Chester, agreed with Mary. She was very unreal, not to say irresponsible, about money. She often gave it away in a most reckless and unreasonable manner, so that not enough was left for the nourishing food so essential in Grave's disease; in a way she even starved herself to death.

*Precious Bane*, finished three years before her death, is generally recognized as her masterpiece. It is also most revealing, as was *Weir of Hermiston* in Stevenson's case, of the point Mary Webb reached in her attempt to re-enter Eden. She tried indeed to write another novel, *Armour Wherein He Trusted*, but after nearly two years' work it

[3] *Ibid.*, p. 111f.

was barely half done. She became so discouraged that she rang up Mr. Adcock, the editor of *The Bookman* and a great friend, to tell him that she had destroyed all there was of it.[4] Unknown to her, however, it had been rescued from the fire and was published after her death. But it in no way represents an advance over *Precious Bane,* rather a regression—a point we will return to later. In the same telephone conversation with Mr. Adcock she sobbed that she "would never write any more," which—though he, of course, did everything he could to reassure her—turned out to be almost literally true. Presumably she had unconsciously already written her "testament" in *Precious Bane.*

Mary Webb lived from 1881 to 1927, but the background of *Precious Bane* is placed a century earlier, in the Napoleonic Wars. The book is so well known that I will summarize the story in the fewest possible words.

Prudence Sarn, the heroine, is, according to her mother, "the best girl in the 'orld . . . very jimp and slender, with a long silky plait to the knees, and dark meltin' eyes and such pleasant ways, merry and mocking and pitiful,"[5] but she is cursed with a harelip, regarded in those days as the hallmark of a witch. Gideon, her ambitious, money-loving brother, uses this handicap to get her to swear to obey him in everything, and promises to buy her a cure. He proposes unremitting work for the purpose of making a large fortune out of Sarn, their ancestral farm, and then leaving it forever. Prue knows she is doing the wrong thing, and, when she makes the vow, she feels "as if Sarn Mere was flowing right over us" and shivers as if she has an ague. But Gideon can "make you feel as if you wanted what he wanted, though you didna'," so, as always, Prue gives in.

For some years Gideon works his sister like a slave on the farm. Then something happens which might have saved the situation: Gideon falls in love with Jancis, the daughter of

[4] *Ibid.*, p. 259f.
[5] *Precious Bane* (Sarn Edition), p. 159.

Beguildy, the local wizard. Prue tells us that Janis has "a very white skin, creamy white—and her face was dimpled and soft and just the right plumpness. Sh'd got a red smiling mouth, and when she smiled the dimples ran into each other. Times I could almost have strangled her for that smile."

Prue first sees Kester Woodseaves, the Weaver, at Jancis' "love spinning." [6] She falls in love with him at first sight but is afraid for him to see her on account of her harelip. But it soon becomes clear that Kester will not allow this to deter him. In spite of many ups and downs, everything seems set for a double wedding and for the establishment of an enduring symbol of the quaternity. Gideon's goal—the large fortune—is even realized, the result both of a phenomenal harvest and of the Corn Laws. Gideon and Jancis are to be married in a week and Kester and Prue in a year.

Then things go wrong. Jancis' father, the old wizard, sets fire to the ricks, and Gideon's fortune is burned up in a single night. Every bit of the humanity that his love for Jancis has given him is also burned out. He abandons Jancis and even kills his own mother because she can no longer work for her keep. When, nine months later, Jancis brings him their child, he rejects them both and Jancis drowns herself and the child in the Mere.

From now on Gideon is haunted, partly by the mother he has murdered, but even more by Jancis and her child, until, four months later, he follows them into the Mere. Prue is left alone on the farm that her ancestors had owned for centuries. But after one night there she decides to leave Sarn to its fate and "flee away as they did from the cities of the plain." [7] But she cannot leave the animals, so, since it is the day of the yearly fair at Sarn Mere, she takes her "flocks and herds" there to be sold.

Her harelip has always laid Prue open to the accusation

[6] A provincial custom: whenever a girl was engaged, the neighbor women gathered to do a day's spinning for the bride-to-be, for "love."
[7] *Precious Bane,* p. 275.

of being a witch. Now the villagers, partly puzzled and frightened and partly out of revenge, slowly reach the decision that the terrible happenings at Sarn have all been Prue's work. Ably worked up by Prue's enemies, the crowd shouts: "Hare-shotten, a witch. Three times a murderess . . . 'Suffer not a witch to live'." Prue finds herself tied to the ducking-stool and already in the water. At the last moment she is rescued by the Weaver. She then marries the Weaver and writes the story as an old woman at the bidding of the parson who knew "of the lies that were told" about her and wanted "the whole truth and nothing else." [8]

These are the bare bones of the story. The quaternity motif is very clear in the two pairs—Gideon and Jancis, the Weaver and Prue—clear as it was in "the incident at the window" in Stevenson's dream and book, and clearer than in *Weir of Hermiston* where it only appears for a moment in the theme of the Four Black Brothers who were planned to rescue the whole situation. The quaternity is most adequately represented by the symbol of the *marriage quaternio*, consisting of two pairs, one of which usually represents the real man and woman, the other the animus and anima in projected form, although sometimes both pairs are real. This is an age-old social pattern which one can trace back to the "cross-cousin marriage" of the primitives.[9] A man, for instance, must marry his "mother's brother's daughter and give his sister to his wife's brother," or whatever the tribe's endogamous arrangement is, to avoid incest between brother and sister and yet keep the tribe together. One also meets this pattern in alchemy, depicted as the marriage of the personified substances in the retort, the *mysterium coniunctionis*, and the alchemist and his *soror mystica* on earth. One of the best examples is to be found in Jung's

[8] *Ibid.*, p. 16.

[9] A full account of the cross-cousin marriage can be found in Layard, "The Incest Taboo and the Virgin Archetype." Cf also Jung, "Psychology of the Transference," in *Practice of Psychotherapy*, pars. 433ff.

paper on "The Psychology of Transference" [10] where a series of pictures from the *Rosarium Philosophorum* depicts the whole process. The opposites of male and female are thus united and the two marriages include the projected wholeness of man. Such a constellation appears clearly in *Precious Bane*, is almost achieved and then rejected, mainly because it would involve more acceptance of evil than Mary Webb could achieve.

Another book in which it is equally clear and where it also disappears for similar reasons is *Mansfield Park* by Jane Austen. Jane's books usually end with three marriages, of which at least one and usually two are vitally important. In *Pride and Prejudice* there is even a complete marriage quaternio in the double marriage of the four principal characters. But in *Mansfield Park*, although the whole stage is set for a double marriage, Edmund and Mary Crawford and Fanny and Henry Crawford, it breaks up and ends in the one very dull marriage between the cousins, Edmund and Fanny. The dual pairs are truly each other's opposites. They have already had a considerable influence on each other, leading in the direction of a real transformation, when, most unusual in the case of Jane Austen, she ends the book, as if caught against her better judgment, in a conventionally moral and, to me, very unsatisfactory way. I mention *Mansfield Park* merely as a parallel and not in order to draw any conclusions about Jane Austen herself.

Mary Webb also very nearly brought off a quaternity, in which the relationship between the two pairs could have resulted in the transformation of all four figures and in a firm symbol of the quaternity. But, as was the case in *Mansfield Park*, though very differently, Mary Webb yielded to the same temptation to shut out the dark and doubtful and to allow the *privatio boni* [11] philosophy of the Weaver

[10] In *Practice of Psychotherapy*, pars. 353-539.

[11] The *privatio boni* is a doctrine of the Roman Catholic Church, already in evidence with the Church Fathers, according to which all real substance is denied to evil and it is defined as the mere absence of good.

to triumph. The Weaver would never even speak of anything so dark as winter, but always referred to "summer sleeping."

One can see two levels clearly at work in *Precious Bane*. It is as if the Self were spinning the pattern of the process of individuation, attempting to lead Mary Webb back to Eden, to her totality. But our shortsighted conscious egos are always pulling threads out of this pattern and thus spoiling the design. This is all the more deadly because we do not always keep in mind the ego demand we are determined to satisfy. And we do not keep it in mind because of what Jung called "compartment psychology," a very widespread phenomenon. It is very much what Christ meant when He spoke of the right hand not knowing what the left hand is doing. As we shall see, Prue is perfectly aware, in one compartment, or in Christ's "left hand," that she is determined to marry the Weaver at all costs, but at other times in other compartments, or when she is using her "right hand," she regards it as absolutely impossible or even as something she would never do. The great danger of compartment psychology is that, during those times when we are unaware of our ego demand, we leave its accomplishment to the unconscious, which is usually far more efficient but utterly ruthless and inhuman. I will try to make this clearer as we study Mary Webb's novel.

But to understand the disasters that broke up the quaternity in *Precious Bane*, we must go into more detail. The Sarns have long been said to have "lightening in their blood," and "sullen as Sarn" is a countryside saying. At seven years Gideon has already declared: "And the devil shall have my soul." When his father dies, from sheer miserliness, he refuses to pay for a "sin eater"—an old custom still in force at that time—and takes his father's sins on his own shoulders, not from pity but on condition that his mother give him undisputed possession of the farm. Thus from the start Gideon identifies with the dark side.

Not so Prue, who, on the contrary, identifies with the light side from the beginning. The figure of Prue clearly carries the conscious ego of Mary Webb.[12] Her vision in the attic and her stall at Lullingford Market, if not much more in the book, were experiences of Mary's own. Prue is, moreover, the narrator of the story; we hear everything from her point of view, as we do from the author's. The shadow is not entirely carried by one figure, as it was in Stevenson's books, although the local sexton's daughter, Tivvy, whom Prue hates and rejects, is her true shadow *par excellence*. But Jancis, whose beauty makes her very jealous, and Felena, the shepherd's wife who is her rival for the Weaver's love, each carry other aspects of Prue's shadow.

We have already seen very clearly in *Jekyll and Hyde* how dangerous it is to identify with the white side. The issue in Stevenson's story is comparatively simple; the author separated good and evil to the best of his ability, producing the worthy doctor with his "imperious desire to carry his head high," and his inevitable double, the infamous Mr. Hyde. The simplicity of this representation of the opposites is largely the result of Stevenson's excluding the feminine principle entirely from his story. A man whose anima is quiescent will always see life much more simply that a woman who—one frequently hears from men—raises such unnecessary complications. Undoubtedly a woman often does; yet in her attitude to the opposite, she is hampered, in Stevenson's last written words, by "the ambiguous face of woman as she is." To man her reactions often seem "a wilful convulsion of brute nature."

Woman is nearer to nature than man, her whole being is more closely woven into it. Moreover, it is only in comparatively recent times that she has shared man's education and learned to differentiate herself at all from nature. And there she has been handicapped by the fact that the education she received has been for the most part masculine and therefore

[12] See above, p. 20.

not directly adapted to the needs of her nature, much more related to the dark side than that of man's. We see this already in our image of Eden. Left to himself Adam would probably have gone on indefinitely obeying God's command; it was Eve who opened negotiations with the serpent which represented the enemy of God in Jewish and Christian tradition, but more probably was really the first personification of God's own dark side. Therefore, we must expect a more complicated interrelation between good and evil in women's books than we have seen with Stevenson.

This is especially the case in *Precious Bane*. It is a wonderful example of how dangerous a charming girl can be who is quite sure of her own good motives. Although it is not often realized, it is very common to find quite destructive things in the unconscious of particularly positive girls and women. We find this theme in the age-old story of Tobit.[13] The girl, Sarah, is possessed by a devil who brings about the death of seven men, as, one after the other, they marry her and each is killed on his wedding night. Naturally her reputation in the neighborhood is exceedingly bad and Tobias, Tobit's son, is very unwilling to marry her and be added to her victims. Yet the Archangel Raphael says of this girl of ill repute: "The maid is wise, steadfast and exceedingly honourable." We cannot have a pronounced virtue without a corresponding vice, and, if we seriously intend to find our own totality, we must sooner or later deal with its opposite.

In spite of all Prue's undoubted virtues it is very dangerous for a Sarn, with the "lightening in his blood," to identify with the light side, and especially so for Prue with her harelip, still widely regarded as the devil's mark. Gideon, identified with the dark side, is clearly Prue's animus, the masculine figure in herself (and, ultimately, in Mary Webb) who is prepared to sacrifice everything for money and power. It is a constellation very like the one in the *Book of Tobit*

[13] Charles, *The Apocrypha and Pseudoepigrapha of the Old Testament*, Vol. 1, p. 174ff.

where the arch-demon Asmodeus is the polar opposite of the "exceedingly honourable" Sarah.

As Sarah was possessed by Asmodeus, so Prue, on the very evening of her father's funeral, allows her evil brother to possess her. Gideon, having obtained full possession of the farm through being his father's sin-eater, unfolds his wildly ambitious plans to his sister. He will make a fortune from the farm, then sell it and buy a gentleman's place where he can be "first among ten thousand." These plans alone would not have bought Prue, though a few words that she drops show her to be far more caught by them than she allows; but then Gideon plays a master stroke, one that is very typical of an ambitious, unscrupulous animus who just wants to possess the woman.

Like most country girls of her age, Prue is counting on getting married and having a babe, "grand and solemn" in a "rush cradle," as she expresses it. Gideon shatters these hopes with a single stroke by suddenly confronting her with the effect of her harelip on her chances of marriage. Until now Prue has bothered very little about it; she is used to the moans of her mother who keeps repeating, "Could I help it if the hare crossed my path?" But Prue had never really been conscious of what it meant to have the mark of the witch in those days until Gideon delivers his shattering stroke.

At first Prue's instincts react perfectly. She replies, "Not wed, Gideon? Ah, ah! I'll wed for sure." This turns out to be true, for the Weaver never thinks of her harelip as an obstacle. If *only* Prue could have stayed with her sound instinct she would not have deviated from the pattern the Self was weaving. The instincts are always on the side of totality and, if allowed to develop naturally, will surely lead us to the goal of individuation. But Prue makes the fatal mistake of believing what Gideon tells her; in other words, she allows a rational, typically animus opinion to win the day. He convinces her that she is inferior as a woman, that no man will accept her harelip. She is then lost, because a man and children are honestly and truly the one thing she wants of life, her purely feminine and legitimate goal. But once she accepts the opinion of her animus that this can only be achieved through him and his ambitious plans, it is no longer legitimate, for she wants to *force it*, whether it belongs to her pattern or not. She even gives herself wholly to Gideon's plans, although she is conscious that he can "make you feel as if you wanted what he wanted though you didna'." She never once wavers in wholeheartedly working with her whole strength for what Gideon wants until she learns that Gideon has murdered their mother, and even then she only threatens to leave him.

Gideon reinforces his position by making her swear an oath which is strangely reminiscent of the medieval witches' oaths to the devil:

> "I promise and vow to obey my brother, Gideon Sarn, and to hire myself out to him as a servant, for no money, until all that he wills be done. And I'll be as biddable as a prentice, a wife, and a dog. I swear it on the Holy Book. Amen."

Gideon swears in return to share all their gain with her and to buy her a cure at the end. Then Prue feels "as if Sarn Mere was flowing right over us, and I shivered as if I had an ague."

This is a wonderful description of how one feels when one deviates from the pattern of individuation, when one pulls out a thread, as it were, for an ego purpose. For this is what Prue has done here. Marriage may or may not be part of a woman's process of individuation; to live the pattern of her individuation she *must* accept whichever it is. But once Gideon has placed a doubt on the subject in Prue's mind, she is willing to go to any lengths to obtain what she wants. Her harelip *must* be cured so that she will be beautiful and marry. She even says later, "If I do well and go to heaven I shall be made all new, and I shall be lovely as a lily on the mere. And if I do ill and go to hell, I'll sell my soul a thousand times but I'll buy a beautiful face, and I shall be gladsome for that though I be damned." [14] Such an ego demand is the hook by which the negative animus, or even the Devil, can possess one.

It hurts Prue particularly that Gideon is only interested in making money from the farm, after which he intends to leave it. She is forbidden to be "house proud," something she would dearly love to be. There is one point in Gideon's cheese-paring tactics, however, that means a great deal to Prue. To save the expense of employing an accountant and scribe—the peasantry and farmers and most of the squires' ladies of England were illiterate in those days—she is to learn reading, writing and arithmetic from Beguildy, the old wizard and Jancis' father, paying him by working on his land as well as their own. Even the negative animus is not wholly negative, and Prue says it makes her "gladsome to be getting some education, it being like a big window opening."

We can see that, in spite of Prue's vow to her negative animus, the Self has by no means given her up or stopped weaving the pattern of the process of individuation. To be able to read, reckon and write represents an enormous gain in consciousness for an illiterate girl, and, as Emma Jung made so clear in her excellent study of the animus,[15] nothing is so helpful in overcoming animus possession as working with the conscious mind. Prue is quick to seize this point, for she thinks that writing will give her a hold over Gideon. "If he is too harsh with Mother or me, I could be a bit awkward about the writing."

The following years, however, she works like a slave for her vow, grows "lanky as a clothes prop," wearing only old sacks and clogs, until people call her "the barndoor savage of Sarn." But then she thinks of the beautiful house and lovely clothes they are to have, and this gives her fresh heart

[14] *Precious Bane*, p. 57.
[15] *Animus and Anima*, pp. 1-43.

to persevere. Still the time seems long and the work endless. So one evening Prue has the idea of bathing in Sarn Mere at the "troubling of the waters," with the curious ancient prayers which the Parson still keeps in an old book from the days when everyone believed that the waters of Sarn, like Bethesda,[16] could cure all ills. But Gideon, and even her mother, are dead set against such a public display and forbid her to do it. She runs to the attic and cries a long time.

The very idea of weakening her vow to Gideon and finding another way of dealing with her harelip, her feeling of inferiority as a woman, has its effect on Prue. While still in the attic that evening she has a vision, or rather an experience of the Self,[17] which, in her own words, "was a great miracle, and it changed my life; for when I was lost for something to turn to, I'd run to the attic and it was a core of sweetness in much bitter."

The experience is very beautifully described and Mary Webb admitted that it was her own. She had her "harelip" in the staring, protruding eyes that usually accompany severe cases of Graves' disease and which, in her case, never cleared up. I will not attempt to describe the experience except by quoting a few of Prue's own words: "A most powerful sweetness . . . as if some creature made all of light had come on a sudden from a great way off and nestled in my bosom. On all things came a fair and lovely look, as if a different air stood over them." Later she writes that it was as if the nuthatch had come to its own tree and found it "all to the nuthatch, and this was all to me." Above all, she herself likens it to love, which she has already detected in the singing of the many birds, as a "weaving of many threads with one master-thread of clear gold, a very comfortable thing to hear." And now she describes her experience as "a seed from the core of love." [18] The Self is manifesting here on the Eros side.

[16] St. John, 5:2.
[17] *Precious Bane,* p. 58ff.
[18] *Precious Bane,* p. 160.

Prue's own buried feminine principle is breaking through, and for a while it looks as though it will succeed in winning back the leading role and in driving out the animus and the goals of ambition and money to which Prue has been sold by her vow to Gideon.

In a way it does succeed. Prue never loses touch with this experience, which then gives a meaning to her life. Moreover it helps her to cultivate and hold firm to her positive qualities and prevents them from being destroyed by her vow to Gideon. But unfortunately it does not alter her firm adherence to her ego demand for marriage at all costs. If the experience were really "all" to her, as the nuthatch's tree is to it, then she could give herself wholly to it, to the Self's pattern, without pulling this one thread out of place. Nevertheless her experience not only provides an unforgettable experience for the conscious ego, but it also has an effect on the figures of the unconscious, for it is just after this that Gideon falls in love with Jancis. Realizations by, or enlightenments of, the conscious personality, always do have an effect on the figures of the unconscious, whether we know it or not. Prue's experience has even reached Gideon and, against his will, love has overcome him. He realizes at once that, Jancis being lazy and feckless, his love for her will endanger his whole ambitious plans. But his love is too strong for him, and for a long time he is wholesomely torn between the two urges.

At Jancis' "love spinning" yet another factor enters the scene. Prue sees Kester Woodseaves, the Weaver, for the first time and falls in love with him at first sight. Thus her love *for him* becomes "the one master thread of clear gold" for her. He is in every respect the opposite of Gideon; he is the purely positive side of the animus; so an immense step towards wholeness is taken when Prue becomes conscious of his existence and of her own love for him.

The shepherd's wife, Felena, also falls in love with the Weaver at first sight. Felena, who is compared to Mary Magdalene, is described as a woman willing to sleep with any man who attracts her. She is, as mentioned, an aspect of Prue's shadow, and she has a faith in her own attractions that would have been very helpful to Prue if the latter could have brought it into her own consciousness. On the whole, Felena is a good-natured woman who is helpful to Prue, but unfortunately a strong rivalry breaks out between them for the love of the Weaver. They play against each other in the game of "Costly Colours" and Prue, playing like a demon, wins against all expectations. During the game she has a vision that becomes a leading motif in her inner drama. It is a foreknowledge of the end of the book, when the Weaver passes by Felena, takes Prue up onto his horse and rides away with her from a crowd of people by Sarn Mere, till the sound of the people is "less than the hum of a midge." [19]

This vision leaves Prue with too narrow an idea of her love for the Weaver. Only he and she matter, everyone else seems "less than the hum of a midge." Though she really loves him, he becomes too much of a monomania for her, and all her conscious thoughts, as well as her largely unconscious demands, are consequently directed to that *one thread* in the pattern of her life. The larger design of the Self is therefore unable to break through, and this is why the one-sided goal of her ego alone succeeds. From this moment on—the moment of her vision and her first sight of the Weaver—the goal of her ego, marriage to the Weaver, is *the* thread. Joined to the thread of the longing for a beautiful face, these two are the threads in the whole wider design that are always pulled out of place.

Even though she wins the game of "Costly Colours" against Felena and knows that the Weaver is her chosen partner, she is still completely possessed by her *idée fixe*: Gideon's opinion that her harelip will be a fatal barrier with any man. So she hides from the Weaver and leaves the room whenever he is in it. This is a very fatal and dangerous course,

[19] *Precious Bane*, p. 107.

because it means that consciousness surrenders, so to speak, and leaves all the activity in the matter to the unconscious. Once again, and almost as fatally as in her vow to Gideon, she delivers her goal over into the hands of the other figures in her psyche. They begin at once to work on her ego longing. Old Beguildy, the local wizard, decides to invite young Camperdine, the Squire, to his house the very same evening, on the pretext of "raising the goddess Venus." He intends to raise his daughter, Jancis, through a trap door, with only her face veiled, and hopes that when the young Squire sees her without clothes he will be willing to pay handsomely for a night with her. But Jancis goes crying to Prue, telling her it will ruin her chances with Gideon should he ever hear that the young Squire has seen her naked body. Prue agrees to take her place, as she is well able to do, having a beautiful figure. When she is raised, with only her face veiled, she sees that not only the Squire but also the Weaver are in the room. Half deadly ashamed, half triumphant, she sees the desire she is kindling in the Weaver and asks herself: "Was it all of the flesh . . . or did my soul, that was twin to his, draw him and *wile him*, succor his heart and summon his love, even then?" [20]

This incident is a marvelous example of why people, and particularly women, tend to glance in only one compartment of their heart's desire, leaving the rest to the unconscious which, as we see here, is far more efficient in a girl like Prue than the conscious. The amazing subtlety of showing her beautiful naked body, only the face with its harelip veiled, within two or three days of first falling in love would conflict so incompatibly with Prue's traditional morality that only the unconscious could achieve such an end.

Nevertheless, from the point of view of individuation and establishing a totality, the very unconsciousness gives the story a fatal twist in the next few days. The Squire offers Beguildy a large sum of money for a night with "Venus,"

[20] *Precious Bane*, p. 116. Italics added.

whom they both believe to be Jancis. The old wizard gives his daughter the choice of accepting the Squire's offer or of being hired out as a servant for three years at the hiring fair. She comes crying to Prue and Gideon and implores the latter to marry her at once as her only escape. Gideon is very much in love, but he is highly suspicious of the Squire's passion for Jancis and also afraid of marrying her out of hand, "in the teeth of young Camperdine's longing after her." Jancis' eyes implore Prue to let her explain the whole Venus matter to Gideon, and indeed, although Jancis is bound to secrecy, there is a condition in their arrangement that in "utmost need" Gideon may be told. Prue refuses to allow her. It is "too much," and it might get round to Kester Woodseaves. So Gideon, left with his suspicions, decides against love and for his ambitious plans, and poor Jancis is doomed to three years slavery as a servant, hired at the hiring fair. Moreover, Gideon chooses a particularly unpleasant situation for Jancis, partly because the wages are higher, but mainly because it is a long way away and she will be beyond the reach of the young Squire.

Prue definitely breaks her word to Jancis here. She knows and has said more than once that it is "Gideon's hour of choice," so it certainly comes under the heading of "utmost need." Yet she refuses, partly, no doubt, as she says, for fear of the Weaver hearing about it, though she instinctively recognizes that he knows already and often reveals that she knows, though only in one compartment, it is true. Partly, however, it is undoubtedly also out of jealousy. As in her animus opinion she is debarred from marriage, she somewhere begrudges the state to Jancis, for she often admits how jealous she is of the latter's beauty. Moreover, the fact that she only sees it as Gideon's hour of choice is a projection. It is really Prue's hour of choice. To tell Gideon would be to further the Self's pattern of totality, the double marriage, whereas keeping silence, for fear of hurting herself with the Weaver, pulls the thread still further out of place and uses all of the energy of the union of the double opposites for the *one* marriage that matters above everything to the ego. Jealousy often distorts such a decision, because it robs the woman of any wish to help its object and makes any means seem fair to further one's own ends.

But there is another reason, also very characteristic of such situations. As Jancis is going too far away for Gideon to see her, he plans for Prue to write to her for him, and for the Weaver, who goes regularly to the place he has chosen for Jancis, to answer for her. Thus Prue is provided with an opportunity for writing regularly to the Weaver. Since neither Gideon nor Jancis can read or write, the letters soon become love letters between the two writers. Now of course Prue's conscious mind cannot know of this favorable result, for her, of Jancis being sent away. Yet the unconscious, in which time is so relative, does know such things in advance, as we experience again and again, and these letters—as in the matter of Venus—bring about a great advance in Prue's personal goal with the Weaver. When we examine such situations later, we can often see that we ourselves really brought about what seems to be a gift from the gods.

On the day of the hiring fair, Prue does take a great step forward, this time from the conscious side. By amazing foresight and the greatest presence of mind she saves the Weaver's life when he is attacked by a huge, fierce dog. She manages to keep out of sight until he is presumably unconscious; nevertheless he owes his life entirely to her, and she learns later that he heard everything she said to him.

This has quite a direct result on the unconscious, for when her mother hears what Prue did to save the Weaver, she realizes that Prue must be in love with him and, spinning day and night, she persuades Gideon to send for the Weaver to weave her yarn. Prue sticks to her *idée fixe* and goes off to the meadows for the day, but her mother praises Prue to the Weaver till he says: "Well, single I am, and single shall stay, I do believe. But if ever I did think of asking to wed, it 'ud be just such another as that'n." Her mother implores her that night: "Now dunna you hide from him, Prue. Be well plucked and risk all, like a good player in the game of Costly Colours."

Prue here gets the full support of the mother in herself, of the good earth, for Mrs. Sarn, though weak with Gideon, is a good mother to Prue who now has a wonderful chance here to return to her instinct as a woman and to trust herself to its sure guidance. Had she been able to take it, or rather to remain with it, she might yet have finally given up her ego demand and let the Self, rather than the ego, weave the pattern. Indeed, there seems to be every hope during the next two or three years that the pattern of totality will work its way through. All four are bound together by the regular letters in whch all four are concerned. This hopeful time even survives when Jancis breaks her contract and runs away, thus losing all her wages. Gideon forgives her and promises to marry her next harvest time. For Gideon to forgive the loss of three years' wages is sure proof that he really loves Jancis.

The harvet is phenomenally good that year. Gideon and Prue, through unremitting hard labor, have got practically all the farm ploughed and under grain. The Corn Laws have raised the price of corn to such an extent that Gideon has actually made the great fortune he coveted. And just before the "harvest love carriage" [21] for Gideon and Jancis' marriage, Prue at last meets the Weaver face to face. She tries to run away, it is true, even to jump into the Mere to avoid being seen, but he is near enough to prevent her. He thanks her for saving his life, discusses the letters and makes it quite clear that he loves her. Together they watch the dragonflies emerging from their shrouds, "ether's mon or ether's nid" as they were called at Sarn, for it was supposed that where the adder, or ether, lay hid in the grass, there above hovered the

[21] A custom similar to the "love spinning." The neighboring farmers gather the crops of the future bridegroom for "love," not money.

ether's mon (or dragonfly) as a warning.[22] Happy as the day is, it yet contains a fatal mistake—indeed a mistake made through the influence of the Weaver who is far too much on the positive side, just as Gideon is too far on the negative. The Weaver holds the fatal doctrine that if you think of sin rightly, it just isn't there,[23] and is so optimistic that he never speaks of winter, but of "summer sleeping," nor of caterpillars, but of "butterflies to be." So both he and Prue identify with the dragonflies, fly with them to heaven and forget all about the adder hidden in the grass. In short, they identify with an attitude which corresponds to the doctrine of the *privatio boni.*

But the adder is far from sleeping and takes the form of old Beguildy, the wizard. Prue has always underestimated evil, particularly in Beguildy, although she admits he has no heart. She always makes excuses for him. While thinking of him, however, she comes very near to a philosophy, strangely Eastern in character, that would save the whole situation if she could live it in actuality. She realizes, namely, that evil as well as good is part of God's design. She says, for example: "We are his mommets that made us. He takes us from the box, whiles, and saith: 'Dance now.' . . . Then he puts it back in the box. . . . The play is of His making. So the evil mommets do His will as well as the good, since they act the part set for them. How would it be if the play came to the hour when the villainous man must do evilly, and see! he is on his knee bones at his prayers. Then the play would be in very poor case." [24] But she could not carry it through and did land her story in "very poor case," as she forsees here so clearly. The very name of the book has this problem in it. "Bane," according to the Oxford Dictionary, means "a slayer or murderer, anything which causes ruin or destroys life." It is also a poisonous herb, widely distributed in the

[22] *Precious Bane,* p. 189.
[23] *Ibid.,* p. 213.
[24] *Ibid.,* p. 157f.

north temperate zone and found frequently in North England. Prue often refers to this plant and blames it for Gideon's mistakes, but I have not been able to find out if "Precious Bane" is a local way of referring to it or if Mary Webb herself supplied the adjective. At all events, the very title of the book indicates the value that lies in the dark, evil, destructive element. If only Mary Webb had been able to hold to this insight, the Self's pattern could have worked itself through, and the light and dark quaternity could have been established as an enduring symbol of the quaternity. But she was unable to hold to her own philosophy concerning the evil mommets.

In the meantime, the entire countryside comes to the "love carriage," and about fifty men successfully stack all of Gideon's wonderful corn. The Weaver comes too and tells Prue that he is going to London to study the colored weaving for ten months and will then return with a question for her. Prue knows that he definitely means marriage. Gideon and Jancis are to be married within a week. Everything seems set for a double marriage of the four principal figures.

Then a mistake is made, one of those mistakes into which we are lured by our unconsciousness, which seem at the time not to matter and yet in the long run are so fatal. We are constantly blind to such situations because we only see them in one compartment. At the feast with which the love carriage ends, the young Squire turns up again with his request for "Venus." Gideon is once again so suspicious that he insists on sleeping with Jancis *before* the wedding, so as to "make sure of what's mine" and to make sure that the young Squire has not slept with Jancis. Prue overhears his demand and knows that it is the Venus incident which has prompted it. Once again, and far more fatally this time, she holds her tongue, leaving Gideon to his fear that Jancis has yielded to the Squire.

Now the Weaver, who has promised Prue to come back for her in a year, has also told her that he knows she was

Venus. Although Mrs. Beguildy has lured the old wizard away, Prue knows that he always returns when least wanted. Yet she allows Gideon to go down to sleep with Jancis in the old wizard's very bed, dismissing it with the thought that "maybe it was no harm, for they would be wed so soon." She then withdraws with the moral reflection that she is overhearing a conversation not meant for her and that she cannot "abide an eavesdropper."

If Prue could only come out of her egotistical dreaming here and recognize the situation of Gideon and Jancis as well, she would never leave Gideon at this fatal hour with his illusion that Jancis was Venus. But unfortunately his and Jancis' affairs are no more important to her than the "hum of a midge," so his jealousy of the young Squire does not seem important to her. Yet it is her attitude that directly brings about the catastrophe which an unseen ego demand often releases, apparently as a bolt from the blue. Beguildy hears of the matter, returns, finds the pair in his bed. He has always hated the wedding, for he hopes to make more money in "nights with Venus." Now he has an excuse to wreak his vengeance on Gideon. He sets fire to all the ricks and in a single night everything that Gideon owns is destroyed. It is quite clear that Beguildy, although he has always hated Gideon, would never have dared to fire the ricks without the excuse of avenging his daughter, for at that time arson was still a capital offence, punishable with hanging. But with the excuse of "extreme provocation" concerning his daughter, he gets off with a very light sentence.

But the unseen adder—unseen because of the *privatio boni* attitude of the Weaver who does not believe in the absolute character of evil, and because of Prue's repeated omission in clearing up the Venus situation with Gideon—has disrupted the whole process of individuation and, to use alchemistic language, has broken the retort and scattered its contents. Gideon completely identifies Jancis with her father. He not only refuses to marry her but to see her at all. As Prue says,

"The milk of human kindness in my poor brother has been scorched up in the fire" and his face has become like "the face of one without hope, spent and foredone, a lost face." The only thing that rouses him is the thought of vengeance on Beguildy; Prue prevents such an encounter by telling him that Beguildy would be taken to prison and that he must not have murder on his soul. Gideon replies: "It would have eased me. It is all dammed up within. Choking, choking me. . . . I'll never mend of it now."

One cannot blame Prue for fearing such an encounter. Gideon, however, murders someone else; his remark that he "never mended" of the blow comes true. The animus regresses to a state far worse than at the beginning. Jancis, together with her mother, leaves their home, from which they are evicted, like a "dead maid," and goes to the small town, Silverton, where, without money or hope, she awaits her father's fate at the assizes. Nothing is left but Prue's real dream: she knows that the Weaver loves her and that her marriage with him will be the one thing saved from the burning.

The thread that has been pulled out of the design has indeed led Prue onto the path towards her heart's desire, but at the cost of the whole process of individuation. It is really worse, from the point of view of the totality, for the ego to succeed in its goal, for it will then seize the prize and do no more, whereas if it fails another effort may be made. But worse is to come, and Prue says that she can hardly write of that time of "grief and bitter woe." Gideon decides to start all over again with the work; Prue, still bound by her vow, is forced to help him. The old mother becomes more and more bedridden, and one of the most amazing things in the whole book is Prue's blindness to her brother's intention to rid himself of the burden of his mother's keep. But again she sees the situation in one compartment. Her mother begs her not to let Gideon come to see her, for he always makes her feel that she is a burden. The old woman even tells Prue that Gideon has no love for her and would be better pleased to have her dead and buried. This could hardly be clearer, yet Prue lets Gideon go to see her every evening and listens passively to his efforts to get her to say that she would sooner be dead than alive. The old mother holds out bravely for several months. Gideon finally wears her down, however, and at last she says wearily that maybe she would sooner be dead than alive. Having attained his object, Gideon ceases visiting his mother and Prue records only that this is a great relief to the old woman. Moreover she knows her brother will do anything for money; he constantly complains to her of the expenses of getting "the doctor's man" and of the food they have to give Sexton's Tivvy to get her to look after their mother while they are both in the fields.

Now Tivvy is Prue's blackest shadow. She is a miserable creature, everything that Prue in consciousness is not. She is lazy, deceitful, untruthful and above all abysmally stupid. Yet Prue quietly leaves her mother to Tivvy's tender mercies, though she knows very well that Tivvy only comes to further her own plot to marry Gideon. She hates and despises Tivvy, but she is nevertheless quite willing to make use of her.

Now Prue is really fond of her mother and consistently kind to her. Why then is she so blind to Gideon's intentions? When he poisons her with foxglove tea, Tivvy knows it. Prue has even heard Gideon talking to "the doctor's man" about the effect of foxglove tea, but she has no suspicions whatever, even when the doctor makes it clear that he believes her mother has been poisoned. She just thinks that he is "a peculiar man."

Prue certainly has no conscious wish to kill her mother, but she is so wrapped up in her own desire to marry the Weaver that everything that goes on around her is less to her than the "hum of a midge." She even tells us that when Tivvy comes running to tell her that Mrs. Sarn is dying, she is lost in thinking about the Weaver's promise to return. Tivvy tells her it was the tea but Prue fails again to register what Tivvy is saying, although her ears hear it and she records it quite naively. Such side effects are only too common when all energy and attention are taken up with the attainment of the one goal which is important to the ego. Prue is only indirectly responsible for the death of her mother. Yet, in one compartment, she recognizes her responsibility, for when Tivvy admits quite brazenly that she is using the murder of his mother to blackmail Gideon into marrying her, Prue is not surprised and realizes at once that it is true. In this case the consciousness of what is happening drops into the unconscious and is picked up by the shadow, Tivvy, to use for her own ends. As Dr. Jung once remarked in a seminar, when we leave things to the shadow they get done, but they are done against us instead of for us. Prue's painful knowledge is left to the shadow who almost destroys her, and does destroy everything else as a result.

Just as the goal can be furthered by leaving it to the unconscious—as we saw when Prue appeared before the Weaver as Venus and, as he tells her himself, lights a fire in him which will be very hard to put out,[25]—so it also can lead to the reverse. Killing the mother is killing the creative, the one who bears the seed; and Prue, like Mary Webb herself, has no children.

A single passionate desire, such as Prue has for the Weaver, can be and often is satisfied by such methods, but not only does such a success break up the process of individuation, it also kills the creative seeds. Prue's original longing was for a child, but such a creative solution cannot be achieved by such means. This is seen very clearly in our story in Prue's abysmally unconscious inability to prevent the murder of her mother, and thus allows her feminine creativity to be destroyed.

A month or two later another tragedy takes place at Sarn. Jancis brings to Gideon the child she has borne him and risks everything in an attempt to awaken his paternal feeling and

[25] *Precious Bane*, p. 241.

reawaken his love for her. Gideon repulses her cruelly and mocks at his son who is indeed a weakly half-starved creature. Tivvy, terrified that Jancis might yet succeed and herself pregnant by Gideon, tells Prue that she is going to denounce him for the murder of his mother. Understandably horrified, Prue loses sight of Jancis and the child, and Jancis drowns herself and the child in the Mere. Thus the last weak creative seed is lost, and another mother is allowed to die through Prue's unconsciousness.

Prue never sees her own contribution to these disasters; they seem to her to be bolts from the blue. Such unawareness is another characteristic of these mainly unconscious goals that use the forces of the unconscious for *personal* ends. The ego is blind and unconscious, it would never commit murder itself, yet it allows murder to take place under its very nose when a little more consciousness could have prevented it.

The ghosts of his mother and of Jancis begin to haunt Gideon, and before many months have passed he follows Jancis into the Mere. Prue's failure to register the danger signals is, in this instance, even clearer than ever. Gideon speaks more and more of Jancis' ghost, even telling Prue that it has beckoned to him from the boat on the Mere. One evening, when he is more than usually haunted, he goes out to see to the stock, telling Prue not to wait up for him if he is late. Something tells Prue to follow him, but she decides it is "too queer" to do so. Instead she searches in Beguildy's book and in the Bible to see if there is any cure for such bewitchments. While she is reading, two children come running to tell her that Gideon has gone into the Mere. She runs fast enough, but it is too late. Gideon's body is never found, for he plunged into the deepest part of the Mere, from which, we are told, no body is ever recovered.

The most important characters that represented the figures of Mary Webb's own psyche [26] have thus vanished into the Beyond, and only the conscious ego remains. Such a condi-

[26] See p. 20 above.

tion presents a complete break-up of the process of individuation, but the process might yet be retrieved if it were possible for the ego to remain with the ruins and suffer the anguish of what has happened, particularly the pain from recognizing its own guilt. Such tragic crises do occur, at least once, in most deep analyses that involve the whole personality. It is possible, however, to pick up the broken pieces and begin all over again, as the alchemists did when their retorts blew up or broke. One also sees such a development in *Wuthering Heights*; although everything is blown sky-high by the death of the elder Catherine, the broken pieces are gathered together again and brought to a satisfactory conclusion in the younger Cathy.

Mary Webb was not made of the same courageous substance as Emily Brontë, although there are points of similarity in their fate. So, faced with complete disaster, Mary's Prue gives up the fight. Sarn now belongs to her but she immediately decides to leave. Since she knows that she will find no purchaser after what has happened there, she decides to leave the old ancestral home to ruin and its ghosts and the land to return to nature, "not for any fault in the place," she says, "but for what Gideon had made of it." Gideon is blamed for everything, so Prue experiences nothing of the "enrichment" or "new spiritual dignity" which finding her own guilt would have provided, as Dr. Jung put it in "After the Catastrophe." [27] Prue simply walks out on everything. It is only too easy for us to do the same when the disasterous consequences of our too unconscious goals become manifest, but the initial suffering of recognizing our own part in such guilt is as nothing compared with the slow disintegration of the whole process of individuation and the loss of the meaning of our life.

But Prue retains enough humanity to look after the animals, realizing that they cannot be left on the farm which she is leaving to its fate. The next day is Sarn Fair, the day

[27] In *Civilization in Transition*, pars. 400-443.

that Kester has promised to be back. Although she tells us this specifically, it now suits her to say that he has forgotten her; indeed, why should he remember a "hare-shotten woman, in danger of being accused of witchcraft." [28] No, she says, he will have taken up with another woman by now. She even maligns him by saying that it will be a woman he has written of most disparagingly. This is also characteristic of compartment psychology: one convinces oneself that the goal one only knows in one compartment is completely unobtainable, even losing trust in the person one loves. If Prue had said to herself, "It is today he promised to come," it might have struck her that it was very convenient, to say the least, that her vow to Gideon—the great obstacle to her marriage—had been cancelled just in time by his death. And once she had realized her own advantage, the way would have been open to seeing her own guilt. But by choosing to say that the Weaver had "forgotten her," she can still see herself as Gideon's innocent victim.

But to doubt the word of the man she loved was perhaps the worst of all Prue's sins, for it was undeniably conscious and she knew what she was doing. The results of her unconsciousness are at least not deliberate and are so far from consciousness that it would have needed unusual self criticism, I admit, to see them. But if she had now said to herself, "The Weaver promised to come today," she would have had to see that she must wait quietly at home for him and do nothing irrevocable till he comes. But this course does not recommend itself to her, because she is still unconsciously influenced by the vision she had when she first saw him: she would go only with the Weaver, throwing off all of her past life, so that it would be less than "the hum of a midge." So she chooses to burn her boats. She decides to take all of the animals to the fair and sell them.

But her failure to see that her own unconsciousness is largely responsible for everything that has happened comes

[28] *Precious Bane,* p. 277.

back to her at the fair *from outside*, as those things always do if our eyes are open to see the connections. At the fair she is denounced as a witch. The actual outer accusations are all false, or grossly exaggerated; she has done none of the things she is accused of, at least she has not consciously done them. But, as we have seen, her unconsciousness has offered her enemies hooks on which to hang their accusations. The worst of these comes from Tivvy, Prue's blackest, most completely rejected shadow. Prue had boxed her ears and declared that she hated her, on the occasion of Jancis' return with the baby. Now Tivvy revenges herself by accusing Prue of having murdered her mother and prevented her marriage to Gideon out of sheer jealousy, and declares that Gideon "loved her right well." This turns the scale. Prue finds herself in the water, tied to the ducking stool. She is to be drowned as a witch. Her unconsciousness of her own dark side has pinned her down. She is within minutes of paying with her life, when the Weaver, true to his word, appears and saves her.

Mary Webb was unable to bring the two opposites as close together as Stevenson did. Already in *Jekyll and Hyde*, Stevenson realized that "these polar twins" in our nature *must* "be continuously struggling," that this "doom and burthen of our life is bound forever on man's shoulders, and when the attempt is made to cast it off, it but returns to us with more unfamiliar and more awful pressure." Prue does not realize this, so she has to suffer the fate of the witch and be bound to the ducking stool, even to know the crowd really intends to drown her.

It is true that an enantiodromia takes place. When Prue is rescued from her terrible predicament by the Weaver, the dark opposite is replaced by the light; this, until some effort is made to unite the opposites, is the eternal law of nature. As the night is replaced by the day and the day by the night, so as long as we are unconscious our lives will always obey the law of enantiodromia, swinging from one opposite to the other.

Prue begins by allowing herself to be completely possessed by the negative animus, going so far as making a conscious vow. She ends by marrying the positive animus, the Weaver. It is an advance, a great advance, but all of the negative side has disappeared into the unconscious, and in the worst possible way—by self-destruction. The Weaver denies its very existence: he maintains that if you think of sin rightly, "it just wunna there."

In mythology weaving is above all a feminine activity and is in the hands of female goddesses (above all, the three fates, the Parcae) or far-famed women (Penelope). Weaving symbolizes creative Eros, making meaningful connections between separated people or things—in short, the feminine principle of Eros or relatedness. In Mary Webb's story, however, weaving remains in the hands of Kester Woodseaves, that is, in the hands of the animus. Gideon represents egoism, ambition, inordinate love of money and is therefore, as we saw, purely destructive. But Kester is the polar opposite; he opposes all cruelty and destruction, and even learns the "colored weaving," a novelty in those days—in other words, he is purely creative. Perhaps this was the net result, so to speak, of Mary Webb's own life. She escaped from the negative destructive animus, which was necessarily present as the shadow of her own truly kind and positive father, and won through for many years by using all of her energy creatively in her work—for some of her earlier work and, above all, *Precious Bane*, are truly creative achievements, and this is a step, perhaps the most important step, in a woman's individuation. Like Moses, however, she seems to have viewed the promised land, but not to have been fated to enter it.

To return to our simile of paradise, the only gate by which it seems possible to re-enter paradise is the one opposite to and behind the one through which we left. Mary Webb undoubtedly left by a way that led to unusual virtues. We know this from many facts in her own biography but most particularly from the character of Prue in *Precious Bane*. Prue is a girl of sterling character and charm, yet she carries "the devil's mark." Moreover, as the story develops, it becomes more and more clear that she can only reach her totality—symbolized by the two pairs: Gideon and Jancis, the Weaver and Prue—by accepting both sets of opposites completely and by reconnecting with Eden through the dark region of Gideon's unusual vices.

As we have seen, Mary Webb went a long way towards realizing this. She saw that God's play needed evil mommets as well as good, and that it would be "in very poor case" without them. But she could not quite hold to her own realization and allow her "evil momments" to have their share in the ending of her novel. At the last moment she went back, as it were, to the gate through which she had come out, to the virtues which even denied the existence of the evil she had so nearly accepted: if you thought about sin rightly it was just not there. We do not yet know enough about Mary Webb's life to know whether she came anywhere near realizing this. Two short biographies were written within five years of her death.[29] Everyone close to her was still alive and not enough time had elapsed to give the necessary perspective. But one can gather that the three years she lived after publishing *Precious Bane* were not happy years for her, for they were a time when she could not write, when she became more and more sleepless and when the terrible depression of Graves' disease reasserted its power. Her health failed more and more, although, like Emily Brontë, she refused to recognize this fact until it was too late.

Although it can be no more than a tentative hypothesis, one wonders whether she herself was not consciously or unconsciously disappointed and dissatisfied with the outcome of *Precious Bane*. Probably not outwardly, for though many of the reviews disappointed her, the book was awarded the yearly prize of the "Femina Vie Heureuse" Committee, and Prime Minister Baldwin's appreciative letter of January 14th, 1927, pleased her enormously. The depression that overtook

[29] Addison, *Mary Webb*; Moult, *Mary Webb, Her Life and Work*.

her more probably came from within. In *Precious Bane* she had been very close to finding her way back to the totality; she had seen that the play of life would be "in very poor case" without the evil mommets who "do His will as well as the good," and she had four good and evil mommets at the point of a marriage *quaternio*, an enduring symbol of the totality. But her task then apparently proved too much for her. She reverted to traditional morality, allowed the two evil mommets to destroy themselves and ended with the one marriage of the two good mommets. She attempted indeed to give the book a fairy tale lived-happily-ever-after end, but it is not very convincing. Prue speaks with adoration of her Weaver, it is true, but the few places in the story when she speaks of their long marriage do not sound very full or complete. Apparently there were no children, and Prue mentions the optimism of her husband more as if it were a pleasant quality of his than if she really shared it. Furthermore, speaking of writing her book, she says: "I sit here by the fire with my Bible to hand, a very old woman and a tired woman, with a task to do before she says good night to the world."

If I am right that Mary Webb was unable to stand up to her amazing realization of the place of evil in the pattern of the world, it would explain the curious fact that her last and unfinished book, *Armour Wherein He Trusted*, was placed right back in the time of the Crusades. She would have been forced to go back to an era when the ending of *Precious Bane* would have been the only right and fitting solution, a time when good still had to be differentiated from evil, and when this was so vital that Crusades were fought for it. But we cannot return to an earlier age; we must remain in our own, however dark and hopeless it seems to us. So it is not surprising that Mary Webb fell into despair while she was writing her final book.

We cannot tell how far she had fulfilled her appointed pattern, but it certainly looks as if life had disappointed her in the end. In the last three years after finishing *Precious*

*Bane*, she was unable to write as before, and she became more and more depressed and ill. The fact that she would see no doctor until it was too late looks as if she had lost her zest for living and as if the goal of wholeness and her hopes of paradise regained had moved into the Beyond. We cannot possibly answer these questions; we can only regret her early death and wonder very tentatively whether perhaps, if she could have found another and more complete end for *Precious Bane*, it might not have opened her eyes to a yet further "task to do before she said goodnight to the world."

# 5 THE BRONTË CHILDREN

AMONG THE CLEAREST and best examples of the original Eden's influence on subsequent life are the members of the Brontë family. The sojourn in paradise of all four children was unusually prolonged and they had the greatest difficulty in finding their way into the outside world.

It is true that the outer circumstances of the Brontës, looked at from the extraverted point of view, were rather grim. Growing up in the lonely village of Haworth on the Yorkshire moors, they lost their mother before the eldest of the originally six children was ten years old; and the two eldest girls had died by the time Charlotte, the third child, was nine. Their father was a very strong, exceedingly introverted, character who had a tremendous impact on all of them. The wildness and violence of his temperament were evidently much exaggerated by earlier biographers, particularly Mrs. Gaskell, but this myth was exploded by a scholarly and well documented book published in 1958.[1] He emerges as a very unusual person, extraordinarily broad-minded for a clergyman, with an original attitude to the opposites. He took two newspapers, one Tory and one Whig—the two great political parties of the time—in order always to study both sides before making up his mind on any question. And he used to impress on young clergymen that preaching the word

[1] Hopkins, *The Father of the Brontës*. Seven years later a much longer and more detailed life of Mr. Brontë appeared: Lock and Dixon, *A Man of Sorrow*.

was useless unless they themselves lived it, and that they should always strive "*to keep the golden middle way.*" [2] He also had a very broad and tolerant attitude towards love and sexuality, a fact which largely explains the "amoral world of Angria," as Fannie Ratchford refers to a large section of the childhood writings, to say nothing of the later books, particularly *Wuthering Heights*.

It is above all their relationship to evil that makes the Brontës so very interesting to us today, when evil has broken all bounds and has become modern man's problem *par excellence*. Evil burst into their writing, particularly into the juvenilia, to an extent that was rare in the first half of the 19th century. By no means did they dismiss it as something which could be overcome by good: they were fully in agreement with Stevenson's much later opinion concerning the dual nature of man. They even called the world of imagination, in which they lived as children, their "infernal world" and "the world below." It is obvious, therefore, that the Brontës would each be called upon to meet the serpent of the Garden of Eden and to have it out with him again and again.

No doubt a great deal of this realistic attitude towards the dark and evil came from their father, originally an Irish peasant whose family had lived on the land for generations. When Patrick Brontë broke away from this tradition and, through his own efforts, succeeded in going to Cambridge and being ordained in the Church, he did not by any means shed his realistic peasant nature. But he had little or no understanding of children. He treated them as grownups, and this had a peculiarly forcing effect on their minds, making them all ardent politicians and extremely well informed on world affairs even before they reached their teens. But, as mentioned, he was very introverted. He took almost all his meals alone, and the children thus saw very little of him.

[2] Hopkins, p. 55.

Their maternal aunt, who came to live with them after Mrs. Brontë's death, was also not companionable. The children were therefore thrown entirely on their own resources, for they had no friends in Haworth.

In 1924, Mr. Brontë did indeed make a great effort to enlarge their horizon by sending the two eldest girls to a school which had only recently been opened at Cowan Bridge in Lancashire, and which offered a good education to the daughters of clergymen on very reasonable terms. Mr. Brontë was so delighted to be able to afford this opportunity that he sent Charlotte about a month later, and even Emily, who was then only six, joined her sisters before the end of the year. There has been a great deal of controversy about this school, but as far as one can gather, Charlotte's account of it as Lowood in *Jane Eyre* was a fair enough description of the terrible physical conditions which prevailed at the time the Brontë girls were there. (It was greatly improved later but too late for the Brontës.) The two eldest, who had been in bad health even before they went to Cowan Bridge, became so ill at the school that they had to be sent home, where they both died shortly afterwards. Mr. Brontë took alarm at this double tragedy, and Charlotte and Emily, to their great relief, were finally also allowed to come home. Maria, the eldest, who had been a second mother to the others, was almost as great a loss to the whole family as Mrs. Brontë herself had been.

Under such ciicumstances, it is no wonder that the four surviving children remained within their inner worlds, in the "web of childhood," as Fannie Ratchford calls it.[3] They have left records of their inner adventures in quantities of tiny volumes in tiny handwriting or print. Although Mrs. Gaskell and Clement Shorter, among the earlier biographers,

[3] *The Brontë Web of Childhood*, p. 110. Fannie Ratchford got this term from a verse manuscript of Charlotte's, written when she was 19, in which she likened their earlier "Young Men's play" to a "web woven in childhood," expanded to all-embracing proportions.

saw a great many, perhaps all, of these little volumes, even they failed to realize their importance, so the juvenilia were sold to collectors and widely distributed throughout England and America. It is largely due to the great and enduring merit of Fannie Ratchford, who traced almost all of them and published a great many, that these documents are available. She writes: "In contrast to the oft-repeated, tragic picture of the four little Brontës, frail, neglected, and prematurely old, crouching in terror before the ever-threatening monsters of disease and early death, the *juvenilia* shows us singularly happy beings, possessed of an Alladin's lamp through whose magic power they transcended time and distance, walked with kings and swayed the destinies of a mighty empire."[4]

If we were to express the same idea in Jungian language, we could say that they escaped from the narrowness of their outer world into the collective unconscious, where space and time seem to obey totally different laws, the world in which we all spent our earliest childhood. I have tried to convey an idea of this realm by likening it to the Garden of Eden.

The written records of the children's games, plays and magazines seem to have begun when the eldest surviving child, Charlotte, was nine years old. Mr. Brontë brought Branwell a box of twelve soldiers and these soldiers then became the center of endless adventures, the beginning of the whole written Brontë juvenilia. Interestingly enough, they each chose one special soldier and named him in a very characteristic way.[5] Charlotte called hers the Duke of Wellington and identified with him for many years; "I *am* the Duke of Wellington," she even declared. Emily selected a "serious-looking fellow, derisively dubbed 'Gravey' by the others." Anne's was called Waiting Boy, characteristic of much of her subsequent life. Finally, Branwell named his

[4] *Ibid.*, p. xv.
[5] *Ibid.*, p. 6.

favorite Buonaparte. The battle of Waterloo had been fought several years before and Napoleon banished to St. Helena; so from the beginning Branwell identified with brief brilliance and ultimate failure.

After many early exploits, the twelve soldiers land on the coast of Africa where there are further endless adventures, battles and the like. But the important point for us is that soon after the landing in Africa, the children, according to Fannie Ratchford, "hit upon a new fascinating self-dramatization. They became the Chief Genius Talli (Charlotte), the Chief Genius Branni, . . . Emmi and . . . Anni and under their powerful protection the little band of shipwrecked adventurers proceeded to explore the country." [6] Ratchford attributes this development to reading the *Arabian Nights*.

Be that as it may, a very powerful archetype thus broke into, or manifested itself in, the children's lives, an archetype that was to have the most far-reaching effect on all of them, although—as we shall see—a totally different effect on each.

The term "archetype" [7] is perhaps easiest, though inadequately, explained by the familiar term, "pattern of behavior." The quaternary character, exemplified by the *four* genii, points towards wholeness, and the fact that the genii represent superhuman figures, not bound by the laws of space or time, shows that they come from the unknown basic essence of man. This fundamental pattern—which is the nucleus that regulates a process of individuation—is the most vital and essential human "pattern of behavior."

It was very dangerous, however, for the children to identify with these supernatural figures. That such figures should appear as helpers and guides, or, on the negative side, as misleaders or even destroyers, would be a relatively normal state of affairs with introverted and lonely children. But calling the genii by their own names, and, as is recorded

[6] *Ibid.*, p. 12.
[7] See above, p. 25ff.

again and again, performing supernatural actions in their own persons is—in spite of the fact that the layman may dismiss this as mere fantasy!—a dangerous weakening of the boundaries between the human mortal side of man and his immortal counterpart. We have noted in Charlotte a tendency to this identification with something beyond herself when she stamped her foot and declared: "I *am* the Duke of Wellington," and all four of them were inclined to people their imaginary islands and kingdoms with the most famous men of the time. But this was still within human bounds and was very much less dangerous than identification with the Chief Genii. Such identification usually leads to inflation and to a corresponding deflation, to a swing between megalomania and perilous feelings of inferiority.

For at least six or seven years all four children shared their fantasy world. It should be mentioned, however, that Charlotte destroyed all of her sisters' papers [8] after they had died, so that unfortunately we have hardly any record of either Emily's or Anne's juvenilia. On the other hand, Charlotte's and Branwell's records, of which the former are by far the most valuable, are exceedingly voluminous. The tendency towards megalomaniacal ideas and feelings of inferiority is already evident in much of this early material and later becomes far more marked. Whereas Charlotte slowly but surely fought this tendency with increasing success, Branwell gave way to it more and more. In Charlotte it was checked by her excellent common sense and an increasing dislike of extremes. She says, for instance, in her introduction to *The Professor*: "I had got over any such taste as I might once have had for ornamented and redundant composition and come to prefer what was plain and homely. . . . As Adam's son he [the hero] should share Adam's doom and drain

[8] In fairness to Charlotte, it is not *quite* certain that it was she who destroyed these papers. We know for certain only that Mr. Nichols handed over Charlotte's and Branwell's juvenilia some time after Charlotte's death, and that Charlotte had herself obliterated many names and titles from Emily's poems.

throughout life a mixed and moderate cup of enjoyment. . . . 'He that is low need fear no fall.' " But the less Branwell achieved, the more inflated he became and the further the swing into a too-well-justified sense of terrible inferiority. When we come to consider his short, sad and unsatisfactory life, we shall see only too clearly a classical example of the dangers of identifying with a figure such as Chief Genius Branni.

The negative aspect of the Genii was indeed already exceedingly apparent in the juvenilia. For example, when Charlotte was thirteen she wrote in one of their magazines: "Sir, - It is well known that the Genii have declared that unless they [the Young Men] perform certain arduous duties every year, of a mysterious nature, all the worlds in the firmament will be burned up, and gathered together in one mighty globe, which will roll in solitary grandeur through the vast wilderness of space, inhabited only by the four high princes of the Genii, till time shall be succeeded by eternity."

The "one mighty globe" rolling through the vast wilderness of space, the archetypal *four* represented by the supernatural Genii, is an awe-inspiring image of the process of individuation turned negative and autonomous. In our text it is definitely a warning; the image of the archetype of the totality had broken into the Brontë family and was bound therefore to take its fateful course. But this need not be a fatally negative course, for we are definitely informed that this will occur only if "arduous duties . . . of a mysterious nature" are not performed and maintained every year.

Can we hazard a hypothesis concerning the significance of these "arduous duties"? When there is an invasion from the collective unconscious into the conscious life of man, experience tells us it can be met in one of two ways: (1) *creatively*, that is, every effort is made either to understand, become conscious of its meaning, or at all events to give it the best form we can achieve; or (2) with sterile *passivity*, ignoring it as much as possible, thus allowing it to take its purely autonomous and therefore negative course. In the first reaction, the "arduous duties" would be performed to the best of the individual's ability; in the second they would not, with the result foretold in Charlotte's vision. Each of the three girls chose, in her own way, the former alternative: whereas Branwell, who in many ways had the least chance of them all, more and more omitted the "arduous duties" and was thus unfortunately swept away and possessed, as we shall see.

It is important to realize that, although the Brontës saw the most extraordinary images in the collective unconscious, they had no idea what they were seeing. They realized, even as children, that things visited their minds which were entirely unknown to other people, and to this they had the creative artist's approach. They eagerly apprehended whatever they saw or heard to the best of their ability and gave themselves infinite pains to formulate it within the dimensions of the concrete world. But the subsequent step, that of asking the meaning of what they had formulated and thus becoming really conscious of it, was naturally entirely beyond them, although, as we shall see, they sometimes made infinitesimal steps in that direction.

At this time, however, they were still children, and it is amazing enough that they had sufficient instinct to write and draw unceasingly, thus holding fast to some very strange contents from the collective unconscious which invaded their conscious minds. One of the most extraordinary was written by Charlotte in *The Young Men's Magazine* when she was fourteen, a year or so after her vision of the solitary globe rolling through space.[9] She wrote in the name of Lord Charles Wellesley, the younger son of her early hero, the Duke of Wellington. Lord Charles says that he has fallen "into the strangest train of thought that had ever visited his mind."

[9] The story is entitled "Strange Events." It is dealt with in more detail in *Harvest*, Vol. 10, p. 1ff.

> It seemed as if I was a non-existent shadow—that I neither spoke, ate, imagined, or lived of myself, but I was the mere idea of some other creature's brain. The Glass Town seemed as likewise. My father, Arthur, and everyone with whom I am acquainted, passed into a state of annihilation; but suddenly I thought again that I and my relatives did exist and yet not us but our minds and our bodies without ourselves.[10]

This idea of the three-dimensional body and mind being the "mere idea of some other creature's brain" reminds one vividly of the dreams reported by Jung in *Memories, Dreams, Reflections,* published after his death:

> The thorny problem of the relationship between eternal man, the self, and earthly man in time and space was illuminated by two dreams of mine.
>
> In one dream, which I had in October 1958, I caught sight from my house of two lens-shaped metallically gleaming disks, which hurtled in a narrow arc over the house and down to the lake. They were two UFOs (Unidentified Flying Objects). Then another body came flying directly toward me. It was a perfectly circular lens, like the objective of a telescope. At a distance of four or five hundred yards it stood still for a moment, and then flew off. Immediately afterward another came speeding through the air: a lens with a metallic extension which led to a box—a magic lantern. At a distance of sixty or seventy yards it stood still in the air, pointing straight at me. I awoke with a feeling of astonishment. Still half in the dream, the thought passed through my head: "We always think that the UFOs are projections of ours. Now it turns out that we are their projections. I am projected by the magic lantern as C G. Jung. But who manipulates the appartus?"

[10] Ratchford, *op. cit.*, p. 40.

> I had dreamed once before of the problem of the self and the ego. In that earlier dream I was on a hiking trip. I was walking along a little road through a hilly landscape; the sun was shining and I had a wide view in all directions. Then I came to a small wayside chapel. The door was ajar, and I went in. To my surprise there was no image of the Virgin on the altar, and no crucifix either, but only a wonderful flower arrangement. But then I saw that on the floor in front of the altar, facing me, sat a yogi—in lotus posture, in deep meditation. When I looked at him more closely, I realized that he had my face. I started in profound fright, and awoke with the thought: "Aha, so he is the one who is meditating me. He has a dream and I am it." I knew that when he awakened, I would no longer be.[11]

The idea is the same in both: *the human being is entirely dependent on the eternal*. But whereas Charlotte "annihilates" our present world—it is a non-shadow—Jung points out its great value. He continues:

> I had this dream after my illness in 1944. It is a parable: My self retires into meditation and meditates my earthly form. To put it another way: it assumes human shape in order to enter three-dimensional existence, as if someone were putting on a diver's suit in order to dive into the sea. When it renounces existence in the hereafter, the self assumes a religious posture, as the chapel in the dream shows. In earthly form it can pass through the experiences of the three-dimensional world, and by greater awareness take a further step toward realization.[12]

Here, as in other places, Jung emphasizes the great (really equal) importance of our reality, for it seems that only in

[11] *Memories, Dreams, Reflections*, pp. 322-323.
[12] *Ibid.*, pp. 323-324.

the three-dimensional world can "clear and decisive cognitions" [13] be attained and "greater awareness" thus take a "futher step towards realization."

Charlotte continues:

> Then this supposition—the oddest of any—followed the former quickly, namely, that WE without US were shadows; also; but at the end of a long vista, as it were, appeared dimly and indistinctly, beings that really lived in a tangible shape, that were called by our names and were US from whom WE had been copied by something—I could not tell what.[14]

Here Charlotte began to see the other reality, something of "the other creature," though still "dimly and indistinctly." But her observations bear out Jung's later empirical discovery of the objective psyche, particularly in her pronouns "we" and "us." "We" the subject are nothing without "us" the object. And the fact that these eternal beings are called by our names and are the originals from whom we have been copied, contains the same idea as the yogi in Jung's dream who had the same features as his earthly body. "The relationship between eternal man, the self, and earthly man in time and space" is indeed a "thorny problem," but this vision of a fourteen-year-old girl, one hundred and thirty years ago, is very enlightening and becomes still more so as it proceeds.

After a short, rather confused passage which ends, "But I am lost, I cannot go on," Charlotte continues:

> For hours I continued in this state, striving to fathom a bottomless ocean of Mystery, till at length I was roused by a loud noise above my head. I looked up and thick obscurity was before my eyes. Voices—one like my own but larger

[13] *Ibid.*, p. 308.
[14] Ratchford, *op. cit.*, p. 40.

and dimmer (if sound may be characterized by such epithets) and another which sounded familiar, yet I had never, that I could remember, heard it before—murmuring unceasingly in my ears.[15]

As she gets lost in her attempts to see, another sense is appealed to—hearing. At first it is only a loud noise, and sight is blocked by thick obscurity. But then she hears voices and learns that "us" have voices like "we" and that these voices are "familiar," although, as far as memory goes, they had never been heard before. She did not, however, distinguish more than an "unceasing murmur," so that fantasy returns to sight:

I saw books removing from the top shelves and returning, apparently of their own accord. By degrees the mistiness cleared off. I felt myself raised suddenly to the ceiling and ere I was aware, beheld two immense sparkling bright blue globes within a few yards of me. I was in a hand wide enough almost to grasp the Tower of All Nations, and when it lowered me to the floor I saw a huge personification of myself—hundreds of feet high—standing against the great Oriel.[16]

That it is books she saw is very understandable when one remembers that even then writing was her only way of dealing with the strange phenomena that appeared from the unconscious, phenomena which might easily have led to insanity had she been without a creative medium to lend them form. Moreover she was destined to become one of the most famous of English novelists. The fact that the images moved of their own volition indicates that it was the unconscious itself which was to give her the spiritual motivation for her books. In

[15] *Ibid.*
[16] *Ibid.*

his essay on "Psychology and Literature"[17] Jung divides works of literature into two classes, "psychological" and "visionary." The first comes primarily from the conscious, the second from the unconscious. Most of Charlotte's works belong to the latter class.

After the moving books she finds herself raised far above the ground by a huge hand. We had heard before that the "us" beings "really lived in a tangible shape," and now we have proof of this tangibility in that human beings—"we"—can actually stand in the hand of an eternal being. By doing so the former's standpoint is completely altered.

Now this whole vision seems to be concerned with what Jung calls "the thorny problem of the relationship between eternal man . . . and earthly man." Therefore, when the elevation in standpoint reveals "two immense sparkling bright blue globes," exactly equal to each other, it seems a likely hypothesis that the globes represent the two realities, one of which Charlotte, when on the ground, was inclined to annihilate as a "mere shadow." We shall see that this led to an enantiodromia, i.e., it turned into its own opposite, as Charlotte later attempted without success to annihilate the world of fantasy, the eternal world, and to dismiss it as "mere shadow," in contrast to the only real, outer concrete world. But for the moment, from the standpoint of the eternal man, she sees both as equally important. One is reminded of old Mr. Brontë's "golden middle way" and of the lifelong tension between the opposites to which the whole family was exposed.

When she is lowered to the ground of everyday reality, she has a clear vision of the Self, no longer seen "dimly and indistinctly," but quite distinctly, with the same features as the earthly man and hundreds of feet high. This is a very remarkable clarification of what went before, and the image agrees with many modern dreams which also represent the Self as an infinitely larger figure than the ego. We find similar

[17] In *The Spirit in Man, Art, and Literature*, pars. 133-162.

images in many cultural areas, both East and West, of which I mention only the Indian Purusha who is cosmic man and the essence of each individual and who is called "greater than great and smaller than small."

> This filled me with a weight of astonishment greater than the mind of man ever before had to endure, and I was now perfectly convinced of my non-existence except in another corporeal frame which dwelt in the real world, for ours I thought was nothing but idea.[18]

The "nothing but" again reveals the tendency to depreciate the everyday world, which passes again into a "state of annihilation" as it did at the beginning of the vision. The two equal globes represent only a brief insight as indeed, at Charlotte's age and in her circumstances, it was bound to be.

Fannie Ratchford says that this "story," as she calls it, towers over and above all other interests in *The Young Men's Magazine* for December 1830. These invasions from the collective unconscious are indeed of a significance far superior to the rest of the material, which is for the most part more like the "make believe" of many other children who find an "imaginary" compensation for a lack of sufficient interest in their outer lives. It is much better formulated, however, than the efforts of most children, for the Brontë genius for writing showed itself early. Nevertheless the majority of the juvenilia is a kind of endless serial story in which the same characters, though they sometimes change their names and environment, appear again and again. Branwell met every difficult situation by declaring another war or by killing off the girls' characters. But the other three Genii countered this by miraculously bringing their favorites to life again! Charlotte's stories are somewhat overburdened by titles and by the magnificence of their settings, whereas the little we know of

[18] Ratchford, *op. cit.*

Emily is characterized by a much greater simplicity. Lord Charles Wellesley—whom we have already met as the "author" of "Strange Events"—has only a "pitying contempt for the Caledonian poverty" of Emily's domain. (Each child had a separate kingdom in Africa, arranged according to his or her individual taste and presided over by his own Genius.) Lord Charles is immediately struck by the change as he crosses the border into Emily's "Parrysland." Instead of "strong, tall, muscular men, going about seeking whom they might devour," he sees only "shiftless little milk and water beings in clean blue linen jackets and white aprons." All the houses are small and very much alike. There are no castles, splendid palaces or factories and no high-born noble to claim the allegiance of his vassals. Even the King's palace is "a poor enough dwelling in Lord Charles' eye," rather like a farmhouse where there is only one cow to give milk, butter and cheese to the family and one horse to draw their Majesties' gig. The food is very simple, of the roast beef and Yorkshire pudding variety, so Lord Charles only stays at "Parry's palace" one night and then departs, "having found his visit intolerably dull." [19]

Apparently no records of Anne's kingdom remain. Presumably, however, since the four were beginning to divide up into two pairs, her kingdom would have been more in sympathy with Emily's simplicity than with the overpowering magnificence favored by Charlotte and Branwell. At all events, when Charlotte was sent to school at the age of fifteen, the two younger girls left the common African venture and set up for themselves on first one, then two islands in the Pacific. Even when Charlotte returned home after eighteen months, no entreaties would move Emily and Anne to return to the African kingdoms. For several more years Charlotte and Branwell played on the old territory and produced the so-called "Angrian Chronicles," while the two

[19] Ratchford, *op. cit.*, p. 38f.

younger girls evidently produced the "Gondal Chronicles," a fantasy or game continued till shortly before their deaths.[20] Unfortunately all of these chronicles were later destroyed, presumably by Charlotte, except for the poems which Fannie Ratchford has taken great pains to fit into a kind of Gondal Saga. Even in the poems, however, Charlotte often destroyed the Gondal titles. Ratchford's effort has certainly given a rational explanation to many questions raised by Emily's poems and made a fairly convincing consecutive story, but there is very little data and a good deal remains conjecture.

The separation of the original four into two pairs makes a suitable point for moving from the common childhood of the Brontë children to the individual development of each.

[20] In the so-called "birthday notes of 1845" (which Emily and Anne used to write on Emily's birthday and of which 1841 and 1845 are still extant) Emily refers to the first long journey—to York—which she and Anne had ever taken alone, during which they each identified with Gondal characters. Emily says: "We intend sticking firm by the rascals as long as they delight us, which I am glad to say they do at present." Anne is less enthusiastic in her notes, but the game was thus evidently in full swing in 1845, three or four years before their deaths.—Ratchford, p. 167.

# 6 ❧ CHARLOTTE

CHARLOTTE WENT to Miss Wooler's Roe Head School when she was nearly fifteen and found herself at last outside the gates of Eden. She retained an unusually definite memory of the latter, though, and was only happy when creating something to keep that memory alive. However, from the time she reached Roe Head, she never wavered in her conviction that she must do the best she could to find roots and a place in the outside world.

Fannie Ratchford describes the transition as follows: "Chief Genius Talli, ruler of spirits, who created and destroyed worlds by the power of her word, traveled to Roe Head in a covered cart as plain Charlotte Brontë, arriving very cold and miserable." [1] It was a very difficult transition, for there was not only Chief Genius Talli to deal with but also the fact that Charlotte had been very much the despotic ruler of her younger brother and sisters at home —at least as far as they had permitted. The real rebellion of the younger girls against her authority took place only during and after the time at Roe Head. The little girl who declared, "I *am* the Duke of Wellington," was very ambitious and fond of power, a fact one must keep in mind, for it was covered over more and more by a very modest and unassuming persona.

We hear from Mrs. Gaskell, who was able to get her information from Charlotte's still living headmistress and school-

[1] Ratchford, *op. cit.*, p. 51.

fellows, that at school Charlotte was regarded as "well read but not well grounded." In fact, her schoolfellows at first "thought her very ignorant, for she had never learnt grammar at all, and very little geography." [2] This must have been a very galling state of affairs for Chief Genius Talli; for the first time she began to see herself and her family with the eyes of an outsider. On the other hand, the same friend reports: "She would confound us by knowing things that were out of our range altogether." However, the Parsonage set-up was seen by this same school friend as similar to "potatoes growing in a cellar." At first Charlotte talked about their magazines and even told a few of the stories to her friends. But when she discovered that they were blind and deaf to the world of fantasy, she shut up like a clam and refused to mention the subject again. Later she even kept her best friend, Ellen Nussey, not only uninformed about the publication of *Jane Eyre* but even denied it furiously when Ellen heard a rumor that she was the author of that famous book!

Charlotte was a great believer in education and fervently applied herself to learning everything the school had to teach. But perhaps the most important result of her time at Roe Head was the formation of two life-long friendships—with Ellen Nussey and Mary Taylor. Both these friends were very practical. Mary Taylor even remarked, "We had a rage for practicality and laughed all poetry to scorn," and it was mainly through Mary and Ellen that Charlotte learned the importance of outer events. In fact their influence went so far that Charlotte even tried to deny the inner world. But the latter was so strong in her that, however vehemently it was repudiated, it always broke through again. She came to regard it as a secret sin which she fought with all the "strength of a tyrannical conscience."

Although this struggle led to what Fannie Ratchford calls

[2] *The Life of Charlotte Brontë*, p. 79.

"a fifteen years war" between her two natures, such a development was absolutely necessary if she were to find her way out of Eden into the outside world. We saw in "Strange Events" how near she was to dismissing the outer world as a "mere shadow" and to allowing it to be entirely annihilated, which would have meant missing the whole point of her earthly existence and wrecking her chance of greater wholeness. The eternal being, the Self, would also then have been unable to increase its awareness or to take a further step towards realization through Charlotte's three dimensional existence.[3]

During her eighteen months at Roe Head, Charlotte kept in touch with the inner world only through her correspondence with Branwell and an occasional few minutes when her companions were playing games. Her abnormally short vision absolved her from this side of school life; otherwise she gradually fitted into the school pattern. Roe Head was very small, only seven to ten girls, and was wisely run by Miss Wooler. Charlotte remained there as long as she felt there was more for her to learn. Then in 1832 she returned to Haworth, where once more the inner world triumphed over the outer. According to Miss Ratchford 1833 was the "most prolific year of her life." For the most part she produced novels in which her earlier characters slowly develop, but Chief Genius Talli, who had by no means disappeared, again opened the way for strange invasions from the collective unconscious.

One of the strangest has a markedly alchemistic character and is to be found in the longest novel of this period, *The Foundling*[4] (34,000 words, begun May 31st, finished June 27th, 1833). It describes the "Philosopher's Island," which lies at a distance of nearly six hundred miles from the coast of Africa (Charlotte and Branwell's realm was still situated

[3] Cf. Jung, *Memories, Dreams, Reflections*, p. 323f.
[4] Ratchford, p. 67ff.

in Africa) and where the only building is a university for "the rising generation," staffed by the "most learned philosophers of the world." An association (a sort of secret society), founded "amongst the professors and tutors of the university . . . is said to have dived deeply into the mysteries of nature and to have revealed many of her hidden and unthought-of secrets."

The President of this society, Branwell's old favorite Crashie,[5] "after long and arduous effort [one is reminded of the indispensable "arduous duties"] succeeded in compounding a fluid so pure, so refined, so ethereal, that one drop of it distilled in our mortal clay penetrated to the soul, freed it from all grosser particles, raised it far above worldly troubles, rendered it capable of enjoying the calm of heaven amid the turmoil of the earth, and . . . forever warded off the darts of death. But those high and unseen spirits, to whom even the potent Crashie must yield, observed his beneficent work and controverted it, so that his liquid changed its nature, and 'instead of dispensing immortality and holy delight, it would bring the horrors, the darkness of inevitable death.'" This represents exactly the same idea as the *lapis philosophorum* of the alchemists. The *lapis* is an elixir, a universal medicine, but also a most deadly poison which destroys everything it touches. It is unlikely that Charlotte Brontë knew anything about alchemy, certainly not enough to produce such an exact parallel. As mentioned before, there seems to be no time (or a totally different time) in the unconscious, and it is very interesting that not only does the fluid seem to come from the past, but Charlotte also had a "truth drug"[6] which, as far as my knowledge goes, was first discovered in the next century.

This very productive period was of short duration, for two years later Branwell's future had become an immediate

[5] See below, p. 151.
[6] Ratchford, pp. 22 and 201.

concern, and in order to find money for his training at the British Academy schools, the girls decided to take up teaching as a career. At this time only Charlotte was qualified to teach; she returned to Miss Wooler's as a teacher, taking Emily (who was later exchanged for Anne) with her as pupil. It was during this period at Roe Head that Charlotte began to suffer the terrible depressions which were to last during the "fifteen years war" and which are described particularly vividly in *Villette*. Mrs. Gaskell tells us, on the authority of Mary Taylor, that Charlotte went through an experience exactly similar to that of Jane Eyre when Jane was locked in the Red Room by Mrs. Reid. "From that time," Mary adds, "her imagination became gloomy or frightful, she could not help it, nor help thinking. She could not forget the gloom, could not sleep at night, nor attend in the day." Jane Eyre's agony was due to her knowledge that her uncle—who had always been kind to her—had died in the Red Room, and she feared that his ghost might come back to protest against his wife's ill-treatment of herself.

Mrs. Gaskell also says:

> One night I was on the point of relating some dismal ghost story, just before bedtime. She shrank from hearing it, and confessed that she was superstitious and prone at all times to the involuntary recurrence of any thoughts of ominous gloom which might have been suggested to her.[7]

I draw attention to this rather surprising fear of death and ghosts because it seems very characteristic of Charlotte's attitude to the unconscious. Miss Ratchford says:

> It has become the fashion to exalt Emily and debase Charlotte, in utter ignorance that their genius—the ability to realize the imaginative with the vivid intensity of the actual

[7] Gaskell, p. 445.

—was identical, and that Emily's one point of superiority was her full surrender to the creative spirit which Charlotte fought with all the strength of her tyrannical conscience.[8]

This is one of the most discerning statements I have read about the Brontës, but while fully agreeing with Miss Ratchford I would also suggest that, whereas Emily had complete confidence in the "creative spirit," Charlotte was afraid of it and that her lack of surrender to it came just as much from fear as from conscience. Whereas Emily, as we shall see, rejoiced in personified visitations from the unconscious, Charlotte found them almost more than she could bear, and any undeniable autonomous manifestation of the unconscious always filled her with gloom. It was not only ghosts that she feared, any undeniable proof of a completely irrational event had the same effect on her. For example, she told Mrs. Gaskell that when Jane Eyre heard Mr. Rochester calling her a hundred miles away and he heard her actual reply, not only the time and the words but even the impression of the place in which they were uttered being correct, it dramatized an event which had really happened, evidently to herself. Yet, although the result was wholly positive, Jane "made no disclosure in return" for Mr. Rochester's account because "the coincidence struck (her) as too awful and inexplicable to be communicated or discussed." Mr. Rochester, she thought, was "already too prone to gloom" and did not need "the deeper shade of the supernatural."

Charlotte had good reason to be afraid of the unconscious. As we saw,[9] Clement Shorter failed to realize the importance of the juvenilia, but he did print one early story of Charlotte's, called "An Adventure in Ireland," [10] containing a long dream

[8] Ratchford, p. x.
[9] See above, pp. 107-108.
[10] *The Brontës, Life and Letters,* Vol. 1, pp. 74-76.

which reveals the danger particularly well. (He almost apologizes for doing so and makes the remarkable statement that it was "perhaps the only juvenile fragment worth anything"!) In the most revealing scenes of the dream, Charlotte found herself "encompassed with clouds and darkness. But soon the roar of mighty waters fell upon my ear, and I saw some clouds of spray arising from high falls that rolled in awful majesty down tremendous precipices, and then foamed and thundered in the gulf beneath as if they had taken up their unquiet abode in some giant's cauldron. But soon the scene changed, and I found myself in the mines of Cracone." These mines are then described in "all their splendour" which "was never excelled by the brightest fairy palaces." But we soon hear that in the midst of all this magnificence, there is "an indescribable sense of fear and terror, for the sea raged above us, and by the awful and tumultuous noises of roaring winds and dashing waves, it seemed as if the storm was violent. And now the mossy pillars groaned beneath the pressure of the ocean, and the glittering arches seemed about to be overwhelmed. When I heard the rushing waters and saw a mighty flood rolling towards me, I gave a loud shriek of terror."

The ocean is one of the most frequent symbols of the collective unconscious. This dream therefore gives a vivid picture of the great danger that it could break through and drown everything in an irresistable flood. In fact, one could say that this is just what it did, when death swept first Branwell, then Emily and Anne away in less than nine months. The fact that Charlotte was able to survive must have been due not only to her valiant efforts to make roots in the outer world, but also to the probability that she alone of the family to some extent realized thc danger that was constantly threatening them from within.

Although Charlotte could report amazing things, such as "Strange Events," objectively and faithfully, and could declare that eternal beings "really lived in a tangible shape," she was nevertheless profoundly disturbed when they showed their tangibility by upsetting the outer rational order of life which, like most of us, she regarded as fixed for all time. We all move in the direction of panic when we are confronted with something we cannot explain, as the primitives do when a nocturnal animal shows itself by day. Under her quiet and unassuming exterior, Charlotte was very ambitious and fond of controlling her world ("I *am* the Duke of Wellington"), and nothing makes a human being feel more completely helpless than an undeniable supernatural event. But such things were also a threat to her most laudable effort to leave Eden and get right out into the outside world, so that the gloom and depression they produced also had a healthy effect.

All steps on the road towards the process of individuation are necessarily characterized by suffering, and this suffering is particularly important for women. Jung often spoke of the "night sea journey" (of which the best-known example is Jonah's journey in the whale) as a symbol of the process of individuation; in a seminar he once remarked that whereas men overcome by slaying the monster, by an active deed, women overcome by accepting their suffering, by a voluntary passivity. Charlotte's ambition and strong will to power (although these also played a positive role in enticing her out into the world) could not be overcome without great suffering. So the "frightful gloom," so deplored by her practical friend, Mary Taylor, was nevertheless an inevitable stage in her individual effort to come to terms with the archetype of wholeness which broke in so early on all these children.

Charlotte did indeed realize the value of suffering to a far greater degree than did Mary Webb, or even Stevenson. Both of her best known heroines, Jane Eyre and Lucy Snowe (in *Villette*), suffered continually, the latter having the same seasons of unrelieved gloom that beset Charlotte herself. Mrs. Gaskell tells us that she was determined to end *Villette* with the death of Paul Emanuel, because she did not want a happy end for Lucy Snowe. "I am not leniently disposed towards Miss Frost; from the beginning, I never meant to appoint her lines in pleasant places," she wrote to her publishers. (Originally Lucy's surname was Snowe, then Charlotte change it to Frost, but subsequently asked her publisher—after he had already received the first two volumes—to go back to Snowe "if not too late.") [11] It is interesting that Charlotte was determined to have a cold name for Lucy. One is reminded of her own statement that her "veins ran ice." Actually she ended *Villette* with a question mark. Mrs. Gaskell felt she should record the fact that Charlotte had told her that "Mr. Brontë was anxious that her new tale should end well, as he disliked novels which left a melancholy impression upon the mind and he requested her to make her hero and heroine (like the heroes and heroines in fairy tales) 'marry and live very happily ever after.' But the idea of M. Paul Emanuel's death at sea was stamped on her imagination till it assumed the distinct force of reality, and she could no more alter her fictitious ending than if they had been facts which she was relating. All she could do in compliance with her father's wish was so to veil the fate in oracular words as to leave it to the character and discernment of her readers to interpret her meaning." [12] And indeed it is impossible to make oneself believe that M. Emanuel escaped that Atlantic storm. Charlotte certainly suffered a great deal in her brief life but it was meaningful, not barren, suffering, and there are signs that, in spite of her moans—her letters are often one long complaint—she slowly realized its meaning.

When she left Miss Wooler's and went as governess to first one and then another family, it was just the same. It is true that she was not very fortunate in the families she worked for, especially the first, but, as even Mrs. Gaskell

[11] Gaskell, p. 426-8.
[12] *Ibid.*, p. 427.

suggests, she was probably a very inefficient governess, for she seems to have had little relation to and no control over small children. There may have been more to be said for her employers therefore than one would think from her letters. For many years she was still comparatively happy in her intervals at home and suffered from homesickness, as all the Brontë girls did, whenever she was away. This led to a plan for establishing their own school at Haworth Parsonage, and for this purpose—in order to be able to offer French and German instruction—Charlotte went with Emily to school in Brussels when they were in their middle twenties.

The first nine months with Emily was a comparatively happy period for Charlotte, during which time she made great progress with French. But when both girls were recalled to Haworth by the death of their Aunt Branwell, Emily remained at home and Charlotte returned to Brussels alone. This was probably the unhappiest period of her life but one which in the end led to the most positive results.

Her feelings for and her relation to M. Héger in Brussels are very controversial questions among Brontë specialists. (It was to Madame Héger's *pensionat* that the Brontë girls went. M. Héger was her husband and the Professor who taught them. They are both admirably and vividly described in *Villette* as Madame Beck and Prof. Paul Emanuel.) Undoubtedly M. Héger had a profound influence on Charlotte. The differences of opinion among the specialists arise primarily from a doubt as to whether she was in love with him or not. The proponents of the former opinion base their facts, for the most part, on six letters to him, written after Charlotte returned to England for the second and last time. C. W. Hatfield was probably nearest to the truth when he wrote to Fannie Ratchford as follows:

> It is useless to say that the letters are not love letters. They are; but they are just as certainly not the kind of letters that a woman writes to her lover. . . . Had M. Héger not

been a married man, Charlotte Brontë would not have written the letters. It was because he was a married man that she allowed herself to write such letters to him. That seems paradoxical, does it not? Yet . . . I feel sure that you . . . will see the truth of it.[13]

I do not know if Miss Ratchford did see the truth of it; I doubt it, as she is a strong partisan of Charlotte *not* having been in love with M. Héger, basing her opinion on earlier prototypes for the letters in the juvenilia. But it seems to me to be the exact truth. Like most girls with a strong father complex, Charlotte always experienced great difficulty in her relationships with men. More than one man wanted to marry her, but we have her own written evidence that her "veins ran ice" [14] when one of them approached her as a lover. It is most probable that Hatfield is right when he says that it is just because M. Héger was married that Charlotte hoped he "would understand and reciprocate" her feeling for him, *without* turning her blood to ice by approaching her as a lover. Not that Charlotte Brontë was incapable of passion; on the contrary, passion was evidently such a burning force in her that she was terrified of it. Therefore she needed some guarantee—such as Hatfield finds in the fact that M. Héger was a married man—before she dared to admit even some of her own feeling.

What then was Charlotte's feeling for M. Héger? No one doubts that he made an enormous impression on her. "To the only master I have ever had—to you Monsieur," she addresses him in one of her letters, adding that if only she could write a book [15] she would dedicate it to him. To

[13] Ratchford, p. 164.
[14] Letter of Charlotte's, reported in Gaskell, p. 387.
[15] The first effect of Brussels on Charlotte was an inability to write at all and a neurotic fear of losing her eyesight (Ratchford, p. 161f). But such a *reculer pour mieux sauter* is a frequent prologue to a tremendous creative effort.

indicate the tremendous emotional involvement, she writes in a letter: "When day by day I await a letter and when day by day disappointment comes to fling me back in overwhelming sorrow, and the sweet delight of seeing your handwriting and reading your counsel escapes me as a vision that is vain, then fever claims me—I lose appetite and sleep—I pine away." She asks in another letter: "You will tell me perhaps,—'I take not the slightest interest in you Mademoiselle Charlotte'. . . . Well, Monsieur, tell me so frankly. . . . It will be less dreadful than uncertainty." [16]

No letter ever came from M. Héger, and Charlotte was forced to come to terms with her feelings for him entirely alone. Writing of the people who condemned *Jane Eyre*, May Sinclair says:

> What did poor Jane do, after all? Nobody could possibly have had more respect for the ten commandments. . . . And yet Jane offended. She sinned against the unwritten code that ordains that a woman may lie until she is purple in the face, but she must not, as a piece of gratuitous information, tell a man she loves him, not, that is to say, in as many words. . . . She [Jane] had done it.[17]

Charlotte's letters to M. Héger also do just this. Yet Jane knew deep within herself that Mr. Rochester loved her before she told him. Did Charlotte know the same of M. Héger? The jealousy of Mme. Héger makes it possible, and a poem, written in an exercise book which Charlotte herself brought back from Brussels, also rather points in the same direction:

*An hour hence, in my master's room,*
*I sat with him alone,*
*And told him what a dreary gloom*
*O'er joy had parting thrown.*

[16] Ratchford, p. 163.
[17] *The Three Brontës*, p. 117ff.

*He little said; the time was brief*
*The ship was soon to sail;*
*And while I sobbed in bitter grief*
*My master but looked pale.*

*They called in haste; he bade me go,*
*Then snatched me back again;*
*He held me fast and murmured low,*
*Why will they part us, Jane?*

*They call again: leave then my breast;*
*Quit thy true shelter, Jane;*
*But when deceived, repulsed, opprest,*
*Come home to me again!*[18]

But the dramatization of such a scene is also extremely possible, and although no one can answer the question of M. Héger's feelings for Charlotte with any certainty, all of the inner evidence and the complete change in Charlotte's writing after Brussels indicate that she certainly really loved him.

Jung writes in "Woman in Europe":

> It is a woman's outstanding characteristic that she can do anything for the love of a man. But those women who can achieve something more important for the love of a *thing* are most exceptional, because this does not really agree with their nature. Love for a thing is a man's prerogative.[19]

Emily, as we shall see, probably did "achieve something important for the love of a *thing*," all her life, but Charlotte was much more feminine than Emily, and I very much doubt whether she would have achieved anything important in literature had she not loved M. Héger.

[18] Quoted in du Maurier, *The Infernal World of Branwell Brontë*, p. 159f.
[19] In *Civilization in Transition*, par. 243.

Writing at over seventy, I can only say that in my experience such a complete transformation, as is evident in Charlotte's writing before Brussels and after, can only be produced in a woman by the "love of a man," by which I mean that she learns to love herself, not just wants to be loved. We know from the life of the mystics that the "love of God" can produce a similar transformation, but Charlotte was certainly no mystic. Nor is there any evidence of any religious experience during the Brussels period strong enough to produce such a change. And her understanding and wonderful descriptions of Jane Eyre's love for Mr. Rochester and Lucy Snowe's for Paul Emanuel could only have been written, in my opinion, by a woman who had had this transforming experience herself.

Although I have avoided using Jungian terms here, as far as possible, in order to be more comprehensible to the general reader, it is nevertheless necessary to call attention once again to the term *animus*.[20] In almost all of Charlotte's early writing that I have read one could say that her animus, or unconscious mind, speaks through her, with little or no check from the conscious mind. There is a certain unconscious recognition of this in the fact that Charlotte always wrote as a man.[21] There is also an unmistakable "archetypal" style in her early writing. Jung says of such a style:

> Archetypes speak the language of high rhetoric, even of bombast. It is a style I find embarrassing; it grates on my nerves, as when someone draws his nails down a plaster wall, or scrapes his knife against a plate. But since I did not know what was going on,[22] I had no choice but to write everything down in the style selected by the unconscious itself.[23]

[20] See above, pp. 24ff.
[21] As far as my knowledge of her juvenilia goes.
[22] Jung is describing his first efforts to contact the unconscious directly, through "active imagination."
[23] *Memories, Dreams, Reflections*, p. 178.

The first book of Charlotte's in which this style is entirely missing is *The Professor,* written as soon as she had recovered from her total inability to write which was the first result of her time in Brussels. The book is very interesting as a transition. In its preface she repudiates her early writing as "ornamented and redundant composition"—her effort to recognize this rhetorical, bombastic style which the unconscious itself supplies—and she goes on to declare herself the partisan of facts, of what is "plain and homely" and what belongs to the actual fate of a "son of Adam." She still writes as a man, but one can see on almost every page the struggle with her former style of writing in which she allowed the unconscious to use its own language unchecked. She succeeds in her effort, too much indeed for the story as a story, and one can understand why it went the round of the publishers unsuccessfully. Except as a psychological document, is is distinctly dull, and its best parts have all been far better rewritten in *Villette.*

But the actual writing of it was of immense value to Charlotte. She found her own human standpoint in it, to such an extent that she was afterwards able to drop her lifelong habit of writing as a man and to compose *Jane Eyre* in the first person as a woman. As such, both *Jane Eyre* and *Villette* are human documents of the first order. *Jane Eyre,* in particular, is a woman's self-revelation to which I can think of no equal parallel. Moreover it is a most happy mixture of Charlotte's earlier unchecked outpourings of the unconscious and the almost complete repression of the latter in *The Professor.* The unconscious pours into *Jane Eyre,* but—with certain exceptions—the conscious mind of Charlotte Brontë is ever alert to modify its "ornamented and redundant" style, without losing its creative impetus.

The publication of *Jane Eyre* was an instant success, but Charlotte's great pleasure in this fact was damped by increasing anxiety over Branwell. I will leave the details for his own chapter and only mention here that he took more and more to drink, even to drugs, and thus clouded the happiness of this creative period for his sisters. He died at Haworth in September 1848. The door seems thus to have been opened to death, for Emily died in December and Anne the following May.

This must have been an almost unbearable time for Charlotte. Although she had long given up hope for Branwell, she had yet been closest of all to him in their youth. And she was undoubtedly deeply attached to her sisters, so that within nine months she lost all of her closest companionship and sympathy. Moreover, Emily's stoic death, at which Charlotte was unable to do anything, and Anne's longer illness, through which Charlotte nursed her unceasingly, must have been tragic and gruelling experiences.

Although Charlotte suffered almost unbearably, there does not seem to have been any return of the hopeless, almost morbid gloom of earlier years. She exerted herself at once for the sake of her (now old) father and very soon, in spite of the terrible loss of discussion with her sisters, she was writing again. She lived alone with her father for about four years, during which time they became very dependent on each other and fussed about each other rather like married lovers! Charlotte's fame was a great enrichment of their outer lives, bringing not only relief from their life-long poverty but also many visitors to Haworth and many invitations out into the world for Charlotte. She accepted the latter only very sparingly; nevertheless she went to London several times, to Scotland, to the Lake District and so on.

Before we follow Charlotte into the last chapter of her life —her marriage and death—we must take a look at her last three novels, all written before she married, in an attempt to see how the process of individuation manifests itself in them. We must do this more briefly than in Stevenson's and Mary Webb's books, but fortunately, as they have become English classics, most readers will be familiar with their outlines at least.

*Jane Eyre,* as already mentioned, was the first book which Charlotte wrote as a woman. Both it and *Villette* are in a sense autobiographical, rather as Stevenson's unfinished *Weir of Hermiston* is autobiographical. Not that any of the three stories are in any sense the stories of Louis' or Charlotte's own lives, but, just as Stevenson himself said, "Archie was the same kind of fool," so we can see a great deal of Charlotte —beyond the events of her own life that, she admitted to Mrs. Gaskell, she had given to Jane and Lucy—in her two "heroines." I use quotation marks because neither are heroines in the conventional sense. Her sisters both declared that heroines must be beautiful to be interesting, but Charlotte replied that she would write a very interesing story with a plain and unattractive heroine and succeeded in doing so twice, both in *Jane Eyre* and in *Villette*. Now we know that Mary Taylor told Charlotte at Roe Hill that "she was very ugly" which she never forgot, and all her life she believed herself to be plain and unattractive. Therefore in a way she identified herself consciously with Jane and Lucy, and indeed one feels that all their thoughts and reactions come within Charlotte's own conscious experience. Both stories seem to happen to this fixed point of the author's consciousness, just as our own objective psyches happen to ourselves. Jane is, as it were, a younger, more emotional and self-willed Charlotte. Lucy, from the point of view of the story, is much duller and less attractive than Jane, yet she is a riper personality with a great deal of egoism and self-will ground out of her by everything that happened to Charlotte between the two books. (*Jane Eyre* was written during her sisters' lifetime and discussed with them constantly in the fire-lit parlor when the day's work was over. *Villette* was only begun about two years after Anne's death.)

We find only indications of the quaternity in *Jane Eyre*: Jane and her three Reid cousins on hostile terms at the beginning, and Jane and her three Rivers cousins on the most cordial terms at the end. But Mr. Rochester, by far the most important figure in the novel, except for Jane herself, is outside the quaternities. Moreover, there is only one important marriage at the end.

*Villette* also begins with four figures (Mrs. Bretton and her son, Lucy and little Polly), but they are all friendly, there is no hostile tension as in *Jane Eyre*. Lucy soon afterwards falls on evil days and suffers in the end even more than Jane. In Villette (Brussels) she suffers intolerably (admittedly a description of Charlotte's own agony there), indeed a mental suffering which Charlotte regards as far worse than "real material changes." In a letter of April 2, 1845, she says that once the latter are past, "strength, courage, and experience are their invariable result; whereas I doubt whether suffering purely mental has any good result, unless it is to make us by comparison less sensitive to physical sufferings." [24] But she gives the lie to her own doubt by the ripening effect that mental suffering had on Lucy Snowe. It seems to have been the torture which Charlotte herself needed in order to grind out her original self-will and wild ambition. How far it was finally ground out of her is difficult to say, but there was at all events a very great change in this respect.

Unlike Jane Eyre, Lucy Snowe had an earlier "love" before she recognized her fate in Paul Emanuel. But her love for Dr. John is never convincing (as is Jane's for Rochester and Lucy's later love); it resembles more a need to love, born of her terrible loneliness and hung upon a good-looking peg. For Dr. John turns out to be Mrs. Bretton's son and the lonely Lucy finds a welcoming home in the chalet he shares with his mother, who is Lucy's godmother. But when he falls in love with "little Polly," Lucy has already begun to notice that her volcanic but good-hearted Professor means a great deal more to her than Dr. John. The former is admirably described and the scenes between Lucy and him, though totally different, are as convincing as those between Jane Eyre and the far less human Rochester.

[24] Gaskell, p. 228.

*Villette* ends with the marrige of Dr. John and little Polly and the betrothal of Lucy and Paul Emanuel. But the redoubtable Madame Beck and a priest of the Catholic Church have been intriguing heartlessly but efficiently to separate the latter two, the former because she wants to marry him herself, the latter because Lucy is a Protestant. They succeed in sending Paul to the West Indies for three years, but not before he has found and furnished a house for Lucy so that she can leave her post as English teacher at Madame Beck's and not before he has promised to marry her on his return to Europe. She tells us that the three succeeding years were the happiest in her life, for the school—which she regards as a sacred trust from Paul Emanuel—flourishes and his letters are a constant joy. But the storms are the wildest in years the autumn he is due to return, and, though there is the loophole left at Mr. Brontë's request, as already mentioned, there is little doubt that his ship perishes at sea.

Although this quaternity does not eventually materialize, it meets a very different fate from the one in *Precious Bane*. In the latter novel the quaternity disintegrates and one pair disappears through self-destruction. In *Villette* there is the almost usual uncertainty about the fourth, always by far the most difficult to integrate. Jung has pointed out, particularly in *Psychology and Alchemy* and in "A Psychological Approach to the Trinity," that there has always been an uncertainty as to whether the central symbol is characterized by three or four. He shows, however, that the former really represents a completeness which is constructed by consciousness, whereas the latter depicts a natural wholeness in all its aspects. The uncertainity on this point all over the Western world really corresponds to a reluctance to integrate matter and evil into the image of the totality. (This uncertainty, as we shall see, is very evident in *Wuthering Heights.*) Although it is almost certain that in *Villette* the fourth disappears into the unconscious (the sea is the symbol *par excellence* of the collective unconscious), yet the bond of love remains between Paul in the Beyond and Lucy on earth, and one is certain he will never be forgotten by her.

Nevertheless, Charlotte's last book does not end with the integration of the fourth on earth. Charlotte herself was very sure that Paul had perished, because, as a matter of fact, she was "not leniently disposed" towards Lucy. So one may surmise that, as Lucy had so much of Charlotte in her, she was anything but lenient towards herself, in fact she did not really love herself at all. There is ample evidence of this in both her life and letters. Loving oneself is indeed one of the most difficult of all tasks. To spoil and pamper oneself is fatally easy and equally destructive, but to love and respect oneself, in the sense of regarding oneself as a fit vessel for the eternal Self, worthy of consideration as such, is extremely difficult. Yet Christ said, "Love thy neighbor *as thyself*," and it is really impossible to love others unless one loves oneself. To some extent Emily, and even Anne, had better instinctive attitudes towards themselves than Charlotte. In this respect the latter very unwisely gave in to her animus (always ready to depreciate us in our own eyes). Mrs. Gaskell, for example, tells us that Charlotte said: "I notice that after a stranger has once looked at my face, he is careful not to let his eyes wander to that part of the room again." Mrs. Gaskell adds: "A more untrue idea never entered anyone's head," and gives instances proving the contrary.

There is little doubt that Charlotte's attitude towards Lucy Snowe's happiness—"not leniently disposed to" her and never meaning "to appoint her lines in pleasant places"—was ultimately her attitude towards herself. This attitude contributed fatally to the fact that the quaternity was unable to establish itself on earth, for if Paul Emanuel had escaped the storms this development would have been assured. But we cannot tell whether this was the decisive factor, or whether the end of *Villette* was inevitable, forced on Charlotte by the unconscious, so to speak, because it presented a faithful picture of the place where Charlotte had arrived on her way back to Eden.

But before we go into this burning question, we should take a brief glance at *Shirley* which was written between *Jane Eyre* and *Villette*. Charlotte had finished about two thirds of *Shirley* when death broke into the Parsonage and tore the book in two. She took it up again soon after Anne's death with Chapter XXIV, "The Valley of the Shadow of Death." This chapter contains a good deal of what Charlotte herself must have suffered, except that in the novel Caroline recovers at the last moment. Charlotte herself writes of the last volume: "I cannot deny it was composed in the eager, restless endeavors to combat mental sufferings that were scarcely tolerable." *Shirley* is usually considered, with justification, as the least successful of Charlotte's three novels, but it is very interesting from our point of view.

It is totally different from the other two. Painted on a much larger canvas, against a background of world events, including the Napoleonic wars, it has no personal narrator but is written in the third person. Moreover, there is no figure that resembles Charlotte. One feels there is no fixed conscious entity to which the story happens. It has a totally different standpoint from that of *Jane Eyre* and *Villette*. Charlotte as it were stands outside, watches the development objectively from a distance and records what she sees. There are two heroines, the beautiful, lively heiress Shirley and the quiet and pretty Caroline. Mrs. Gaskell writes: "The character of Shirley herself is Charlotte's representation of Emily." Mrs. Gaskell evidently found this hard to believe, for she herself had "no pleasant impression of her." She admits, however, that Charlotte had told her that Emily was "genuinely good and truly great," and that "she had tried to depict her character in Shirley Keeldar as what Emily Brontë would have been had she been placed in health and prosperity." Caroline was probably a fictional representation of Ellen Nussey and Charlotte told her publisher that she had models for several of the other characters. She wrote to Ellen Nussey, however, that she was "not to suppose any of the characters in *Shirley* intended as actual portraits."

One also notices that in *Shirley* Charlotte adopted her sisters' opinion and gave beauty to both her heroines. Their romances, however, are very much less real and convincing than are those of Jane Eyre and Lucy Snowe. They are well worked out, it is true; in fact Mrs. Gaskell tells us that Charlotte took "extreme pains" with *Shirley*; but there is little or no spontaneity, and none of the feeling that Charlotte is writing within her own knowledge and experience which is so evident in her other two novels.

But from the point of view of the achievement of totality it is the most successful of the three, for it ends with the simultaneous double marriage of the two pairs, so that a true *quaternio* is established. Moreover, a sort of epilogue informs us that it was an enduring and fruitful *quaternio*: Shirley and her husband, Louis Moore, staying on at the manor house which belonged to the former, and Caroline and her husband, Robert Moore, at the nearby Mill, both pairs living long, industrious and benevolent lives.

When we consider this triumph of the totality and union of the opposites, it would seem at first as if the end of *Villette*, the later book, must be a regression. But we can soon see why this was inevitable. When Charlotte had distance from her subject, she could allow the *quaternio* to express itself without let or hindrance. (We shall find the same phenomenon in a quite different form in *Wuthering Heights* and even indicated in Anne's *Tenant of Wildfell Hall.*) But when a figure representing Charlotte's own consciousness is in question, then it is far more characteristic of her *own* process of individuation, and she herself is more or less consciously involved. Of course none of the Brontës knew or could know that there was such a thing as a "process of individuation," but the urge of every living creature towards wholeness was unusually strong in all of them (even in Branwell, although in his case it turned autonomous and destructive). This power which operated instinctively enabled the eternal being, the Self, to manifest itself further in the three dimensional world in Charlotte's most objective book. It also does so in *Villette*, but there it is hampered by Charlotte not being "leniently disposed" towards Lucy Snowe, ultimately towards herself, and not meaning (or not being able) to "appoint her lines in the pleasant place" of a happy marriage with Paul Emanuel. Therefore it is *Villette*, her last book or testament, as it were, which records just how far the totality, the Self, was able to advance in Charlotte's own psyche. In *Shirley* she had a glimpse of the promised land from afar, but in *Villette* we learn that, like Moses, she was not destined to enter it *in this life*.

Charlotte had gone far and had apparently arrived, after much suffering, at the door opposite the one by which she had left, the dark and doubtful fourth through which alone we can re-enter the lost Paradise. Mary Webb also approached that door, as we saw, but then took fright at the "evil mommets," drowned them in Sarn Mere and returned, with her one almost too-good-to-be-true pair of mommets, to the door by which she had come out, even denying the existence of evil in the person of the Weaver: "If you think about evil rightly it just isn't there."

Good and evil are very differently constellated in *Villette*. Evil was never rejected by Charlotte, as it was by Mary Webb, but was always accepted from her childhood on as part of the inevitable nature of man. Old Mr. Brontë's ideal of "the golden middle way" was to some extent, though undeniably differently, reflected in all of his children, and the virtues and vices are evenly distributed in the characters in *Villette*. The fact that the quaternity fails to establish itself on earth is by no means due to Charlotte's rejection of evil —as it is in *Precious Bane*—but rather perhaps to her inability to believe in Lucy's happiness because Lucy resembled herself.

Be that as it may, it is certain that Charlotte did not abandon the difficult, even terrifying, country around the fourth gate in horror as Mary Webb did, thereby regressing to a one-sided attitude. The imprint of the archetype of wholeness was too deep for that. It would have been very interesting, had she lived longer, to see how the theme might have been carried forward in her next book. But since that novel never materialized, we are only able to look for indications in the detailed information we fortunately possess about her life during the three years which were left to her after the publication of *Villette*.

It is curious that Mary Webb and Charlotte Brontë each lived three years after publishing her last book and testament, as it were (incidentally Lucy Snowe waited three years for Paul Emanuel's return), but whereas Mary Webb regressed rather than went forward during that time, Charlotte Brontë took a great step forward into the outer world: she at last faced "the ice in her veins," opposed her father for the first time in her life and got married.

In *Shirley*, besides the two main pairs, there are always, in the background, the three curates whom Charlotte endowed with most of the shadow qualities and treated with considerable humor. In her "winding up," she tells us that the infamous Irish curate, Mr. Malone, was replaced by "another Irish curate," Mr. Macarthey. Mr. Nichols, Charlotte's future husband, was the original of Mr. Macarthey and thus represents the fourth curate. In contradistinction to the other three, Charlotte represents Mr. Macarthey as an exemplary clergyman who "labored faithfully in the parish." But she found him very narrowminded:

> The circumstance of finding himself invited to tea with a dissenter would unhinge him for a week; the spectacle of a Quaker wearing his hat in the church, the thought of an unbaptised fellow-creature being interred with Christian rites—these things could make strange havoc in Mr. Macarthey's physical and mental economy; otherwise he was sane and rational, diligent and charitable.[25]

[25] *Shirley*, p. 501.

Many of Charlotte's detractors have accused her of husband-hunting and of being obsessed with the idea of getting married. But after all, Charlotte refused at least three suitors before Mr. Nichols, and had very honestly faced the problem of not being married. In fact she was very much concerned with how women could best deal with the fate of being "Miss" and not "Mrs." and recognized the courage that was needed to avoid feelings of inferiority concerning the social stigma of spinsterhood which was far greater then than now. Many passages in her letters to Ellen Nussey, as well as the chapter, "Old Maids," in *Shirley*, are concerned with this theme.

Ever since she went to Roe Head school, some twenty-five years before, Charlotte had striven valiantly to establish herself in the outer world, to become rooted in it. Such roots are indispensable to the creative genius if he is not to be swept away in his early youth, as Keats was, for instance. This effort was, in Charlotte, always at war with the claims of the inner world, the "fifteen years war," as Fannie Ratchford called it. It seemed as if a truce had indeed been reached: Charlotte had become very famous and was sought after in the outer world and was meeting the claims of the inner world through her creative writing which had as yet shown no signs of abating. But presumably she felt that her outer roots were not yet deep and strong enough to suffice. Objectively, it is clear that she had reason enough for such an anxiety: a strong *unconscious* incest must develop when a father and daughter live together in such lonely circumstances. In itself, this was reason enough for Charlotte to face the "ice in her veins" and break out to an exogamous partner. Moreover, as is clear in almost all her letters of this period, her loneliness was almost unbearable. She missed the cooperation of her sisters more instead of less as the years went by, and she was terribly tempted to live in the past. As I see it, she had to take a step forward if she was not to regress, and fate decreed that this step should be marriage with Mr. Nichols.

There must have been a very strong motive at work in Charlotte to move her to defy her father for the first time in her life, for Mr. Brontë was strongly opposed to the marriage. He thought it the utmost presumption on Mr. Nichols' part and was so upset that the latter resigned his curacy and went elsewhere. Mr. Brontë obviously did not want to share his daughter. He advanced one objection, however, which turned out to be only too true: that Charlotte's health would not stand matrimony. Nevertheless, she remained quietly persistent and Mr. Brontë at last gave in, although at the last moment he did not attend the wedding.

After a honeymoon in Ireland, Mr. and Mrs. Nichols settled down at Haworth Parsonage, where the former subsequently remained with old Mr. Brontë until his death six years after Charlotte's. In fact, therefore, Charlotte's only opposition to her father's will saved him from a completely lonely old age and death! The marriage, which lasted only nine months, seems to have been happy, though it might have become more difficult had it lasted longer. From all accounts, Mr. Nichols would have been likely to oppose his wife's work and, although Charlotte certainly put her duty to her husband very high, she would hardly have been able to repress her creative side which had always broken through any restrictions she tried to impose.

Be this as it may, the difficulty never arose, for six months after the wedding Charlotte caught a bad cold from which she never recovered. Her illness was complicated by pregnancy. Interestingly enough, Charlotte told Mrs. Gaskell that Jane Eyre's dream (of carrying a baby in her arms in some gloomy place and being unable to quiet it) was a life-long recurrent dream of her own and always preceded trouble of some kind. It is, therefore, psychologically very interesting that Charlotte died in the third month of her pregnancy, on March 31st, 1855, after nine months of marriage.

Charlotte made a valiant attempt to leave Eden, to get roots in the outside world, and this was undoubtedly the reason she alone survived when death broke into the Parsonage and swept off the other three. She attempted, in the last year of her life, to send those roots deeper, even to produce a child in order to carry them into the next generation. It was a gallant attempt which, as is all too often the case, was paid for by her life.

In the chapter on "Conscious and Unconscious" [26] I tried to show that entering the unknown country, in the depths of which the fourth gate of paradise is situated, is a psychical equivalent of exploring the unknown territories of the earth and is just as dangerous and demanding, if not more so. In this sense, therefore, one may say that Charlotte Brontë died much as, for example, Scott died in the Antarctic. Each failed in his outer purpose—perhaps the fact that each was unusually ambitious played an indirect part in the failure—but each valiantly sacrificed his life in exploring the unknown. Scott's was a well-recognized, outer unkown and he at once became a national hero. Charlotte's heroism in this respect is only gradually becoming evident, as other people explore the dark, unknown country that guards the fourth gate, the return to Eden and to the wholeness of man.

[26] See above, pp. 15ff.

# 7 BRANWELL

BRANWELL IS PROBABLY the most difficult of the Brontës to estimate. Some of the most important facts are missing and presumably will never come to light. We have no idea, for instance, why old Mr. Brontë, who laid great weight on education and who kept sending his daughters to boarding schools, never sent his son. And we do not know why the long, well-ripened later plan to send Branwell to the Royal Academy to study art never materialized, although Branwell actually went to London. Nor do we have any reliable information concerning Branwell's passion for Mrs. Robinson. And these are only the most important of endless gaps in our information.

An attempt to bring "some measure of understanding for a figure long maligned, neglected and despised" and "to reinstate him in his original place in the Brontë family" has been made by Daphne du Maurier.[1] She makes a valuable effort to show how Branwell remained stuck in the world of fantasy, his "infernal world," and was unable to adapt to the outer world because he always judged the outer by the inner. From the point of view of research into the puzzle presented by Branwell, the book is unfortunately more popular than scientific in character, a fault it shares with a great majority of the many books on the Brontës. For example, although one is grateful for some quotations, she lessens their objective value by providing no reference, only a list of "sources"

[1] *The Infernal World of Branwell Brontë*, p. 10.

for each chapter. And, although she advances a lot of rather seductive theories to fill in the gaps in our knowledge, none of them seems to be founded on factual evidence.

Another difficulty in understanding Branwell is due to the fact that most of our information about him comes to us through Charlotte. Mr. Brontë, it is true, wrote Mrs. Gaskell that her "picture of my brilliant and unhappy son . . . is a masterpiece," [2] but Mrs. Gaskell received most, though not all, of her information from Charlotte. Charlotte's estimate of her brother is evidently much too sanguine in youth, too despairing and moralistic later.

However, we have a few undeniable facts which enable us to see that Branwell had the most difficult fate of all the Brontës. To be the only boy among three—originally five—sisters is a very serious drawback. And to lose his mother when he was only four, then Maria, his eldest sister (who had become his second mother and who evidently understood him much better than Charlotte, who was only a year older), before he was eight, was probably even harder on the boy than on the girls.[3] He was, it is true, the favorite of his aunt, Miss Branwell, but she more injudiciously spoiled him than gave him any real support.

Spoiling and injudicious admiration were indeed Branwell's portion as a child. He was always regarded by all of them as the family genius. Moreover he alone of the Brontës had the dangerous gift of charm. When things wanted en-

[2] *Ibid.*, p. 116. Mr. Brontë would refer, of course, to the first edition in which Mrs. Gaskell laid most of the blame for Branwell's downfall on Mrs. Robinson. She had no factual evidence for this assumption and was forced, therefore, to apologize in print to avoid a lawsuit. This section was omitted in later editions.

[3] As the first projection of animus and anima is always onto the father and mother, psychologically at all events Branwell lacked the original outer foundation for this image, whereas all the girls had a figure in their father that filled the projection of the father-image, or first form of the animus, particularly well.

livening at the Bull Inn, the bar of Haworth's one hotel, the landlord would send to the vicarage for Branwell and he was thus early exposed to the pleasures of relaxation, which the guests had probably earned by hard work but which Branwell just dropped into.

Apparently, it was in his work—or rather in the lack of it—that Branwell failed from the beginning. We have a great volume of material in his juvenilia, it is true; he probably wrote at least as many words as Charlotte. But if one compares the two styles of writing, Charlotte, from the beginning, not only excells in talent but also in industry and effort. When characters got themselves into difficulty, for example, Branwell just declared another war or killed them off, whereas one receives the impression that Charlotte allowed herself no rest until she had found a meaningful solution. Branwell also had a far more facile and superficial style than any of the girls. When the dangerous archetypal image of the four Genii imprinted itself on this family, and the still more dangerous identification of the children with these mighty demons occurred, a ray of hope was provided in Charlotte's vision: if "certain arduous duties every year of a mysterious nature" were performed, it would serve to avert the doom, the complete extinction of all humanity, portrayed in the image of "one mighty globe" rolling in "solitary grandeur through the vast wilderness of space." The girls were indefatigable workers, Branwell unfortunately was not and was therefore from the very beginning far more exposed to the negative side. Indeed, by calling himself "Bany-Lightening" and always bringing their play back "to a game of destruction and war," [4] Branwell even courted the negative side.

It was the purely destructive aspects of Chief Genius Branni that cost Branwell the leadership, so dear to his heart, in their games. The girls hit on the scheme of using their Chief Genii to bring their brother's victims back to life;

[4] Ratchford, *op. cit.*, p. 15.

Branwell could rage and destroy as he would, his sisters just rescued his victims and developed them in their own way.

Most boys go through a destructive stage, but Branwell's destructiveness went a bit further than most. For example, after one battle, won against "overwhelming odds," his forces seized prisoners and crammed them all, soldiers and civilians, including children, into a small room in a castle and subsequently killed them by blowing up the castle. Branwell excused this deed, which he owned that some may think "monstrous and cruel in the extreme," by explaining that they had wounded his favorite soldier, Crashy, "and after this who would think of sparing them?" [5]

We have here, on the one side, a completely primitive psychology—"If I take your woman it is good, if you take mine it is bad"—and, on the other, an anticipation of the Nazis, who, over a hundred years later, would destroy entire villages because of some injury, or even a fancied injury, to one German. Branwell played dangerously with evil in those early games, far more than did the girls who accepted evil but *never* threw their weight on its side. Branwell thus laid the foundations for his later possession.

In his writing, Branwell was always hopelessly outdistanced by his sisters. We have seen more than one of the strange invasions from a deep level of the unconscious that were constellated by Charlotte's industrious and objective attitude. I have never found anything similar in any of Branwell's almost equally prolific juvenilia. The nearest is his description of the Kairail Fish, "a marvelous creature eighty to one hundred feet long with a horn twenty to thirty feet long and hooked at the end, which, when cut off by sailors, grows back in the space of half an hour." [6] This creature is indeed an inhabitant of the deep collective unconscious but, compared with Charlotte's saving "arduous duties" and with the

[5] Ratchford, p. 12.
[6] *Ibid.*, p. 18.

equally positive and negative sides of her (alchemistic) fluid, Branwell's fantasy fish reveals a fatal invincibility. Even if he could have summoned the energy to fight the negative side, his demon possessed all the qualities of the Hydra of Lerna and Branwell was constitutionally unfit to become a Hercules. This, together with his identification at only eight years of age with the already defeated Buonoparte, look as if his defeat were a fatal defeat, as if it were his destiny to play the role of one of Mary Webb's "evil mommets" [7] and that the best he could do was to some extent to realize this fact. Branwell's short tragic life can best be approached from this angle.

Branwell's failure to train as a painter at the Royal Academy deprived him of his only chance for a successful career, as indeed he himself often declared. In painting he was as far ahead of his sisters as they were ahead of him in writing. His few remaining portraits reveal something very different from his facile second-rate style of writing, a true sensitiveness and an ability to penetrate below the surface. The essentials for a very unusual portrait painter are present and there is nothing in the crude and ignorant technique that a few years of hard study could not have improved. Here again it is probably a question of his aversion to hard study, but whether this defect in his character was due to laziness which he could have overcome or whether the ability to work was fatally lacking, part of his destiny in playing the role of an "evil mommet," we cannot presume to judge.

At all events, it is probably here that Branwell's early identification with Chief Genius Branni played its most fatal role. All of the children were in the habit of getting over the difficulties in their play by simply waving a wand. Outer reality, however, taught the girls, as early as Roe Head, the

[7] Mary Webb, it will be remembered, realized that "the evil mommets do His will as well as the good," a strangly Eastern point of view for an English novelist writing in the early 20th century. See above, p. 91.

second school, that the deficiencies in their education—for example, they "had never learnt grammar at all, and very little geography" [8]—were entirely unaffected by the potent powers of the Chief Genii and could only be dealt with by hard, unremitting work. But Branwell was deprived of this discipline. It was much easier for him to remain in the "infernal world" at Haworth Parsonage; the longer the confrontation with outer reality was delayed, the more difficult it became to leave the Parsonage. Branwell was at least nineteen before he went out into the world at all. By that time the fatal conviction that the wand of Chief Genius Branni could obtain him everything he wanted without further effort seems to have been too deeply rooted for the lesson, which the girls had learned comparatively easily at Roe Head when they were several years younger, ever to be learned by Branwell at all.

Although there is no outer evidence for this conclusion, both Ratchford and du Maurier draw attention to a fragment of a story written by Branwell as possibly autobiographical.[9] Written, in all probability, shortly after his trip to London, it describes the first visit of Charles Wentworth, one of his Angrian characters, to Verdopolis (Capital of Angria). When he first beholds the great city, the young man feels "the excitement of anticipation change suddenly to intense depression." He spends the day aimlessly lying on a hotel sofa, listlessly dreaming away his time until dark. "The next day, too depressed to present his letters of introduction or go about the business that had brought him there, Wentworth walked out alone to view the great buildings he had long dreamed of seeing." Of these: "St. Michael's Cathedral moved him more than all else." But he is afraid to enter it "*lest realization shatter the pleasure of anticipation.*" [10] We

[8] Mary Taylor's letter to Mrs. Gaskell.
[9] Ratchford, p. 114f; du Maurier, p. 51f.
[10] Ratchford. The italics are added.

hear later that "strangely enough neither the great libraries nor the picture galleries attracted Wentworth. Restless and aimless he lingered in his hotel, 'feeding his feelings with little squibs of rum', though he was perfectly aware that the drink 'would only depress him more afterwards'."

Miss du Maurier quotes an earlier passage (omitted by Ratchford) which is interesting as confirmation of our surmise that Branwell's attitude toward work was very different from that of his sisters. Wentworth's advisers have been trying to check his idleness and his tendency to build castles in the air by telling him that one can have no real happiness without working for it. "Exertion is the nutshell which holds pleasure, crack it, and it can be found. Otherwise never." Again, "the harder the shell, the better the nut." But Wentworth rejects this advice for he has already decided that "Happiness consists in Anticipation," and says that this latter "argument leads me to the conclusion that I shall have nothing to reward my exertion. Then why should I labour?" [11]

This is a very different conclusion from Charlotte's "arduous duties" which are to save the world from destruction. It seems to me that this "bone idleness," even championed here by Branwell (whether it was his fault or was too deeply ingrained to be conquered), was responsible for his tragedy. This whole account of Wentworth's visit to Verdopolis is very interesting psychologically, whether Branwell was consciously describing his own visit to London or writing it more or less from the unconscious, for it is connected with his own psyche in either case.

The words "lest realization shatter the pleasure of anticipation" show us very clearly how Branwell treasured his inner world, where everything could be dealt with by Chief Genius Branni, and how he consistently turned away from reality. In justice to him, he was not only forced to face reality much later than were his sisters, but also under very much less

[11] du Maurier, p. 51f.

sheltered conditions. There is no evidence that anyone accompanied him to London; if no one did, the great metropolis must have really been a thousand times more intimidating than Roe Head School. When the London experiment failed, he set up, almost at once, as a portrait painter in Bradford—an extraordinary foolishness, presumably brought about not only by his lack of knowledge of the world but also by the short-sighted partiality of his family. Except for a few private painting lessons, Branwell had had no training whatever and was anything but proficient in technique. How could he earn his living as a painter, a much more difficult matter than receiving a salary as a governess? The wonder is that the experiment lasted as long as a year. But it was a year in which he was comparatively happy and, according to a niece of the family he lived with, "was steady, industrious and self respecting." [12] It was a thousand pities that Branwell could not have continued to paint, a vocation in which it is much more difficult *not* to work than in his kind of facile writing. The experiment naturally failed, in spite of some financial help from the Rev. William Morgan, and Branwell returned to hopeless competition in his sisters' field and to writing foolish, vainglorious letters to such people as the editor of *Blackwood's Magazine* and the poet Wordsworth. Branwell suffered, in a particularly acute form, from the inflation that identification with a figure of the unconscious—such as a Chief Genius—naturally breeds. His sisters, each in her own way, succeeded to a greater or smaller degree in dissolving this identification. But Branwell remained naively certain that he was simply a great genius, an opinion his family for many years unfortunately encouraged. He could write quite seriously, to the editor of *Blackwood's Magazine*, such sentences as:

Sir, Read what I write. And would to Heaven you could

[12] du Maurier, p. 77.

believe it but then you would attend and act upon it. I have addressed you twice before, and now I do it again. . . . Now, sir, to you I appear to be writing with conceited assurance, but *I am not;* for I know myself so far as to believe in my own originality. . . . The idea of striving to aid another periodical is *horribly repulsive*. . . . In letters previous to this I have perhaps spoken too openly respecting the extent of my powers. But I did so because I determined to say what I believed. I *know* that I am not one of the wretched writers of the day. . . . Now, sir, do not act like a commonplace person, but like a man willing to examine for himself. Do not turn from the naked truth of my letters, but *prove me*. . . . You have lost an able writer in James Hogg (the Ettrick shepherd) and God grant you gain one in Patrick Branwell Brontë.[13]

Charlotte produced a satirical, exaggerated but good-natured portrait of Branwell in one of her stories. She called him Patrick Benjamin Wiggens and wrote on his tombstone:

As a musician he was greater than Bach, as a poet he surpassed Byron and as a painter Claude Lorrain yielded to him.[14].

On the one hand, there is ample evidence that for many years Branwell implicitly believed his own estimate of his genius but, on the other, his feelings of inferiority grew more and more ominous, a natural, inevitable consequence of his unfounded inflation.

After giving up the Bradford studio Branwell returned to Haworth, where the outer situation must have supported his feelings of inferiority to an increasing degree. A short effort as a tutor, an attempt to earn his living as a clerk and then

[13] Ratchford, p. 112.
[14] *Ibid*, p. 98.

as a very minor stationmaster on the railways all ended in failure. It is not clear when either Branwell's addiction to drink or later to drugs actually started, but the former was certainly to a great extent his master very soon after Bradford. The only post he held for any length of time, and at first very creditably, was his position as tutor to the Robinson boy in the family in which Anne was governess to the girls.

In July 1845, when he was twenty-eight, and after two and a half years of holding the post, Branwell lost his position. Daphne du Maurier has pointed out very rightly—and as far as I know for the first time—that there is no evidence that Mr. Robinson's letter dismissing Branwell as his son's tutor really refers, as has always been assumed since Mrs. Gaskell's spirited assertions, to Branwell's attitude towards Mrs. Robinson. Charlotte wrote to Ellen Nussey that Branwell had "received a note from Mr. Robinson sternly dismissing him, intimating that he had discovered his proceedings, which he characterised as bad beyond expression, and charging him on pain of exposure to break off instantly and for ever all communication with every member of the family." [15]

If this is all the written evidence we have concerning Mr. Robinson's letter, Miss du Maurier is certainly right when she suggests that it could just as well have been intended as a protection of his son as of his wife. We simply do not know what Branwell's "bad beyond expression" proceedings were. Miss du Maurier also points out that, whereas Branwell evidently allowed his family to think that Mrs. Robinson was even the prime instigator in the alleged affair, he increasingly represented her to his friends as a suffering angel and a paragon of all the virtues.[16] It is impossible to disentangle fact from fiction in the story, though it is factually proven that the lady refused to have anything to do with him

[15] du Maurier, pp. 163ff.
[16] du Maurier, p. 209.

after her husband's death and that Branwell's assertion that this was forced on her by her husband's will was absolutely false. Francis Leyland tells us that neither he nor his brother, the sculptor, ever believed the story and that it probably had no "foundation save in Branwell's heated imagination." [17]

After leaving the Robinsons Branwell spent the next three years at Haworth in increasing degeneration, and it is psychologically interesting that his final deterioration was the result of his first strong attachment to a woman. Whatever the facts of the case and however much Branwell dramatized the story, Lydia Robinson, seventeen years older than Branwell, certainly received the full projection of his anima.

I have suggested that the deaths of Mrs. Brontë and Maria were harder on the boy than the girls, and that the reason for this was that Branwell was thus deprived of a firm foundation from which his anima could develop, a foundation that the girls had in their very definite father. For Branwell, the older Mrs. Robinson with her evidently fascinating qualities would be and evidently was a powerful magnet for this long buried figure. Not only his obsession with Mrs. Robinson after the break but also the fact that he had been able to pull himself sufficiently together to retain his post for two and a half years, even giving complete satisfaction at first, speak for the probability of her very strong attraction for him. There had indeed been fantasy equivalents in his own infernal world, as Miss du Maurier points out, but as far as we know this was the first time the image projected itself and appeared in concreate reality. Such an anima figure almost always projects itself onto an unsuitable object—as experience shows us again and again—just as if she were a jealous woman who will brook no rivals.

I cannot help feeling that, in spite of his infantile and absurd behavior in the whole matter, Branwell's feeling for

[17] *Ibid.*, p. 173. The sculptor Leyland and his brother were friends of Branwell.

Mrs. Robinson was probably a very genuine thing, a last attempt as it were to find his way back to an experience of human emotions and of love. The little we know from Anne about Mrs. Robinson clearly indicates that she was an egotistical woman who had not got it in her to help a young man in Branwell's predicament. Bernard Shaw's Candida played this role to perfection with the young Marchbanks, and in real life Madame de Berny did the same for the young Balzac.[18] But such women are unfortunately very rare or fewer Branwells would fall by the way.

Branwell let himself go completely when he returned to Haworth, and the evil which had always been lying in wait for him possessed him more and more. He wrote to Leyland, the sculptor, that he would like to write a novel that would give "a vivid picture of human feelings for good and evil" but realized he could no more do this than he "could jump over the Mersey." [19] Drink and laudanum (tincture of opium) were rapidly killing what was left of any earlier creative urge.

Branwell certainly played the role of an "evil mommet" more and more in his last years. Of this there can be no doubt. The only question is: How much was he forced to do so in the "play" of the Brontë family? As Prue Sarn says: "The play is of His making. So the evil mommets do His will as well as the good, since they act the part set for them. How would it be if the play came to the hour when the villainous man must do evilly, and see! He is on his knee bones at his prayers. Then the play would be in very poor case." [20]

We have seen that the archetype of wholeness imprinted itself on the four surviving Brontë children at a very early age. There is no wholeness without the opposites and these

[18] I owe the latter example to a lecture by Aniela Jaffé.
[19] du Maurier, p. 168.
[20] Webb, *Precious Bane,* p. 158.

were also present from the beginning in all their childhood games and magazine articles. Even their name for their inner realm, the "Infernal World" or "the world below," shows that there was no attempt to shut out evil; in fact it flourished in their "amoral world of Angria" (Ratchford). From the first, Branwell identified with destruction; even in their early games he voluntarily or unconsciously usually played the roles of the "evil mommets." Now such fantasies, even in childhood, have far more effect on the personality than is generally realized, and if evil is thus constellated, it must be faced in later life or it will inevitably emerge into outer reality, "called or not called."[21] So that all four were psychologically doomed to have it out with evil.

None of the girls avoided this problem in their work; each dealt with it in her own way. But in their lives, all of them, especially Charlotte and Anne, took over the roles, for the most part, of the "good mommets." Someone, therefore, was fated to take the evil role and that someone was certainly Branwell. How far such a role is a matter of free will and how much it is a destiny beyond our control we do not know but one doubts whether Branwell had much choice in the matter. With more consciousness, he could have had a choice, but such consciousness was beyond the time or reach of the Brontës.

If this hypothesis is correct, Branwell would not only have been the bane and torment of his sisters' lives, as he is usually represented, but also their indispensable shadow, the Mr. Hyde as it were to their Dr. Jekyll. In a sense, by living the dark side of the constellated totality, he set them free to live the light side. In Mary Webb's words, "the play would have been in very poor case" without him. As Daphne du Maurier points out, Charlotte need not have condemned him quite so strongly, for at the same time as he was breaking his heart

[21] "Called or not called, God will be there"—Delphic inscription.

over Mrs. Robinson, she was writing undoubted love letters to a married man. Christ's saying, "Man, if indeed thou knowest what thou doest, thou art blessed: but if thou knowest not, thou art cursed, and a transgressor of the law,"[22] has never been understood by the proponents of Christian morality; otherwise Charlotte could not have been quite so sure that she was in a position to throw stones at her brother. Moreover, as we shall see in her treatment of Anne, Charlotte carried far more shadow qualities and played more tricks behind her own back than she ever began to realize. Such realization on her part might have relieved Branwell from carrying the *whole* weight of the family shadow. I mention only Charlotte here because she was much the nearest to Branwell, and it is to her letters that we owe most of our knowledge of his last miserable years; we will return to Emily's and Anne's roles in the family "play" later.

But what of Branwell's own individuation process? The achetype of wholeness had already put its imprint upon him in childhood, as it had on all four of them. Such children seem destined to meet the totality subsequently in some form or other. As we have seen, Charlotte met it in her books (to say nothing of her life) where it was able to express itself through the merit of unremitting work. We shall see, in their own chapters, how it manifested in Emily and Anne. But Branwell missed out on the "arduous duties," so that Charlotte's vision fulfilled itself as it were in his fate. The process of individuation became completely autonomous in him, it rolled on "in solitary grandeur through the vast wilderness of space," and Branwell was only present as "Chief Genius Branni," with the human being entirely blotted out.

May Sinclair, who titles her book *The Three Brontës*, thus ignoring the very existence of Branwell, dismisses him in the

[22] From Codex Bezae at Luke VI, 4. In *The Apocryphal New Testament*, translated by M. R. James, p. 33.

following words: "Branwell's case, once and for all, was purely pathological." [23] Miss Sinclair dates her preface 1911; she was therefore writing in the days when even psychiatrists allowed themselves similar (though better-named) diagnoses and thought the matter settled. But since then Jung's works have proven that no such sweeping distinction can be made between the "normal" and the insane. The contents of the unconscious are very much the same in both, but in insanity the human being gets swept away by the unconscious. Thus Branwell must be admitted to have been completely possessed, solitary and unrelated, bereft of all consideration for other people, and therefore over the border of sanity, during his last three years if not earlier. The fluid Charlotte describes as having been discovered by Branwell's beloved Crashie (so beloved that he was willing to blow up one hundred and eighty prisoners as revenge for wounding his hero) was alas changed in Branwell's case by the Genii, "those high and unseen spirits," and "instead of dispensing immortality and holy delight, it would [and did] bring the horrors, the darkness of inevitable death." [24]

Yet, at the last moment, an enantiodromia occurred. Sooner or later an extreme condition always turns into its unrecognized opposite, and although Branwell seemed entirely to have disappeared into the dark opposite, he was allowed a glimpse of the light before he died. Charlotte wrote to her friend and publisher, W. S. Williams of Messrs. Smith and Elder, about ten days after Branwell's death:

> When I looked on the noble face and forehead of my dead brother (Nature had favored him with a fairer outside, as well as a finer constitution than his sisters) and asked myself what had made him go ever wrong, tend ever down-

[23] Sinclair, p. 52.
[24] Ratchford, p. 70.

wards, when he had so many gifts to induce to, and aid in, an upward course, I seemed to receive an oppressive revelation of the feebleness of humanity; of the inadequacy of even genius to lead to true greatness if unaided by religion and principle. In the value, or even the reality of these two things he would never believe till within a few days of his end, and then all at once he seemed to open his heart to a conviction of their existence and worth. The remembrance of this strange change now comforts my poor Father greatly. I myself, with painful, mournful joy, heard him praying softly in his dying moments, and to the last prayer which my father offered up at his bedside, he added "amen". How unusual that word appeared from his lips, of course you, who did not know him, cannot conceive. Akin to this alteration was that in his feelings towards his relatives, all bitterness seemed gone.

When the struggle was over, and a marble calm began to succeed the last dread agony, I felt, as I had never felt before, that there was peace and forgiveness for him in Heaven.[25]

Charlotte tells us here, in Christian, even in Church, language, that the "darkness of inevitable death" was lightened by its other side which dispensed "immortality and holy delight." Branwell had undoubtedly suffered a great deal, not only in his unhappy love for Mrs. Robinson but also in the realization that his whole life had been a failure—he did fully realize this in his last year. "I have done nothing good nor great," was only one of many remarks he made, proving that his earlier inflation had entirely disappeared. This is somewhat similar to Stevenson's cry, "I am a fictitious article," although Stevenson revealed a deeper insight and far more self-criticism, because, as the world judges, Stevenson

[25] du Maurier, p. 231.

was a recognized and even popular author, whereas the complete failure of Branwell was obvious to everyone, even himself. Yet this gleam of light in Branwell's dark last days substantiates a conviction that suffering, that "fastest horse that leadeth to perfection," redeemed a life that the world would judge, and has judged for over a century, to be a completely wasted existence.

# 8 ❧ ANNE

OF ALL THE BRONTËS, we know the least about Anne. Not because there are any relevant gaps in our knowledge of the outer events of her life (as with Branwell and the British Academy), but because she has always been an accompanying figure, overshadowed by her two great sisters. Moreover, even more than Branwell, Anne suffers from the fact that most of our information about her comes through Charlotte, whom Derek Stanford calls, with considerable justification, "Anne's well-wishing Bad Fairy."

A few voices were raised on Anne's behalf during the first century after her death, but they usually made extravagant, even absurd, claims for her work. George Moore, for instance, went so far as to declare that *Agnes Grey* was "the most perfect prose narrative in the English language," and that "If Anne Brontë had lived ten years longer she would have taken a place beside Jane Austen, perhaps even a higher place."

Anne suddenly emerged into the limelight in 1959 when two books in which she was the central figure appeared within a few months of each other.[1] With so many studies of the Brontë already in print and almost every available document published, the authors were unable to offer any sensational new evidence. But both books illuminate dark corners, containing facts that had never struck one before, and all three

[1] Harrison and Stanford, *Anne Brontë, Her Life and Work;* Gérin, *Anne Brontë.*

authors throw new light on Anne's poems. Derek Stanford in particular emphasizes some important dates in Anne's poems, relates them to events in her life in an illuminating way, and more or less reaches the conclusion that her nature was reflective rather than creative. She considered what had happened to her, then wrote a poem to digest the event, so to speak. All three authors seem to agree that Anne's poems are autobiographical. There is so much conjecture, sometimes even fantastic conjecture, about the private lives of the Brontës, that any indisputable facts, such as a date or the existence of the Héger letters, are pure gold.

Anne was the only one of the Brontë girls who seems to have been considerably under the influence of her aunt, Miss Branwell. She was only eighteen months old when Miss Branwell took over at the Parsonage, and she was always her aunt's favorite among the girls. She had to sleep in her aunt's stuffy, over-furnished room until after she was grown-up and was alone with her when her sisters were at Cowan Bridge school and during the catastrophe of the deaths of her two elder sisters who had been sent home to die.

Miss Branwell was always an exile in Yorkshire, pining for the warmth of her native Penzance. The bleakness and loneliness of the Yorkshire moors and the solitude of Haworth, so different from the social round of Penzance, were in no way congenial to her. If she had been able to marry Mr. Brontë it might have been better for everyone concerned, but the Church still forbade a man to marry his "deceased wife's sister," so Miss Branwell remained the duty-doing maiden aunt. Everyone in the Branwell circle in Cornwall had been profoundly affected by Wesley and consequently Miss Branwell's religion was much narrower, more prejudiced and terrifying than Mr. Brontës. Alone of the children, Anne was profoundly and deeply affected by her aunt's religious views; in fact they were probably even more deeply imprinted on her soul than was the "amoral world" in which they all played unceasingly. Branwell may also have been *indirectly* affected by his aunt's narrow and gloomy religion; indeed, it may well have been responsible for his later complete rejection of anything to do with religion. But the two elder girls, particularly Emily, remained amazingly free from the influence of her doctrines. Their creative genius could work on and try to formulate the amazing things they met in their "world below," but the constellated opposites were much more difficult for Branwell and Anne. The former, as we have seen, eventually fell victim to the evil that was so conspicuous in the "infernal world," whereas Anne tried to solve the problem in the frame of the Christian religion, complicated by her aunt's narrow animus opinions on the subject.

In her childhood, Anne was very much the baby of the family, much as she describes Agnes in *Agnes Grey*, admittedly an account (thinly disguised) of parts of her own life. Ellen Nussey says of her when she was fourteen: "Anne, dear gentle Anne, was quite different in appearance from the others. . . . Her hair was a very pretty light brown and fell on her neck in graceful curls. She had lovely violet blue eyes, fine pencilled eyebrows and clear, almost transparent complexion." [2] Plain elder sisters are seldom quite objective about their much prettier younger sisters, and this probably enters unconsciously into a good deal of Charlotte's blindness concerning Anne. Ellen Nussey also tells us that Emily and Anne "were like twins—inseparable companions, and in the very closest sympathy which never had any interruption." [3]

The sympathy probably was really uninterrupted, though we have very few *facts* that would enable us to get a reliable impression of their companionship. However, they were separated more than is generally supposed. Their years apart, adding Anne's longer times away and Emily's briefer absences, must have amounted to nearly a third of their short lives.

[2] Harrison and Stanford, p. 19.
[3] Gérin, p. 67.

This was probably fortunate for Anne's development, always a bit threatened by her symbiosis with Emily. Winifred Gérin strongly emphasizes, with considerable justification, that Emily saved Anne from falling completely under the influence of her aunt's gloomy religion. Emily's well-known poem, "No coward soul is mine," with its bold statement, "Vain are the thousand creeds that move men's hearts," lay indeed far in the future, but such an attitude seems to have been innate in her and no late acquisition. Anne was never able to base her religion on overwhelming direct experience, as was true with Emily; religion was always a problem for Anne, but she could and did experience nature almost as deeply as Emily.

Anne's chief problem in her girlhood was being the youngest child and thus never being trusted to do anything at all. But she had a certain quiet endurance and, whereas Emily only put up with Roe Head School for three months, Anne, who took her place, stayed well over two years. Directly afterwards, she horrified her family by insisting on becoming a governess. She undertook the profession full of illusions for, as she describes in *Agnes Grey*, she thought, "How charming to be entrusted with the care and education of children. Whatever others said, I felt I was fully competent to the task: the clear remembrance of my own thoughts in early childhood would be a surer guide than the instructions of the most mature people." [4]

Her first charges soon disillusioned her. As Winifred Gérin expresses it: "The little Inghams were not only the naughtiest children she had ever met, they were a *revelation* in naughtiness." [5] Anne must have been accustomed in the Brontë's "world below" to encountering much worse evil, but I doubt whether she was ever as wholeheartedly engaged in this inner world or as committed to it as were the others. Moreover

[4] *Agnes Grey*, p. 400.
[5] Gérin, p. 128.

it is a very different matter to meet concrete evil in the outer world, particularly for a girl of Anne's type.[6] The little Inghams were her first and a comparatively mild taste of a problem that was to follow her all her short life. Mr. and Mrs. Ingham had imbibed some notions ahead of their time about not crossing children, and they gave Anne no support whatever with their demonic offspring, so it is not to be wondered at that she was dismissed after two very miserable terms. She was deeply humiliated but not discouraged, and during the year or two she remained at home she never wavered in her decision to try again.

When she arrived home she found an addition to the family circle in the person of her father's new curate, William Weightman. It is difficult to form a reliable picture of him, as Charlotte's account differs materially from old Mr. Brontë's, but he must have been a very cheering influence to the girls at the Parsonage, for during the fifteen months after Anne's return they lived a far more social life than ever before or after. He was the original of Mr. Sweeting in *Shirley* and appears a great deal in Charlotte's correspondence with Ellen Nussey. He was evidently very good-natured, he did not resent his nickname of "Celia Amelia," but, from Charlotte's account, he had a heart like a hotel and was always in love with someone else.

According to her biographers Anne was undoubtedly in love with William Weightman. Although Derek Stanford regards the point as irrelevant to his own purpose, he offers some convincing proof when he says: "Most of the evidence points that way, for he died in the October of 1842 and all the love poems which speak of their subject being dead are dated later." [7] This certainly is evidence, as is the wording of some of the poems. And Charlotte, who coupled him with every girl he knew, particularly Ellen Nussey, but had never

[6] Anne Brontë was probably a feeling type.
[7] Harrison and Stanford, p. 183.

previously mentioned Anne, did say on almost the last occasion she saw him: "He sits opposite to Anne at Church sighing softly and looking out of the corners of his eyes to win her attention—and Anne is so quiet, her looks so downcast—they are a picture." But she continued: "He would be the better of a comfortable wife like you to settle him, you would settle him I believe—no one else would." Anne was always more or less invisible to her eldest sister except in regard to her health which Charlotte guarded zealously. Emily is spoken of as a great comfort in Brussels, but as far as I know, Anne is ignored in Charlotte's letters from Roe Head where Charlotte was really in worse need of a companion. Also she arbitrarily decided in favor of Emily for her Brussels scheme, giving neither of her sisters any choice. So it is quite possible that even if Anne were in love with Mr. Weightman, it might escape Charlotte's notice or possibly be willfully ignored.

But for internal reasons, I rather doubt that "Celia Amelia" was any more to Anne than a very welcome opportunity to realize every young girl's dream of falling in love. I cannot believe that Anne had had the transforming experience of *really* loving a man when she later wrote the scenes between Agnes Grey and Mr. Weston, or the early scenes between Helen and Huntingdon, or any of the scenes between Helen and Gilbert Markham. To me they entirely lack the authentic, genuine, empirical note that is so evident in Charlotte's Jane Eyre and Lucy Snowe. But one thing does emerge that seems beyond doubt: in contradistinction to her sisters, Anne wanted to marry and have children *more* than anything else in the world, far more than she wanted to be creative or to win literary fame. To marry a good clergyman—like her own Mr. Weston in *Agnes Grey*—was evidently the summit of her hopes. Whether or not Mr. Weightman was the man into whom this fantasy poured, his death, while Charlotte and Emily were in Brussels, must have been a great shock to Anne. That their young, cheerful daily companion should die at the early age of twenty-eight must have reawakened memories of the catastrophe of her sisters' deaths when Anne was five, and must also have reinforced her aunt's dismal teachings of the Methodists who, as Gérin puts it, tried "to disgust their followers with this life and speed them to the next." [8]

Anne, however, had taken a new situation with the Robinsons of Thorpe Hall eighteen months before Mr. Weightman's death and was therefore away for more than half of the latter's three-year stay at Haworth. She had always meant to redeem her failure with the Inghams, and this time she met with considerable success. But one thing is strange and has never been satisfactorily explained. When Charlotte and Emily went to Brussels, it was arranged that Anne should give the Robinsons notice and live at Haworth; but against all expectation she returned to Thorpe Hall, missing the opportunity for several months of Mr. Weightman's company and being away from home when he died. The reason she gave to Charlotte—that the Robinsons could not spare her—seems thin, when we have documentary evidence that she did not like the place or the family and wanted to change.

We shall presumably never know her conscious reasons for this decision. Nor can we know why her unconscious—the entity "that really lived in a tangible shape" of Charlotte's early vision and that certainly knew far more than her conscious ego—allowed her to do so. But the fact that Anne probably attached herself to a man fated to die early looks as if it was her own fate never to be granted her heart's desire for a happy life as a wife and mother. On the face of it, it seems very sad that pretty, gentle Anne should have been denied a role she was apparently so well-fitted to play: as she put it in a poem: "The heart that Nature formed to love/Must pine, neglected and alone." But it is usually misleading to judge a life by such outer traditional standards.

[8] Gérin, p. 35.

For one thing, we should not forget that Charlotte's considerably stronger constitution proved too weak to bear a child, and that Anne, like the rest, had in her childhood received the stamp of the archetype of wholeness with its tension between the opposites. The course of such lives seldom runs smoothly or along traditional lines. Moreover, in Anne's last book, *The Tenant of Wildfell Hall*, certain qualities come to light that make one wonder whether Anne would really have made such a satisfactory wife for Mr. Weightman—he would hardly have curbed his roving fancy the moment he was married—as the surface might lead one to expect.

Another puzzle is why Anne introduced Branwell at Thorpe Hall. No doubt the Brontë girls were at their wits' end over what to do with their brother, as he had just been dismissed from his railways job. Furthermore, the Robinson boy, who was then handed over to Branwell, had always been the most trying of Anne's pupils. Still Anne did not like the Robinsons (she became rather fond of the girls later, but at this time she badly wanted to find another place for herself) and she was highly critical of the worldly standards of the Thorpe Hall family. More than one of the Brontë biographers have suggested that Anne's descriptions of the drunken orgies in *Wildfell Hall* were those of similar scenes she had witnessed at Thorpe Hall. But would Anne have risked introducing her brother, who she already knew had a drink problem, into such a milieu? It is more probable that she overestimated her own influence for good over Branwell. At all events Thorpe Hall—as we have seen—turned out to be a disastrous failure for Branwell.

That Anne—gentle, virtuous Anne—was fated to have it out with evil is the one thing that seems certain from all we know of her life. The process began in the nursery when Miss Branwell succeeded in implanting her gloomy notions about sin and judgment and set Anne an impossibly high standard of virtue. Such a standard was a historical necessity in the early days of Christianity, when the opposites were still unseparated and hopelessly mixed up with each other. Only centuries of striving exclusively after the light opposite could possibly have differentiated it and led to our current level of civilization. There could never have been any science, for instance, if man had not learned to be undeviatingly honest. No individual, of course, has ever reached the standard set, for it is impossible to do so. I would remind the reader, for example, of St. Augustine, who thanked God that he was not responsible for his own dreams, and of the fantasies of naked women that beset the anchorites in the desert. But striving towards such a standard developed consciousness as nothing else could have done.

The dark opposite cannot be imprisoned forever. Christ was well aware of this; therefore he advised his followers to be wise as serpents and gentle as doves and told the parable of the unjust steward. The compilers of the New Testament, however, fell into the error of excluding those parts of Christ's teaching that included both opposites, as even a superficial examination of the evidence reveals.[9] (One feels that the parable of the unjust steward must have escaped their notice!) Of course evil was recognized as existing (except in the psychologically disastrous doctrine of the *privatio boni*), but it had to be resisted and repressed on every occasion. Since this worldwide repression went too far, it more and more broke its bounds, until it should be obvious today to everyone but the willfully blind or hopelessly stupid that we *must* find another solution or we will perish.

Evil also broke its bounds within the "infernal world" of the Brontë children, to such an extent that each of them was forced in later life to find some answer to the problem beyond the conventional ready-made solutions that had not yet

[9] Cf. for instance, *The Apocryphal New Testament*, where particularly in "Agrapha" (p. 33-37) it is clear that passages were omitted which show that Christ had a far greater appreciation of the opposites than the New Testament would lead one to suppose.

(except for the intermezzo of the French Revolution) fully revealed their weaknesses. Charlotte and Emily eventually found their own creative solutions in the writing of their books, Branwell became possessed by evil and had to suffer the consequences. Anne alone tried to meet the problem head-on, as it were, in her own daily life. But she, even more than the others, was ahead of her time. There was no psychology in her day and she was forced to try to solve the problem within the confines of the Christian religion, thus attempting to repress the dark side of the constellated archetype of wholeness into the old traditional, conventional pattern that, on a worldwide scale, was to prove so impotent a century later.

More than any other Brontë, Anne realized the value of knowing oneself. When she was twenty-one she wrote in her 1841 "Birthday paper":

*How little know we what we are*
*How less what we may be.*

her own work

One cannot doubt that Anne would have welcomed help in learning what she was. During a severe illness while she was still at school, she did send for a Moravian bishop, instead of one of the many clergy she knew.[10] Undoubtedly he helped her, for the Moravians were more broadminded than the Methodists, with less emphasis on the law and sin and more on the grace of God. But of course he demanded faith from Anne, and Anne, like so many of us since, found it terribly hard to believe what she did not *know* from experience. The result was years of agonizing doubt and of a self-criticism that always fell just beside the mark.

In addition to her life-long preoccupation with evil in the form of sin, Anne also met evil three times in long-drawn-out problems in the outer world: in the demonic Ingham children, in the worldly dishonesty of the Robinsons and, worst of

[10] Gérin, pp. 98-102.

all, in the degeneration of her own brother. The first two encounters—really no worse than everyone meets from time to time but a great shock to the hypersensitive, innocent and very young Anne—are described minutely in *Agnes Grey*. Although the externals of the novel's beginning have been changed from her own childhood, and the two places she served as governess are slightly disguised, the book is undoubtedly autobiographical throughout. Anne only deviates from essential reality in giving the book a happy end. Happy endings were not in her own experience, and there we see how very weak her creative ability was. Looked at from the psychological point of view, Anne wrote almost entirely from the conscious.[11] The unconscious did not pour through her, as it did into all of her sisters' work, with the possible exception of *The Professor*, which explains why her books are so much duller and less significant than theirs. Emily and Charlotte wrote because they were driven by the creative spirit, and they wrote for the most part as the spirit decreed, but Anne wrote because she had a *conscious purpose:* to help other people by relating her own experiences. She worked very hard at her writing, the "arduous duties" were punctilliously performed according to her lights, but she knew little or nothing of their "mysterious nature." Although it seems absurd for George Moore to compare her writing with the genius of Jane Austen, he appears to be much nearer the truth when he goes on to say: "*Agnes Grey* is a narrative simple and beautiful as a muslin dress." The novel *is* a conscious creation, like a frock, every stitch carefully put in from her own experience, and it is refreshingly simple and unpretentious. It has indeed a purpose, stated in its opening sentence, "All true histories contain instruction," and Anne offers her own experience in the hope that "it might prove

her own views

[11] Unlike her sisters, Anne definitely belongs in the first class of writers mentioned by Jung in his essay on "Psychology and Literature." See above, p. 117.

useful to some, entertaining to others." Later, in her preface to the second edition of *The Tenant of Wildfell Hall*, in reply to criticisms of the unvarnished way vice is represented, she goes much further and declares that she will not limit her ambition to amusing the reader nor "even to producing 'a perfect work of art': time and talents so spent I should consider wasted and misapplied. Such humble talents as God has given me I will endeavour to put to their greatest use; if I am able to amuse, I will try to benefit too; and when I feel it my duty to speak an unpalatable truth, with the help of God, I *will* speak it, though it be to the prejudice of my name and to the detriment of my reader's immediate pleasure as well as my own."

At the time she wrote *Agnes Grey*, Anne had met evil only in outer everyday life, in the Ingham children and the Robinson family. A governess gifted in discipline could have wheeled the former into some sort of shape easily enough, and we all have to come to terms with the worldly and dishonest standards of the Robinsons. I have emphasized these encounters of Anne's with evil, because they show how more than usually difficult evil was for her and how helpless it made her feel. But it was a very different matter by the time she wrote *Wildfell Hall*, for by then she had encountered evil face to face in Branwell where it naturally shook her to the core. Moreover in her later years at Thorpe Hall—after Branwell came as tutor to the Robinson boy—she was probably exposed to far worse conditions than those in *Agnes Grey*. At all events she certainly wrote *Wildfell Hall* in a missionary spirit and with a strongly moral purpose.

Although Charlotte always saw Anne as a little sister, barely grown-up, and was inclined to be far too pitying and apologetic in everything she said to Mrs. Gaskell and published about Anne, she was probably near the mark when she wrote: "(Anne) had, in the course of her life, been called on to contemplate, near at hand, and for a long time, the terrible effects of talents misused and faculties abused. . . . She brooded over it till she believed it to be a duty to reproduce every detail (of course with fictitious characters, incidents, and situations) as a warning to others. She hated her work, but would pursue it. When reasoned with on the subject, she regarded such reasonings as a temptation to self-indulgence. She must be honest; she must not varnish, soften, or conceal."[12]

This statement and her preface to the second edition of *Wildfell Hall*[13] leave no doubt that Anne wrote her second book with the avowed purpose of warning the public against the kind of fate which befell her brother. She even remarked: "Let it not be imagined, however, that I consider myself competent to reform the errors and abuses of society, but only that I would fain contribute my humble quota to so good an aim." The fact that she "hated her work" shows very clearly that in her case the conscious got little inspiration from the unconscious, a relationship which is responsible for the joy of all really creative work.

Nevertheless, the unconscious is always present in any piece of writing, however unaware of it the working conscious may be, and *Wildfell Hall*, Anne's last book and her testament, so to speak, does reveal her own projected psychology and the stage that her search for wholeness had reached. Though written from Anne's experience, it is not autobiographical as *Agnes Grey* is, but is rather a very courageous attempt to have it out with evil. Although it does not seem to me in any way a great novel from the literary point of view, it is most unusually interesting as a psychological document.

Two thirds of *Wildfell Hall* is a first-person narrative by a man, the young farmer Gilbert Markham, but the middle

[12] C. Brontë, "Biographical Notice of Ellis and Action Bell."

[13] The complete text of this preface is usually omitted in reprints of *The Tenant of Wildfell Hall* but can be found in Gérin, p. 276f.

third consists of the diary of the heroine, Helen Huntingdon.[14] Unlike Charlotte, Anne only wrote as a man *after* the novel in which the narrator, Agnes Grey, is really herself. This would suggest that the animus, instead of losing ground, as it did with Charlotte, was gaining ground in Anne. (This is not meant as a negative criticism, for it was almost certain to happen when Anne ventured into the unknown land of evil.) Helen is in no way Anne herself, so, although in *Agnes Grey* we have, in a sense, an ego from whose standpoint everything is seen, there is no such figure in *Wildfell Hall*. Anne rather attempts an objective outside standpoint, as Charlotte did more successfully in *Shirley*.

Since *The Tenant of Wildfell Hall* is not nearly as well known as Charlotte's or Emily's novels, perhaps a short synopsis is necessary. It is the story of Helen, a beautiful girl whose mother died when Helen was an infant and whose father drinks. For these reasons she is brought up by an uncle and aunt. The uncle is a reformed roué, the aunt a religious and opinionated lady, reminiscent of Aunt Branwell. Against the advice of this aunt and of her nearest friend, Helen marries a cheerful, irresponsible young man-about-town, certain of her own power to reform him. She fails miserably. He degenerates rapidly and his occasional drinking bouts become habitual. He spends more and more time with his old cronies, has drunken parties at home—described in minute detail—and finally starts to teach his four-year-old son to drink and swear. When Helen discovers that he is the lover of Lady Loughborough, her *béte noire* and shadow, she slams her bedroom door in his face and never sleeps with him again. She finally succeeds in running away, with her son and a maid, and takes refuge as "the tenant of Wildfell Hall," a derelict old house belonging to her brother.

[14] The construction of *Wildfell Hall* has certain interesting resemblances to *Wuthering Heights*, which also has two narrators and also begins near the end of the action and only subsequently relates the earlier events.

In order to escape detection by her husband, she passes herself off as a widow, does not admit her relationship to her landlord, and tries to live as a recluse, supporting herself by selling her paintings. But her sociable neighbors force her to see them. Soon they begin to gossip about her landlord, who only visits her after dark. This difficult situation is complicated by a growing attachment between Helen and a young farmer, Gilbert Markham, the narrator of the book. He does his best to defend her against the gossip, until one evening he sees and hears her together with her landlord in the garden. Not knowing that the latter is her brother, he assumes the worst, and to placate his fury she gives him her diary, from which we learn the foregoing story. Not long after this, she hears that her husband is very ill and voluntarily returns to him. She nurses him with Christian charity till the end, making great but unavailing efforts to induce him to repent. A year or two after his death she marries her young farmer —in other words, a not very convincing happy end.

None of the great religions has torn the opposites so far apart as has Christianity; indeed it lacks all trace of any real unification of the opposites. The dark side of God is unrecognized in Christian dogma; it is seen, but only as God's enemy, Satan, who must be vanquished at all costs. This fatal split, which is threatening to destroy our whole culture, is very evident in Anne's last novel. She tears the opposites apart, with a light heroine and a dark hero, and gives her heroine just one *purpose:* to convert the dark and win it over to her own light side. Anne's own avowed purpose in writing the book was to warn others about falling into the fate which overtook Branwell, but she did not see how much she herself was naturally fascinated by her own dark opposite. The descriptions of the drunken orgies are incredibly detailed and vivid; unpleasant though they are, they have an imaginative and living quality, whereas the rest of the book is somewhat lifeless and insipid, in short, a bit dull. Anne's preoccupation with the dark side she was out to fight is not only visible in Helen's descriptions of Huntingdon and his circle, but it also flames up in the narrator's account of the parson's daughter whom he was courting before Helen dawned on his horizon. Eliza Milward's malice and spite also have a living, even sparkling, quality that is very striking.

But the most interesting element of the novel is the effect the dark hero and the light heroine have on each other. The former is depicted at the beginning as a young man about town, lavishly sowing his wild oats, as was common at the time in which the story is set, several years before the accession of Queen Victoria. He is cheerful, good company and has evidently never bothered his head about right and wrong, about anything but having a good time. Helen, an eighteen-year-old debutante when the story opens, has been brought up in the country and is a healthy, pretty girl with good prospects. Indeed, she has the makings of a prig from the start, but she has enough instinct to reject most of her aunt's preaching and the rich, elderly and boring suitors the worthy lady wants her to marry.

Arthur Huntingdon seems a God-sent rescue and Helen is fascinated by him at first sight. He takes longer to make up his mind but eventually decides to marry her and settle down. Helen's aunt is horrified and does all she can to dissuade her. When her arguments regarding their future in this life fail, she turns to the next and asks Helen how she will feel when she finds herself parted from Arthur forever, for perhaps she "will be taken into eternal bliss" and be cast "into the lake that burneth with unquenchable fire." Even then, just engaged and supposedly in love, Helen seems to have no doubt that she is destined for heaven and Arthur probably for hell, for she disputes only the "forever." She is convinced that Arthur will join her when "he has paid the uttermost farthing" and announces that she has found nearly thirty passages in the Bible to support this theory, against her aunt's conviction of *eternal* damnation!

Were it not for Helen's *idée fixe* about saving Arthur's soul, the two young people might well have been able to establish a durable marriage. Arthur has a delightful country house, Grassdale Manor, where they settle down after their honeymoon, but Helen has no talent for making it a home and is soon preaching, even nagging at her husband, "to fortify himself against temptation," "to think more deeply, to look further and aim higher" than he does.

Such recommendations mean nothing to Arthur but they soon make him feel dangerously insecure. He comes to the conclusion that his wife does not love him and tries to convince himself that it is all her fault. Since she loves to read she is quite happy at home in bad weather but when they quarrel she notes that he is unutterably bored if he cannot get to his outdoor life and that he even takes "an unusual quantity of wine, but not enough to loosen his tongue" (to apologize to her!). She takes no notice of these danger signals, however; she only notes them *en passant*. It is interesting, as modern psychology has proven, that women with fathers who drink, as Helen's did, very often marry men who either drink already or take to it after marriage. Arthur had loved to take part in drunken orgies long before his marriage, but his habitual drinking, which begins only after he marries, soon increases rapidly.

From then on the battle is lost. Arthur seeks comfort and reassurance with the boon companions of his bachelor days, and Helen retires more and more into her role of the suffering innocent, the victim of a devilish husband. Indeed Arthur gives her more and more outer reason to see and depict him in such a light, for he definitely, and in order primarily to compensate for the saintliness of his wife, identifies with evil, so that in the end, like Branwell, he becomes completely possessed by it. Anne spares no detail in order to warn the reader how bestial and vicious such a man can become; she is admittedly copying her data from the degeneration of Branwell. What Anne did not see—could not see with her upbringing—was that identification with good necessarily calls for its opposite and that if Helen is determined to qualify as a saint, Arthur can answer adequately only by becoming the worst of sinners.

Charlotte has long been criticized for her too censorious attitude toward Branwell after his degeneration, but our complete ignorance of the external facts has so far spared Anne from any share in the blame. The evidence in her last book, however, at least prompts the question: Did Anne, whom no one criticizes but always praises for her gentleness and modesty, go too far in her identification with virtue and thus unconsciously oblige, or at least help, Branwell to identify with vice? Such a situation may well have arisen during their two and a half years together at the Robinsons and may then have increased and continued during the subsequent three years at Haworth. We simply do not know whether Anne preached at Branwell as Helen did at Huntingdon, but the fact that she evidently thought her heroine was doing the right and laudable thing makes it possible. I think anyone who reads the scenes between Arthur and Helen carefully will agree that such an attitude on Anne's part would make Branwell's point of view at least much more understandable. At all events Anne, alone of the three sisters, was with Branwell when the Robinson catastrophe took place and must have observed many warning signs.

When Helen voluntarily returns to her husband, to nurse him in his last illness, he is horrified, and, insofar as he is able to recognize her at all, can hardly believe she is there. He begs her to cease tormenting him. When convinced it is really Helen and that she means to stay, he says with a bitter smile: "Oh. I see, it's an act of Christian charity, whereby you hope to gain a higher seat in heaven for yourself, and scoop a deeper pit in hell for me." Of course she denies this quite justifiable assumption, but even then she adds that she wishes she could benefit his soul as well as his body and awaken some sense of contrition in him. She carefully nurses his body, eventually making herself indispensable in this way, but she never ceases to worry him about his soul. She has no success whatever in the latter effort; she only embitters his last months.

It is interesting that Anne depicts Helen's great friend, Millicent Hattersley, as gaining a decent, even happy country-house existence, with a husband just as bad or even worse than Arthur, by *never* reproaching or criticizing him at all. She simply suffers everything in silence. Consequently Hattersley's ground is never taken from under his feet by criticism or nagging; he can go on believing in his wife's love and is thus able eventually to pull himself together. Yet Helen is held up as an example to Millicent, instead of vice versa, so that probably Anne never realized how much her heroine contributed to Huntingdon's downfall.

In considering the *results* of the marriage, it is striking that the effect on Arthur is one of complete disaster—he dies miserably in his thirties—while Helen loses only a few years of her youth and is left a rich widow in her twenties. Of course both were to blame. Arthur made no secret of his wild oats, even before marriage, and Helen preached at him whenever he referred to them; so that each was fairly warned in time about the other. But whereas Arthur did make an effort at the beginning of his marriage to leave his wild bachelor friends and settle down at Grassdale Manor with his wife, Helen never made—or intended to make—any concessions to him. It was the purpose of her life to save his soul, and saved it must be, willing or unwilling! He went far beyond the bounds of good taste in describing scenes from his past life to her, but when it did at last penetrate to him that she hated it, he desisted. He explained to her again and again that he was *not* religious, that he did not know what it meant; she never wavered however, nor tried to understand his points of view, because she was rendered completely inhuman by her possession by "good" and her unshakable opinion that she knew all the basic truths about God and man. It is quite as destructive to be possessed by good as by evil; either destroys the balance of the opposites, that condition that old Mr. Brontë discerned when he spoke of the "golden middle way." The ancient Greeks also expressed this truth when they said: "Exaggerate nothing, all good lies in right measure." [15]

What can we learn from this last book of Anne's concerning her own effort to reach the goal of wholeness? Apparently, like Mary Webb, she also repressed evil, for the novel ends with the triumph of good over evil. Anne makes as clean a sweep of her evil mommets as Mary, for they all come to a bad end, except for two who are reformed by their wives. Nevertheless, there is a great difference between these two solutions. The one denies evil, dismisses it as a mere *privatio boni*, endorsing the Weaver's conviction that: "If you think of evil rightly, it just isn't there," and thus retires entirely from the unknown country round the fourth gate; whereas the other does nothing of the kind. No one was ever more convinced of the reality of evil than Anne Brontë, so convinced that she regarded it as a sort of maelstrom that would inevitably draw you under if you got too close to it. Nevertheless, she never thought of leaving the unknown country just because it was full of evil, but felt obliged to remain right there, diligently writing her epic warning in order to help prevent others from falling into its trap as she had observed in Branwell's case.

I trust the reader will not take the foregoing as a criticism or depreciation of Anne. The opposites exist equally in us all and it is obviously more meritorious to work hard at building up one's virtues than to allow oneself to be possessed by one's evil. The Christian religion has recognized this fact in its great insistence on sin. I once heard a very interesting discussion between Professor Jung and a very intelligent and good-hearted Catholic priest about analysis and confession. Their experiences in their two fields were identical in the most important point. The former remarked that all the un-

[15] Jung, *Psychology and Alchemy*, par. 37.

important guilt is brought consciously to analysis, but that it takes a very long time and a most painful process for even the most honest of analysants to see their *real* guilt, deeply buried because of its painful nature or because it has never been recognized as such. The latter agreed that it is exactly the same in the confessional; the penitent often keeps harping on and exaggerating very minor transgressions, while the priest knows that there is something else behind. He pointed out that it was very difficult—sometimes impossible—to discover the nature of those real sins which were consciously, or more likely unconsciously, lurking in the background. Here psychology has an advantage over the confessional, for it is usually the analysant's dreams that probe these hidden regions and reveal the truth. The Christian religion by no means denies the value of dreams—*somnia a Deo missa*. Catholic priests as well as many Protestant ministers are therefore beginning to investigate psychology, particularly the psychology of dreams, although it is still often made difficult for them by the prejudice or ignorance of their superiors.

Anne's heroine behaves in the same way as analysants and penitents; she worries a lot about her small transgressions; she is very distressed, for instance, that she slowly becomes more accustomed to vice, so that it no longer shocks her as before. But that her preaching may be having a destructive effect on her husband seems never to have reached her consciousness at all. Anne was conscious enough, in fact almost too conscious, of sin, but she was blinded by opinions as to what was really having a destructive effect and what could cure the evil. These opinions were branded on her in childhood, probably very largely by Aunt Branwell, and became immovable convictions, entirely beyond question.[16] Anne probably went as far as she could, in her time and with

[16] What Jung calls "animus opinions" usually have some such origin and are characterized by their absolute nature.

her upbringing, towards a toleration of evil when she made Gilbert Markham a very mixed character. He was a decent enough man, but violent and prejudiced, and also not too honest, for he succeeded in concealing from everyone, including Helen, that he had beaten up her brother and left him on the road "to live or die as he could." That Anne permitted such a man to marry her saintly heroine is a considerable concession, and she even predicts a long and happy marriage for them.

We must consider the year or so that elapsed between the time Anne finished *Wildfell Hall* and her death. She was absolutely amazed when the novel was declared by the critics, with few exceptions, to be "brutal and coarse." [17] She immediately wrote a defense, as a preface to the second edition, in which she made her purpose overwhelmingly clear. She stated that she was "little prepared to accept" such censure, for she intended to warn the public by telling the truth and that she was determined to contribute her quota to reforming "the errors and abuses of society." This purpose was so strong in her that she was willing to go on living, even after Emily's death, which must have been a bitter grief to her. She did everything she could to live and she wanted to live in order to pursue her purpose, as the following verse in her last poem indicates:

*I hoped amid the brave and strong*
*My portioned task might lie,*
*To toil amid the labouring throng*
*With purpose keen and high.*

When she learned from a specialist that, in spite of all care, death would be the outcome of her illness, she went through hell before she was able to accept the fact that God

[17] Harrison and Stanford, p. 125f.

was not as interested as she was in her high purpose to reform society,[18] and that she must prepare instead to face death and its final accounting. At first it was more than she could bear:

*A dreadful darkness closes in*
*On my bewildered mind.*

She felt that she could not depart with so little of her life's purpose accomplished, but slowly it dawned on her that a higher purpose exists: to accept God's will *whatever* it is and however much it destroys one's certainty that it is God's will to pursue one's chosen mission. Might it be true that God is not so interested in reforming society as one had always assumed? In psychological language, Anne was confronted with the necessity for sacrificing the ego to the Self. Meister Eckhart probably expressed an understanding of this most difficult of all problems better than anyone who ever lived in his constantly repeated advice to "*sich lassen.*" [19]

Anne faced this problem before she died and won the battle. Therefore there was no enantiodromia on her deathbed as there was on Branwell's. Even though she still could not see that to be possessed by good was destructive, she had nevertheless taken the first step towards it in realizing that she could not claim the right to live in order to pursue her own aims (however high) but must submit completely to the eternal decrees. Her acceptance was evidently sufficient, for she died very confidently, even happily. Her doctor at Scarborough was so struck by her attitude that he kept

[18] A great many women are completely convinced that their will and God's will are identical. As the French say: "*Ce que la femme veut, Dieu veut.*"

[19] This untranslatable phase, for which the literal meaning is to "leave yourself," includes a complete sacrifice of all ego demands and wishes in favor of the eternal being that is living in us.

returning, because, he said, "in all his experience he had seen no such death-bed and that it gave evidence of no common mind."

Anne did not succeed in rooting herself as deeply in the outer world as Charlotte. But she did manage to overcome her dependence as the little sister and, after one failure, succeeded in her profession as governess. She was not granted her heart's desire, to become a wife and mother, and we do not know how much she herself contributed to this fact by her inflexible opinions.[20] But we can imagine that if William Weightman was the man she would have liked to marry, as her biographers think, the inflexibility of her opinions on conjugal fidelity might well have given a man with such a roving eye cause to hesitate. In *Wildfell Hall*, as soon as Helen discovers that her husband is unfaithful to her, she deprives him, as a matter of course and until the end of his life, of all his conjugal rights and feels herself free to leave him and to conceal their son from him. Anne must have been very sure of herself in this respect, for, as May Sinclair has pointed out, this ultimatum, and one or two other scenes in *Wildfell Hall*, "for sheer audacity stand alone in mid-Victorian literature. . . . Thackeray, with the fear of Mrs. Grundy before his eyes, would have shrunk from recording Mrs. Huntingdon's ultimatum to her husband." [21]

Anne, like Charlotte, most certainly entered and tried to explore the unknown country round the fourth gate. She had not the genius of either of her sisters and is rather an example of how a more mediocre mind reacts to such an invasion of the collective unconscious, with its obligations to deal with the opposites. Anne's many inflexible opinions and her narrower outlook hampered her terribly; yet perhaps they

[20] Jung used to say that when women were too set on marriage they often defeated their own end.
[21] Sinclair, p. 54.

also saved her from drowning in the high tide of the unconscious to which all the members of this family were exposed. At all events, she certainly made her contribution to our scant knowledge of the unknown country round the fourth gate.

# 9 ❧ EMILY

ALTHOUGH I DO NOT WANT to explore the subject of typology to any great extent in this book, it is necessary to consider briefly the attitude types of the Brontës, as they contribute considerably to an understanding of the individuals in this family, particularly Emily. Moreover, the terms "introvert" and "extravert" have become such household words that practically everybody knows, at least approximately, what they mean.

Through their preoccupation with inner figures and events in their games and writings, and because of their isolated outer lives, introversion was almost forced upon them all as children. This was hardest for Branwell who, as far as one can determine from his juvenilia and from what we know of his life, was a true extravert. Charlotte was certainly less extraverted than Branwell. Her shy and retiring character rather suggests an introvert but, if so, the influence of her two extraverted friends, Martha Taylor and Ellen Nussey, must have modified her original introversion to a considerable extent; in fact "the fifteen years' war" could also be considered a war between introversion and extraversion. Anne is the most difficult to type. Her shyness, her evident wish to know herself, and her lifelong preoccupation with religion, all seem to indicate introversion; but her comparative lack of enthusiasm for fantasy life, and her later urgent desire to do all she could to reform society, point more in the direction of extraversion. The only true introvert, who never wavered for a moment all her life in her introverted attitude, was undoubtedly Emily.

This was Emily's strength and her doom, her strength because it enabled her to give herself wholly to her creative spirit, and her doom because it prevented her from rooting herself more adequately in the outer world. As far as we know, Emily made no friends outside her immediate family, and, although she was by far the strongest character of them all, she always failed when she tried to live away from Haworth Parsonage, with the partial exception of Brussels. While in Brussels, however, she seems to have taken as little part as possible in the life around her but devoted herself unswervingly to the things she had come to learn, regarding everything else as a mere means to this end.

We know less of Emily's childhood than of the others; this is probably due to her great reserve. Charlotte always wrote and spoke of her less freely than of the others and often explained that Emily wanted to be let alone. Yet Charlotte probably realized early on that Emily was greater than the other two and she may even have been fonder of her. But she never understood her, particularly not while Emily was alive, and Emily certainly gave her no encouragement to do so. Charlotte's rather apologetic references to *Wuthering Heights* in her preface to the 1850 edition show clearly that she had no idea of the magnitude of Emily's genius. Not that one can blame her for this; according to her own lights she was generous, for *Jane Eyre* had had such immediate success she could not help having a much better opinion of the critics' and public's judgment than either revealed in their reception of *Wuthering Heights*. But in the destruction of all of Emily's papers except her poems—in which Charlotte was most likely to have been the guilty one—one is more doubtful and cannot help wondering if jealousy, of which she was certainly unconscious, did not play a role behind the scenes.

Be this as it may, their disappearance has deprived us of our best opportunity for learning to know the young Emily. One must in justice to Charlotte, however, admit that Emily evidently had no wish to be known. According to Mrs. Gaskell, Ellen Nussey's first impression of Emily and Anne was that whereas the latter, like Charlotte, was shy, Emily was extremely reserved. Mrs. Gaskell continues: "I distinguish reserve from shyness, because I imagine shyness would please if it knew how; whereas reserve is indifferent whether it pleases or not." [1]

In a verse of a poem (of which no manuscript exists) Emily tells us:

*I'll walk where my own nature would be leading;*
*It vexes me to choose another guide;*
*Where the gray flocks in ferny glens are feeding;*
*Where the wild wind blows on the mountain side.*[2]

F. W. Hatfield suggests that this poem is not by Emily at all but that Charlotte wrote it and published it as Emily's in 1850, and that it was intended as "an interpretation of her sister in the guise of Emily's own words." [3] It certainly does confirm Charlotte's frequent comments on her sister's independent nature and her laments that Emily was not more accessible to influence. (As I have frequently noticed in working with translators and editors of C. G. Jung's books, it *is* a human passion to alter the words of geniuses, even to smuggle in something of the translator's own!) Charlotte says: "My sister Emily was not a person of demonstrative character, not one on the recesses of whose mind and feelings even those nearest and dearest to her could, with impunity, intrude unlicensed." [4] It is possible that the temptation thus to intrude after Emily's death proved too strong for Charlotte; nevertheless, printing a poem of her own as Emily's would be going further than I should expect.

[1] Gaskell, p. 99.
[2] *The Complete Poems of Emily Brontë*, p. 256f.
[3] *Ibid.*, p. 255.
[4] In the "Biographical Notice of Ellis and Acton Bell."

However this may be, it must certainly have been true that Emily *did* follow her own nature to a most unusual degree and that, on account of her extreme introversion, she followed it consistently and without ever allowing outside influences to affect her. Her passion for the moors was indeed an outside influence in a way, and one which she fully accepted and encouraged. Very early it became clear that for her the moors were a necessity of life, one which her genius needed and depended on. Therefore she sickened when sent to school at Roe Head and made only one short effort to contribute to the family finances by earning her living as a governess. Then it was established that whoever went away and earned money it would not be Emily.

Now all the girls loved Haworth and hated the drudgery of governess life, so Emily must have been very much aware that she was taking what her sisters also wanted. Had she done this for egotistical reasons, it could not have agreed with her; moreover her sisters would inevitably have resented it. But there is no evidence that this was the case. Anne even wrote in her birthday notes of 1841 that they were "all doing something for our own livelihood except Emily who, however, is as busy as any of us, and in reality earns her food and rainment as much as any of us." [5] Even Charlotte, whose letters are often one long complaint, never as far as I know wrote a word that indicated even the faintest resentment at Emily's lot being outwardly so much pleasanter than her own.

When a fact like this is accepted by everyone concerned, one may be sure that it is fundamentally in tune with something deeper than everyday considerations. Emily seems to have habitually ignored the usual Christian precepts that govern households such as Haworth Parsonage. A few people —M. Héger in Brussels, for instance—allude to her lack of unselfishness, a virtue that Charlotte practiced morning, noon

[5] Ratchford, p. 154.

right, falling into great despair when she thought she failed to do so. But I doubt if such terms meant anything at all to Emily, though to have escaped their tyranny while living in a Parsonage household was almost miraculous.

Let us return for a moment to Fannie Ratchford's remarks about Charlotte's tyrannical conscience that led to the "fifteen years war" with her creative spirit.[6] This terrible battle was the result of the fact that Charlotte, unlike Emily, succumbed to the usual fate of girls brought up in conventional and traditional morality, accepting all these precepts as the authentic, basic truth, laid down for all time and from which there is no appeal. This unquestioned, unquestionable character is a hallmark of the animus. The animus is also inclined to give a subtle twist to these traditional opinions, so that they are even a bit more rigid and tyrannical than the precepts themselves.

One rarely sees the same phenomenon in men. Except in the case of those who have such a strong mother-complex that they are still ruled by the mother's animus, men throw off with comparative ease all the conventionally moral opinions that were taught them as children. A man would not very likely be caught like Charlotte in a conflict between creative genius and opinions as to how, for instance, he should always live for other people and not for himself. (This is conpensated in men, of course, by other conflicts from which a woman escapes comparatively lightly.)

Emily's reaction to the precepts by which she was brought up (no less than were Charlotte and Anne) was far more masculine in character than feminine. They apparently meant nothing to her, no more than the Christian creed in which she was also certainly brought up. In one of her most famous poems she says:

*Vain are the thousand creeds*
*That move men's hearts, unutterably vain,*

[6] Ratchford, p. 105ff; see also above, pp. 122-123.

*Worthless as withered weeds*
*Or idlest froth amid the boundless main*
*To waken doubt in one*
*Holding so fast to thy infinity*
*So surely anchored on*
*The steadfast rock of Immortality.*[7]

Charlotte added a note to this poem stating that these lines were the last her sister Emily ever wrote. However, they are dated more than two years before her death. At all events they reveal the mainspring of her life and explain a great deal that would otherwise be inexplicable in Emily. She actually was "surely anchored on the steadfast rock of Immortality" and seems to have lived her short life in most unusual obedience to this core of her being, in "full surrender to the creative spirit," to quote Fannie Ratchford again.[8]

The creative spirit was unusually personified in Emily's case, and she had a far more intimate, even personal relation to it than most authors. The fact that the creative writer owes his inspiration to something quite other than his conscious mind was well known to all the Brontës. Charlotte, for example, says:

> The writer who possesses the creative gift owns something of which he is not always master—something that, at times, strangely wills and works for itself. He may lay down rules and devise principles, and to rules and principles it will perhaps for years lie in subjection; and then, haply without any warning of revolt, there comes a time when it will no longer consent to "harrow the valleys, or be bound with a band in the furrow"—when it "laughs at the multitude of the city, and regards not the crying of the driver"—when, refusing absolutely to make ropes out of sea-sand any longer,

[7] *Complete Poems*, p. 243.
[8] Ratchford, p. x.

> it sets to work on statue hewing, and you have a Pluto or a Jove, a Tisiphone or a Psyche, a Mermaid or a Madonna, as Fate or Inspiration direct. Be the work grim or glorious, dread or divine, you have little choice left but quiescent adoption. As for you—the nominal artist—your share in it has been to work passively under dictates you neither delivered nor could question—that would not be uttered at your prayer, nor suppressed nor changed at your caprice. If the result be attractive the World will praise you, who little deserve praise; if it be repulsive, the same World will blame you, who almost as little deserve blame.[9]

Emily not only knew all this but, one feels, made an effort, possible only for an extreme introvert, to look into the depths of her own being and to find out—as far as such a thing is possible—what it was that took command of her work, and then she did her best to come to terms with it. She speaks of the figure she thus discovered, again and again, in her poems. I quote only a few passages among many:

*When weary with the long day's care,*
*And earthly change from pain to pain,*
*And lost, and ready to despair,*
*Thy kind voice calls me back again—*
*O my true friend, I am not lone*
*While thou canst speak with such a tone!*
*So hopeless is the world without,*
*The world within I doubly prize.*

Later in the same poem:

*I welcome thee, benignant power*
*Sure solacer of human cares*
*And brighter hope when hope despairs.*[10]

[9] Charlotte Brontë's preface to *Wuthering Heights*.
[10] *Complete Poems*, p. 205f.

In another poem:

*Glad comforter, will I not brave*
*Unawed the darkness of the grave?*
*Nay, smile to hear Death's billows rave,*
*My Guide, sustained by thee?*

*The more unjust seems present fate*
*The more my Spirit springs elate*
*Strong in the strength, to anticipate*
*Rewarding Destiny!* [11]

And again:

*A messenger of Hope comes every night to me,*
*And offers for short life, eternal liberty.*[12]

And yet again she addresses him:
*No—what sweet thing can match with thee,*
*My thoughtful Comforter?* [13]

Sometimes she speaks of him as "Imagination" or as "Fancy":

*Yes, Fancy come, my Fairy Love!*
*These throbbing temples softly kiss;*
*And bend my lonely couch above*
*And bring me rest; and bring me bliss.*[14]

In one poem (which should be read in its entirety) she discusses why she has chosen this path in defiance of the dictates of reason. I quote a few verses:

[11] *Complete Poems*, p. 233.
[12] *Ibid.*, p. 238.
[13] *Ibid.*, p. 196.
[14] *Ibid.*, p. 184.

*Stern Reason is to judgment come*
*Arrayed in all her forms of gloom:*
*Wilt thou my advocate be dumb?*
*No, radiant angel, speak and say*
*Why did I cast the world away;*

*Why I have persevered to shun*
*The common paths that others run;*
*And on a strange road journeyed on*
*Heedless alike of Wealth and Power—*
*Of Glory's wreath and Pleasure's flower.*

*These once indeed seemed Beings divine,*
*And they perchance heard vows of mine*
*And saw my offerings on their shrine—*
*But careless gifts are seldom prized,*
*And mine were worthily despised;*

*So with a ready heart I swore*
*To seek their altar-stone no more,*
*And gave my spirit to adore*
*Thee, ever present, phantom thing—*
*My slave, my comrade, and my King!* [15]

These few quotations should suffice to give us an idea of the path that Emily chose to follow, an exceedingly different choice from those of her brother and sisters. But perhaps "choice" is a misleading word, or rather it can only be used in a limited sense. Emily never really entered the outside world at all; not only were her efforts away from Haworth doomed to failure but even in her beloved home she seems to have associated with no one outside her family. Charlotte says of her:

I am bound to avow that she had scarcely more practical

[15] *Ibid.*, p. 208.

> knowledge of the peasantry amongst whom she lived, than a nun has of the country people who sometimes pass her convent gates. My sister's disposition was not naturally gregarious; circumstances favoured and fostered her tendency to seclusion; except to go to church or take a walk on the hills, she rarely crossed the threshold of home. Though her feeling for the people round was benevolent, intercourse with them she never sought; nor, with very few exceptions, ever experienced. And yet she knew them: knew their ways, their language, their family histories; she could hear of them with interest, and talk of them with detail, minute, graphic, and accurate; but *with* them, she rarely exchanged a word.[16]

How much choice there may have been in such extreme retirement from the world is difficult to say. We know there was a time when worldly values still seemed to Emily like "Beings divine," but that she later found only "pain to pain" in "earthly change," and also that she found the "world without" so hopeless that it taught her to prize doubly the "world within." In a way one can say that the outer world defeated Emily just as completely as it did Branwell, but that their choices were expressed in their different ways of meeting defeat. The captain simply abandoned the ship in Branwell's case. Emily, on the other hand, had the courage to accept the inevitable and turn her ship round to face the uncharted seas within. Above all, Emily performed the "arduous duties" to the limit of her strength and ability, whereas Branwell neglected them entirely.

M. Héger said of Emily during her time in Brussels:

> She should have been a man—a great navigator. Her powerful reason would have deduced new spheres of discovery from the knowledge of the old; and her strong imperious will would never have been daunted by opposition or difficulty; never have given way but with life.[17]

[16] Charlotte Brontë's Preface to *Wuthering Heights*.
[17] Gaskell, p. 181.

This estimation by a man who did not like Emily describes exactly what she did with her short life, but the description is of the *inner* world, not the outer, a world which M. Héger would probably not have recognized as reality at all. Yet for those who have experienced it, the inner world is an inexorable reality, more basically real and more uncompromising than the outer, which is all that most people ever see. It was into this world, which they all had inhabited as children, that Emily deliberately turned back her ship, and it was there that she actually "deduced new spheres of discovery from her knowledge of the old." Children can often play safely with the most dangerous animals, even with snakes, but the world of childhood is very perilous for the grownup. It becomes the night sea journey, on which the hero is so often devoured by the monster; Jonah and the whale is the classical example.

Emily Brontë has often been called a mystic, and with considerable justification. Her complete preoccupation with the inner life was very similar to that of the mystics. The striking difference is that in almost every case the mystics have searched for the inner life *within* the dogma of their faith and have been disposed to reject anything which collided with dogma as "of the devil." A classic example is the vision of St. Ignatius of Loyola in which a serpent covered with shining eyes appeared. At first this image filled him with delight—as indeed illumination from such a deep level as the serpent well might. Then he remembered its connection with the devil, and from that moment on chased it away with a stick whenever it appeared. But by throwing away what appeared to him spontaneously he consequently formulated his famous and in many ways highly psychological and admirable *Spiritual Exercises* far too rigidly, so that no room at all was allowed for spontaneous revelation.

The Swiss saint, Nicholas von Flüe, apparently also had a highly unorthodox vision which he did not deny or reject, though it is said that his face never lost the signs of terror it evoked in him. He was so deeply disturbed at seeing an image outside his faith, outside his dogma's conception of the God-image, that he spent the rest of his life trying to reconcile the two.[18]

Emily Brontë seems to have been quite unmoved by any consideration of dogma or creed in her attempt to find "new spheres of discovery" on her inward voyage. The Christian mystic attempts to unite with Christ or to find out the will of God or the Holy Spirit. Emily was only concerned with *what* it was that demanded so much of her, and in her poems she records what she found. This is a most amazingly modern point of view on the part of a clergyman's daughter who lived over a hundred years ago, and it is what makes her so exceedingly interesting. Her attitude towards good and evil is one that is uncharacteristic of her age and circumstances, as we shall see when we consider *Wuthering Heights*.

Speaking in a seminar of the archetypal myths of the night sea journey, Jung once pointed out that these myths all depend on the hero killing or in some way overcoming the monster, and that this still agrees exactly with masculine psychology; the man must make an active effort in order to overcome his fate. With women, he said, it is different. They overcome their fate by accepting their suffering. And this is exactly what Emily did. Clearly she suffered almost intolerably, between the time when earthly values "seemed Beings divine" and the time she gave up the outer world as "hopeless." Many disappointments, defeats and depressions must have assailed her to produce such a change. For when all is said and done, we cannot get away from the fact that Emily led a most one-sided outer life. *Wuthering Heights* is one of the most complete of *projected* processes of individuation that I know. It follows that of the four Brontës Emily must have had the greatest potentiality for realizing the

[18] von Franz, *Die Visionen des Niklaus von Flüe*, p. 115ff.

e of wholeness that broke into the family. Obedient to the creative spirit, she also produced by far the best image of it. But she lived it less than any of the others; as far as I can see, she also paid the necessary price in suffering.

Once she had chosen—or more likely been obliged—to accept the very narrow limits of her earthly life, she functioned perfectly within them. Her bread was famous for its quality, her cooking in no way suffered from the German grammar propped up on the kitchen table, and we hear no word of complaint from the two old people, her father and aunt, whom she looked after. Though evidently she found relating to people very difficult, her relationship to animals was deep and instinctive. Her dog, Keeper, a fierce mastiff whom she had not known as a puppy and who was said to accept no punishment from anyone, subdued his will to hers and mourned her death to the day of his own. All the parsonage animals seem to have been more closely related to Emily than to anyone else. Charlotte told Mrs. Gaskell that the incident related in *Shirley*, in which Shirley is bitten by a mad dog and cauterizes her own wound, was an actual experience of Emily. She apparently had indomitable courage, and a certain simplicity which is the hallmark of real genius.

The story of Emily's death is a strange one. We read nothing in Charlotte's letters of any anxiety over Emily's health until she catches a bad cold at Branwell's funeral. We hear of no special relationship between Emily and Branwell, either as children or later. Most of the evidence points to the two pairs: Charlotte and Branwell, Emily and Anne. Daphne du Maurier, it is true, points out that Branwell and Emily were at home alone together for some time and she assumes therefore that a great sympathy developed between them. But she offers no facts, other than the time they were without Charlotte and Anne, to support her theory. Nor is there much direct evidence of the way in which Emily met Branwell's degeneration. She certainly referred to him as a "hopeless being" to her sisters, and one can perhaps see something of her attitude toward him in Nelly Dean's attitude toward Hindley Earnshaw in *Wuthering Heights*. Hindley's fate after all was very similar to Branwell's. Nelly saw Hindley completely realistically and made no excuses for his impossible behavior, but she had loved him as a child (her mother was Hindley's nurse and she regarded him as her "foster brother"), so "ancient associations lingered round her heart." Emily probably felt somewhat the same about Branwell; at all events there was no moral indignation on her part, such as Charlotte, and even Anne, seem to have indulged in.

There is a poem by Emily, written in 1839, when Branwell was already taking to bad ways, disappointing his family, but not yet driving them to despair, which has often been thought to refer to Branwell. Hatfield points out that this is impossible, because it was written nine years *before* Branwell's *death*. It is valuable, however, for it reveals Emily's attitude to "such hopeless beings":

*Well some may hate, and some may scorn,*
*And some may quite forget thy name,*
*But my sad heart must ever mourn*
*Thy ruined hopes, thy blighted fame.*
*Do I despise the timid deer*
*Because his limbs are fleet with fear?*
*Or would I mock the wolf's death-howl*
*Because his form is gaunt and foul?*
*Or hear with joy the leveret's cry*
*Because it cannot bravely die?*
*No! Then above his memory*
*Let pity's heart as tender be:*
*Say, "Earth lie lightly on that breast,*
*And, kind Heaven, grant that spirit rest!"* [19]

The fact that Emily survived Branwell for only three months is very puzzling. One cannot see a causal connection, although one could also not deny its possibility. The only

[19] *Complete Poems*, p. 132f.

remote hypothesis I can think of lies in the fact that Emily was exclusively introverted and Branwell was and remained a true extravert. This might conceivably have led to a deep unconscious symbiosis between them on this one point. In that case, when her completely projected extraversion died, Emily would have lost her one connection with the outer world and would naturally disappear into the inner world, which was in any case far more real to her. But it is more likely that the breakthrough of the archetype of death (always near to the Brontës; one thinks of the two elder girls who died within six weeks of each other, only four years after their mother) produced an immediate synchronistic effect on Emily and a shortly delayed one on Anne. Emily had fewer roots in the outer world; she would therefore have the least resistance to offer. Moreover she put up no fight, refusing to see a doctor or even to admit that she was ill.

This attitude of Emily's is very difficult to understand. It certainly caused Charlotte and Anne almost intolerable suffering. The former writes: "The awful point was, that while full of ruth for others, on herself she had no pity; the spirit was inexorable to the flesh; from the trembling hand, the unnerved limbs, the faded eyes, the same service was exacted as they had rendered in health. To stand by and witness this, and not dare to remonstrate, was a pain no words can render." [20]

Charlotte certainly did not think that Emily wanted to die. She wrote in a letter, about four months after Emily's death: "She was torn, conscious, panting, reluctant, though resolute, out of a happy life." [21] Indeed, there is evidence, direct from Emily herself, that her life improved as she grew older and that she had reached some peace of mind. In her birthday notes for 1845 she wrote: "I am quite contented for myself . . . seldom or never troubled with nothing to do and merely desiring that everybody could be as comfortable

[20] "Biographical Notice of Ellis and Acton Bell."
[21] Gaskell, p. 313.

as myself and as undesponding, and then we should have a very tolerable world of it." [22]

On the other hand, Emily had resolutely turned her back on the world and anchored her ship to "the steadfast rock of immortality." In one way it was true that, as she wrote in a poem three years before her death, "A messenger of Hope comes every night to me, and offers for short life, eternal liberty." She had made this pact with her personified creative spirit; on her side she honored it completely and, when the summons of death came, did not hesitate to obey. In Charlotte's words: "Never in all her life had she lingered over any task that lay before her, and she did not linger now. She sank rapidly. She made haste to leave us."

Catherine Linton's words to Heathcliff on the morning before her death illustrate this side of Emily very well:

> The thing that irks me most is this shattered prison [the body], after all. I am tired of being enclosed here. I'm wearying to escape into the glorious world, and to be always there: not seeing it dimly through tears, and yearning for it through the walls of an aching heart: but really with it and in it.[23]

There can be no doubt that Emily Brontë's experience of the inner world was so deep and individual that it amounted to certainty. Yet there is a human ego in us all that says "No" to death, especially at Emily's age. Therefore Charlotte was probably equally right when she said that Emily was torn out of a happy life and was reluctant to go.

I once told Jung about a man's experience at the threshold of death. The doctors had pronounced him dead but, against all expectation, he recovered. He said afterwards that in those moments he had returned to a place which was more familiar

[22] Sinclair, p. 38.
[23] Cf. below, pp. 235-236.

to him than his home on earth, but that he was immeasurably astonished that that could possibly be death. Dr. Jung replied that the experience agreed exactly with his own impression of what death would be like. "But," he added, "the ego will not like it, there is sure to be a protest from that side."

This, it seems to me, is similar to Emily's experience at the end of her life. She foretells and describes it very clearly in a poem which should be read carefully by anyone who is puzzled by Emily's death. I can only quote the first verse:

*Death that struck when I was most confiding*
*In my certain Faith of Joy to be,*
*Strike again, Time's withered branch dividing*
*From the fresh root of Eternity.*[24]

The poem continues with these two themes: her certainty and confidence in the joy of life and the beauty of earthly springs, and her equal certainty that "time for me must never blossom more" and that her mortal body must return to "That from which it sprung—Eternity."

It is not surprising that Charlotte continues the already quoted passage concerning Emily's haste to leave them with these words:

> Yet, while physically she perished, mentally she grew stronger than we had yet known her. Day by day, when I saw with what a front she met suffering, I looked on her with an anguish of wonder and love. I have seen nothing like it; but, indeed, I have never seen her parallel in anything. Stronger than a man, simpler than a child, her nature stood alone.

This terminal conflict in Emily between the eternal Self

[24] *Complete Poems*, p. 224f.

and the ego must have meant intense suffering, not only for her environment but especially for herself. We must consider her great novel, the outstanding and almost the last work of her life, before we can hazard even the smallest suggestion as to the result of this most unusual life.

# 10 ❧ WUTHERING HEIGHTS

WHEN EMILY TURNED her ship into the inner world, she and Anne had already created a parallel to the four earlier African kingdoms, in the form of a large island in the North Pacific which they called Gondal. It was very similar to Haworth in climate, a land "of mists and moorlands drear, and sleet and frozen gloom." [1] Fannie Ratchford has done her best to reconstruct Gondal (mainly from the poems) and, although the records are sparse, she has produced a convincing general picture of it, and even something of Gaaldine, an island in the South Pacific discovered by the Gondals, which was a complete contrast to Gondal in climate and scenery—"tropic prairies bright with flowers and rivers wandering free." [2]

Emily and Anne, and particularly Emily, lived, moved and had their being in these islands. Fannie Ratchford says:

> The people of the northern continent (Gondal) were a bold, hardy, elemental race to whom loyalty was the highest virtue and treachery the darkest crime; freedom was their dearest blessing and prison their deepest hell. . . . Gondal homes were close in view, real and vivid and warm with life. Gondal's chief stage of action, however, was the wide expanse of earth and sea. It was the cool, shady bower of the forest or the white moonlight beach that heard the vows of lovers; the mountain glen that gave a death retreat to the wounded outlaw; and the wild waste of the moor that drank

[1] Ratchford, p. 65.
[2] *Ibid.*, p. 103.

the blood of the suicide and assassin's victim—Earth was mother and nurse to Emily's "Gondolians." [3]

In these rational days, when outer reality has become for most people the only reality, it may be difficult to realize how real and uncompromising such an inner creation as Gondal can be. In the mistaken belief that all experience must have an outer form, a great deal of ink has flowed in wild and unfounded speculation concerning possible outer love affairs of Emily Brontë. It is indeed difficult to imagine that such a poem as "Remembrance" [4] could possibly have been written without an actual, outer experience of losing a lover by death. It is a comparatively late poem (1845), and such an event *might* really have happened. Emily would certainly have kept her own counsel. But there is a great deal in the poem and in *Wuthering Heights* that she could not possibly have experienced, and there is the same ring of empirical reality about them. So we are forced to the conclusion that, for an introvert, inner experience can be just as vivid and gripping as outer experience is for the extravert—which is indeed the case.

Such a life as Emily's and such a life's work make one wonder whether the Buddhist theory of reincarnation may not have some basis in fact. If Emily were an old soul, with many lives behind her, it would be much easier to understand how she could have experienced inwardly what her soul had outwardly already lived once before—and perhaps more than once.

However this may be, Emily certainly did live an eventful inner life in Gondal and, as we have mentioned, she was still fully in it in her birthday notes of 1845, three years before her death.[5] There is even a poem, which Fannie Ratchford attributes to Gondal, dated May 13th, 1848, seven months

[3] Ratchford, p. 65f.
[4] *Complete Poems*, p. 222f.
[5] Ratchford, p. 165f.

before her death.[6] Emily's poems, of which Ratchford has estimated about half to be Gondal poems, certainly prove a deep journey into the unconscious and are an unusually exact record of what she encountered there.

Interesting as the poems are, *Wuthering Heights* undoubtedly represents the crown of what Emily found in the unconscious, for in it we can see an image of the process of individuation, carried as far, I think, as possible in its *projected form*. We see the same phenomenon in several other great masterpieces, but always in works by men. (For example, Goethe's *Faust*, Dante's *Divine Comedy* and several of Shakespeare's plays.) What makes Emily's great novel unique in my experience is that it depicts an image of human wholeness in a *feminine* soul or psyche. There are other examples, as I have shown in *Precious Bane*, but none of them carry the process as far as Emily did and they usually shipwreck sooner or later. As Jung has often pointed out, we find the same phenomenon in alchemy, but also mainly from the masculine side.

The process of individuation can only come into reality in a human being who is *conscious* of it; in fact even then it is uncertain how completely it can be realized in this life. But it is often to be met with in its *projected* form, as in the case of alchemy. Whatever we do not see in ourselves tends to project *itself* into the outside world and we experience it as if it belonged there. This is most easily to be seen in the personal shadow where, if we face the disagreeable revelations concerning unknown parts of our own character, we are able to withdraw most of the qualities that have irritated us almost unbearably in others and recognize them as part of our own totality. When this archetype of wholeness is constellated, but not *consciously* realized by the individual, it will appear in projection in the creative work, as we have seen in Mary Webb's *Precious Bane*, and there it will reveal a great deal of the potentiality for wholeness of that particular

[6] *Complete Poems*, pp. 15, 252f.

individual. Jung has made it possible for those who have the capacity, above all for those who are willing to perform the "arduous duties," to realize consciously this basic human process of individuation and to live it as far as they are able. But Emily Brontë had no such opportunity. She did all she possibly could at that time, she gave her life to having it out with her creative spirit; he rewarded her with a unique formulation of this basic foundation that lies in the unconscious of us all.

There is a verse in Emily's poem, "My Comforter," that describes exactly the psychology of *Wuthering Heights*:

*So stood I, in Heaven's glorious sun*
*And in the glare of Hell.*
*My spirit drank a mingled tone*
*Of seraph's song and demon's moan—*
*What my soul bore my soul alone*
*Within itself may tell.*[7]

Emily's attitude towards the opposites was totally different from the attitudes of her brother and sisters. Branwell allowed the dark opposite to possess him entirely. Charlotte and Anne chose the light opposite and, although they both fully realized the strength of the dark, did all they could to keep it in a subordinate position. Emily made no such choice. She viewed good and evil in a peculiarly pantheistic way, much as nature encompasses cloud and sunshine, dark and light, hot and cold. Nevertheless, although she seems by nature to have adopted her father's "golden middle way" and to have walked this path consistently, she evidently often suffered almost unbearably from the "mingled tone" of Heaven and Hell. But her words tell us that it was not her conscious mind that suffered—as we have seen, it was impossible for Emily in those days to reach consciousness of what was happening *in* her—it was her "soul," or what we

[7] *Complete Poems*, p. 196.

call the psyche. Her soul bore the intolerable pain of the opposites, and in *Wuthering Heights* it actually expressed what it bore. It might indeed only "tell" "within itself," but here we profit by Emily's unconsciousness that she was speaking of her own psyche. She, the most reserved of women, tells us her inmost secrets, secure in their projected form, where she no doubt regarded them as fiction, entirely unconnected with herself.

*Wuthering Heights* comes from a very deep level of the unconscious and is as meaningful therefore in every detail as a dream. Charlotte certainly realized, as is so clear in her preface to the 1850 edition,[8] that an author "who possesses the creative gift . . . sometimes cannot control it at all," and, with all the gaps in her understanding of *Wuthering Heights*, recognized it as such a book. But in many ways Charlotte was much more conscious in this respect than Emily, who was far more identified with the creative spirit. Emily was fully aware of the latter, welcomed it and adored it, but she seems to have had considerable illusions as to how far she controlled it. The passage, already quoted, in which she addresses it as "Thee, ever present, phantom thing,/My slave, my comrade and my King!" continues as follows:

*A slave because I rule thee still;*
*Incline thee to my changeful will*
*And make thy influence good or ill—*
*A comrade, for by day and night*
*Thou art my intimate delight—*

*My darling Pain that wounds and sears*
*And wrings a blessing out from tears*
*By deadening me to earthly cares;*
*And yet, a king—though prudence well*
*Have taught thy subject to rebel.*

[8] See above, p. 195f.

*And am I wrong to worship where*
*Faith cannot doubt nor Hope despair*
*Since my own soul can grant my prayer?*
*Speak God of Visions, plead for me*
*And tell why I have chosen thee!* [9]

Did Emily really "rule" her whole creative spirit or even incline it to her "changeful will"? I should say only very relatively. However, when she writes that she can make its "influence good or ill" she shows a most remarkable insight. This is the secret of the difference between Branwell and his sisters. The latter, each in her own way and to a different degree, influenced the creative spirit to "good" by unremitting hard work, whereas Branwell's self-indulgence and laziness influenced it to "ill." Emily's realization here of the value of pain—"My darling Pain"—is an intuitive anticipation of Jung's later discovery that women overcome by accepting their pain.

Her statement that although she regards the creative spirit as her king, yet "prudence well have taught thy subject to rebel" is also full of insight. Nearly all of Emily's work has the hallmark of the unconscious upon it, and indeed we know from her poems that they were brought to her by the "God of Visions," to use one of the many terms by which she addressed her creative spirit. However, as Jung points out in *Memories, Dreams, Reflections*, "Archetypes speak the language of high rhetoric, even of bombast." [10] As already mentioned, the Brontë juvenilia are full of such language. We know this from Charlotte's and Branwell's many manuscripts; we can assume that although they have disappeared it was also the case with Emily's and Anne's juvenilia. With few exceptions, however, it has disappeared from *Wuthering Heights* and the poems. Prudence had indeed "taught thy

[9] *Complete Poems*, p. 208f.
[10] *Memories*, p. 178; see also p. 134 above.

subject to rebel." The deeper content of all such writing comes from the unconscious, but if the author is to produce a work of art he *must* rebel against the form in which it appears and even "rule" and "change" it to that extent. There seems to be a continual give and take. The conscious cannot write without inspiration from the unconscious, the unconscious cannot formulate in a bearable form without the help of the conscious. Emily seems to have realized this, or at any rate to have practiced it to an unusual degree.

*Wuthering Heights* is one of the great classics of the English language. I think I can assume that readers are familiar with it and therefore will give no plot summary or follow the *peripetia* of the action except where it reveals the process of individuation which Emily found projected into it. When I say "found," I do not mean that she recognized it as such; that, of course, was impossible at that time. She was nevertheless so filled with a passion for wholeness and truth that it came through in an unusually clear form.

Jung has often compared the process of individuation to the formation of a crystal: the framework or lattice is in the solution from the beginning but only hardens and becomes visible much later as the crystal itself. In every human being there seems to be a similar framework or lattice of the process of individuation present from the beginning. It is as if this pattern—although its structure follows its own laws—depends for realization in some way on the individual becoming conscious of it. (We will consider this aspect in the final chapter.) In *Wuthering Heights* we are dealing with it in projected form, and we can easily recognize it at work as the underlying problem of the book. Its four-square structure appears again and again but, through some weakness or incompatibility in its ingredients, always seems to fall apart, only to reappear in another form, until the final and relatively complete image is established.

The complicated form of the book, which has been much criticized from the literary point of view, makes a great deal of sense psychologically. It begins as it were at the end, nearly thirty years after the beginning of the story and only a few months before the unexpectedly happy ending. When Mr. Lockwood rents Thrushcross Grange and goes over to Wuthering Heights, the story is at its darkest, in the stage of the *nigredo*, to use an alchemical term. Everything is in the hands of Heathcliff; the younger Catherine, the rightful owner of the Grange, is his prisoner at Wuthering Heights; and Hareton Earnshaw, the rightful owner of Wuthering Heights, is degraded to the rank of a ploughboy and has no idea how he has been defrauded.

From the psychological point of view, if a dream began with a situation like the one depicted here we could safely assume that the dreamer was animus possessed. Such a state is far more common in women than is generally recognized, and as a rule the woman herself is the furthest from knowing it. To throw off such a state calls for very firm roots in the feminine side and in the instincts, or for great detachment from the drama that is going on in the soul in order to let it work itself out; this is what happens in projected form in *Wuthering Heights*.

From the little we know of Emily's daily life, she must have suffered a great deal from animus opinions. Charlotte describes how, for instance, they had expert advice to sell at once some railway shares they had inherited from their aunt. But Emily, knowing nothing about such things, refused her consent. As a result, they lost all the income they would have received from the sale—although not till after Emily's death. Such hard and fast opinions are typical of the animus, who is always *sure* that he is right and imparts his certainty to the woman. Emily's unbending attitude to the entreaties of her family during her last illness have something of the same character. At all events, the circumstances prevailing at the beginning of *Wuthering Heights* present a marvelous picture of the soul of a woman when the animus is in full possession, of what Emily's soul was bearing within itself.

Mr. Lockwood, the narrator of the novel, is a stranger from the south of England. The whole story takes place in Emily's native Yorkshire, the moor country she adored and which we know was also the country of her island Gondal and can assume fairly confidently was also symbolically the country of her soul. In Emily's psychology, therefore, Mr. Lockwood would represent a point of view just outside the drama taking place in her soul, where it could be observed objectively from a distance. This aspect of her animus does the actual writing and would represent a part of her creative spirit that she really could and even must "rule" and "incline" to her "changeful will." It is something that comes from deeper in the unconscious, something which is brought, so to speak, by that aspect of the creative spirit that often takes complete command of the author, as Charlotte recognized.

In *Psychology and Alchemy* Jung presents a series of dreams in which the process of individuation appears more and more clearly. He says:

> We can hardly help feeling that the unconscious process moves spiral-wise round a centre, gradually getting closer, while the characteristics of the centre grow more and more distinct. Or perhaps we could put it the other way round and say that the centre—itself virtually unknowable—acts like a magnet on the disparate materials and processes of the unconscious and gradually captures them as in a crystal lattice. . . .
>
> Indeed, it seems as if all the personal entanglements and dramatic changes of fortune that go to make up the intensity of life were nothing but hesitations, timid shrinkings, almost like petty complications and meticulous excuses manufactured to avoid facing the finality of this strange or uncanny process of crystalization. Often one has the impression that the personal psyche is running round this central

point like a shy animal, at once fascinated and frightened, always in flight, and yet steadily drawing nearer.[11]

We can see this same process taking place in *Wuthering Heights* although it is the story itself rather than the personal psyche that circles round the central point. And we can see the center—completely unknowable as it is—acting like a magnet on this disparate material, rejecting weak or incompatible ingredients until at last it produces a relatively satisfactory image of itself. I say "relatively" for, as Jung emphasizes in the foregoing passage and even more strongly later, the center itself is unknowable and we are never in a position, therefore, to say how complete an image of it may be.

We may assume, however, that "what my soul bore . . . within itself" was at bottom the terrifying experience of this "uncanny process of crystallization." Meister Eckhart was referring to the same phenomenon in other words when he emphasized the necessity of giving up one's ego will ("*sich lassen*"—leaving onself, as he calls it) in order that God's will may replace it. He says: "Remember, in this life no one left himself so much but he could find something more to leave. Very few can stand it who know what it really means." [12] And: "There is no true and perfect will till, entering wholly into God's will, a man has no will of his own. . . . In fact, unless we do give up our will without reserve we cannot work with God at all." [13] Meister Eckhart uses the religious language of the centuries and was writing some seven hundred years ago; Jung is using more modern and scientific language; but both are describing different aspects of the same phenomenon. Emily naturally could not see it in our psychological terms, but her whole life was spent in try-

[11] Pars. 325-326.
[12] *The Works of Meister Eckhart,* Vol. II, p. 6.
[13] *Ibid.*, p. 16.

ing to accept her creative spirit and fulfill its will. Although she avoids religious terminology, it is quite possible that she could have accepted the language of Meister Eckhart. The further formulation of Jung—which after all makes the characteristics of this mysterious, unknowable center much more distinct—was, in Emily's time, still in the womb of the future.

To return to the beginning of the book: Mr. Lockwood is weatherbound by a snowstorm at the Heights and—most interestingly from the psychological point of view—reads and *dreams* his way into the whole story. Unknown to Heathcliff, the housekeeper has put Mr. Lockwood into the first Catherine's bedroom, where he finds thirty-year-old diaries of hers, which he reads before going to sleep, and glances also at the title of a "pious discourse delivered by the Rev. Jabez Branderham."

His first dream takes up the latter theme. He is wading through the snow to hear this sermon, guided by old Joseph (the man-servant at the Heights), to the chapel on the moors. Joseph reproaches him for having no pilgrim's staff. When they arrive, Jabez Branderham is preaching an interminable sermon on the text, "Seventy Times Seven." The sermon is divided into four hundred and ninety parts, each devoted to a separate sin, which could still be forgiven. But when he comes to the "First of the Seventy-First," the dreamer—goaded beyond endurance—is moved to rise and denounce the preacher as the perpetrator of this sin beyond forgiveness by preaching such a sermon. Jabez denounces the dreamer as being the unforgivable sinner. The ensuing tumult, in which many resounding blows are exchanged, awakens Mr. Lockwood.

This dream, in totally different imagery, also depicts a state of animus possession. One of the most difficult thnigs to overcome is the state of bad conscience in which the animus so often keeps us, suggesting that we have committed one of the four hundred and ninety sins, each of which he tries to persuade us is the unforgivable four hundred and ninety first! It is absolutely necessary for this army of animus prejudices to be overcome, the ground entirely cleared of such opinions, before the voice of the soul can be heard relating what it hears within itself. The prognosis is good in the dream; the writer animus rebels against the preacher, thus putting an end to his interminable sermon. We can see this confirmed in the material. Joseph-Jabez becomes merely an accompanying voice in the dream, somewhat like a Greek chorus, making what mischief he can but never playing a leading role or able to hold up the action while he preaches interminable sermons, as in Mr. Lockwood's dream and as, to a limited extent, he actually does at the beginning of the story. Joseph is a subordinate character, but Emily sketches him in a few strokes with almost the genius of a Rembrandt: "the wearisomest self-righteous Pharisee that ever ransacked a Bible to take the promises to himself and fling the curses to his neighbours."

Mr. Lockwood's rational attempt to attribute the dream to a fir branch tapping against his window is naturally ineffective. He dozes and immediately dreams again: the ghost of a child, who turns out to be the Catherine whose diaries he was reading and whose name is scribbled everywhere, tries to get in at the window. Remembering the fir branch, he attempts to break it off, but his fingers close over the tiny fingers of an ice-cold hand. Almost maddened with fear, he barricades the window against the child's face and answers her entreaties to be let in with the words: "I will never let you in, not if you beg for twenty years." She tells him mournfully, "It is twenty years, I've been a waif for twenty years," and "in a frenzy of fright" he awakens from his nightmare with a loud scream.

On her creative side, Emily was undoubtedly fully adult; there is nothing infantile about her writing, but, as I have pointed out, she seems never to have entered the outer world at all. The continuation of Mr. Lockwood's dream, which introduces him to the drama taking place in Emily's soul, clearly reveals that her feminine side is represented by the ghost of a little girl haunting the moors she loved so well. It is an elemental ghost and when we examine its previous life we shall see that it had lived an elemental, even archetypal, existence on earth.

The time during which this ghost has wandered corresponds more or less with the time that elapsed since the deaths of Maria and Elizabeth Brontë, Emily's elder sisters. Both died as children, when Emily was only five or six. Maria, a most precocious child, as is often the case with those destined to die very young, functioned as a loving mother to her younger brother and sisters and as a companion to Mr. Brontë. This death of their second mother and companion probably made an indelible impression on such sensitive children, and it may well have made it still more difficult for the girls to grow up as women. At all events Mr. Lockwood's second dream announces the leitmotif of the story: the feminine side of Emily's soul which has somehow or other to be redeemed from its childishness and the state of complete animus possession in which the book begins.

Mr. Lockwood's dreams and his account of conditions at Wuthering Heights at the time of his visit are the prologue to the story of the novel. During the long illness brought on by his terrible night at the Heights and by his walk home through the snow the next morning, Nelly Dean, the children's nurse, now housekeeper at the Grange, tells him of the events that have led to Heathcliff's absolute power and to the imprisonment and degradation of the two last descendants of the ancient families of Earnshaw and Linton.

Since she does not belong to either family by birth or marriage, Nelly Dean is slightly outside the story and this gives her a little distance from which to observe; she is not identified with the main actors or events. On the other hand, she is intimately and emotionally involved in everything, as old family servants usually are. She is present throughout the development of the story, from beginning to end, and is therefore singularly well-fitted to recount the events, to be the voice of the soul relating "what it bore within itself."

The conditions she describes at the beginning of the action are very different from those which Mr. Lockwood finds nearly thirty years later. The two families are living the traditional life their ancestors had lived for centuries, the Earnshaws at Wuthering Heights as gentlemen-farmers, the Lintons at the Grange as country gentlemen. From the beginning, it is true, one gets an impression of more dark elemental passions in the Earnshaw family, and of more culture and law-abiding conformity in the Lintons. The houses themselves bear out this hypothesis. Wuthering Heights is built on very high ground, exposed to every wind, so that the very trees have "an excessive slant," stretching "their limbs one way, as if craving alms of the sun." Erected in 1500, it was, happily, strongly built, the windows "deeply set in the wall, and the corners defended with large jutting stones." The Grange, on the other hand, is a much larger house, situated on lower sheltered ground, in the center of a large park, and is comfortably and richly furnished. So from the beginning the former tends to represent the dark opposite and the latter the light. In the present generation there are a boy and a girl in each house, Hindley and Catherine Earnshaw at Wuthering Heights, Edgar and Isabella Linton at the Grange. The continuity of such conditions is very deeply rooted and it requires a major event or events to change them. Two world wars have now somewhat shattered such conditions in England, although they are so ingrained that a surprising number of families still do all their own work and live in the utmost discomfort rather than change their ways. One regrets losing the mellow atmosphere of the old life but must admit that it kept consciousness in the same state, even in torpor, for centuries. If consciousness is to increase, if wholeness is to become more accessible, tradition must suffer some shattering shocks.

Emily's unconscious foresaw this and produced its own bomb. Old Mr. Earnshaw walks to Liverpool, a distance of sixty miles each way, and when he returns three days later he brings with him the element that will explode all of the traditional ways. All of the names in *Wuthering Heights* are symbolically meaningful, and the fact that Mr. Earnshaw finds in the streets of Liverpool a destitute boy who can only repeat "over and over again some gibberish that no one could understand" is no exception to the rule. Although it is the actual name of a famous English port which is definitely referred to here, from the standpoint of unconscious symbolism it can also be understood symbolically. Liverpool, the "pool of life," is the symbol *par excellence* of that place where there are to be found the dynamic new things which tradition does its best to exclude. And Mr. Earnshaw is strangely convinced that this boy is somehow intimately connected with the Earnshaw family, for he not only carries him many of the sixty miles he has to walk home but continues unwaveringly to set a very high value on him. He gives him the name of a son who had died in childhood. The words with which he sets him down prove strangely prophetic: "See here, wife! I was never so beaten with anything in my life; but you must e'en take it as a gift of God; though it's as dark almost as if it came from the devil!" His house is fated to take a beating from Heathcliff, he shows himself for many years as "dark as the devil," yet in the end he does turn out to be a "gift of God," for he awakens everyone from the traditional torpor of the ancestral life and brings them greatly increased consciousness and a big advance along the road towards individuation and wholeness.

Throughout the story, when there are only two or three of the principal characters living together, a state of relative harmony prevails, but, when the fatal fourth appears, conflict and almost insuperable difficulties begin. This is actually the case in every process of individuation, the fourth is the "gift of God," the absolutely indispensable element. But as Christ said of Himself: "I come not to bring peace, but a sword." Unfortunately, conflict and struggle are indispensable and inevitable before there is any chance of the contradictory and fatal fourth finding its way into and then its place within the totality.

The first appearance of Heathcliff immediately shatters the peaceful life of the farm. At this time Nelly Dean, who is the same age as Hindley and whose mother was his nurse and foster mother, is almost always at Wuthering Heights, so the three children play together constantly. Catherine, who is by far the most vital and gifted, easily keeps up with the others, although they are eight or nine years older. But a deadly enmity breaks out at once between Hindley and Heathcliff, and an equally fatal love between the latter and Catherine. At first Nelly takes Hindley's side, but afterwards she goes over to the other: in short, storm and conflict reign among the four children.

What does the advent of Heathcliff mean in the soul (psyche) of Emily? Very often in a dream the age of a dream figure (or a number appearing in some other connection) gives us a hint that something happened in the life of the dreamer at that age which it would be worthwhile to investigate. So we can profitably consider the age (nearly six) of Catherine (the first representation of the feminine side of Emily in the story) when Heathcliff appears on the scene. We notice immediately that this again is exactly Emily's age when her two sisters died. This was undoubtedly a far greater shock to the Brontë children than the death of their mother a few years earlier. Emily and Anne were too young to realize fully the consequences of their mother's death, and moreover they had seen very little of her on account of her failing health. But Maria had been their mainstay. To have both her and Elizabeth torn from their daily life together must have been an unutterable shock. Although Charlotte did everything she could, she was in no way fitted to take Maria's place. The children were probably therefore driven inwards at this point, into the region of the archetypal mother and the Self.[14] Synchronistically they became *four*, so that this image of the Self naturally imprinted itself upon all of their common undertakings. There were four genii, four kingdoms, and so on. Moreover the records of the inward, imaginary life only began *after* Maria's death, and from all we hear of her (her immense interest in politics, newspapers and the like) she probably guided the children's interests into the outer world. Their interest in politics continued, it is true, but the famous men of the time were taken *inside* to become characters in their inner world. It seems exceedingly likely that this was the time when the archetype of wholeness broke into the retired and peaceful life the family lived in the remote moorland village of Haworth and worked upon it in the same bomblike way that Heathcliff worked on Wuthering Heights. To them also it was "a gift of God," yet as dark as the devil and often as destructive as Satan. It was probably not only Emily's soul that was invaded by "Heathcliff" but the souls of them all.

From that moment on none of them was able to avoid the problem of evil, for it had invaded their innermost lives as the dark Heathcliff invaded first the Earnshaw family and later the Lintons. Children though they were, the Brontës were forced to accept it, and they all did, at first completely, as the designation of their inward life as the "infernal world" or the "world below" bears testimony. After childhood they all met, or were met by, the problem each in his own individual way.

I venture the hypothesis that the entrance of Heathcliff into the Earnshaw family depicts or is an analogy of the entrance of a symbol of the process of individuation into the whole Brontë family. The individual characteristics of Heathcliff and the further developments of the story show the individual way that Emily dealt with it, or rather the

[14] The Self in women is often first represented as a Great Mother figure.

way it dealt with her, what her soul suffered within itself and which she here records in a unique document. Her eternal merit is that she learned to deal with the "God of visions," faithfully accepted and never distorted what he offered her, and yet "rebelled" sufficiently to do this in the form of a literary masterpiece. That she was a true introvert turned her entirely inward in her investigation, as it were, into what had hit them, whereas the others were more disposed to turn outward on the same quest, searching for a way to live it, each in his own way.

This childish foretaste of the subsequent quaternities that form the pattern of the novel did not last very long. About two years after Heathcliff's arrival, old Mrs. Earnshaw dies and Hindley's position in the family becomes entirely friendless. Evidently his situation is impossible, for the curate persuades Mr. Earnshaw to send Hindley away to college, which he does with the gloomy prognosis that "Hindley was nought, and would never thrive as where he wandered." It is inexplicable that some writers on the Brontës have compared Heathcliff to Branwell, for there seems no resemblance between them whatever. On the other hand, Hindley's fate and character have a great deal in common with Branwell's. They both founder from lack of a will to work and of all manner of self control, and the final stage, in which each drinks himself to death, begins in both with the loss of the woman he has idolized. Is it possible that Mr. Brontë never shared the girls' early high opinion of Branwell's genius (Charlotte after all is our main informant) but secretly thought, like Mr. Earnshaw thought of Hindley, that he was "nought."

In Hindley's case, although his father's lack of hope for his son can hardly have helped him, the judgment is amply justified by the sequel, for when Mr. Earnshaw dies, apparently six or seven years after Heathcliff's arrival, Hindley returns, after four years absence, with a wife whom he has kept secret from his father, and proceeds to prove himself

ght" in every sense of the word. His revenge on the
l Heathcliff, who is certainly less than twelve at the time, is immediate, petty, mean and cruel, and when he fails to break the tie between Heathcliff and Catherine, he also treats her abominably. There is also no sign of the old friendship with Nelly, who is banished to the kitchen and from this time on becomes a servant, although she is not cruelly treated as Heathcliff is. At the same time Nelly ceases to function as a main character in the drama and is forced into the role of observer, which admirably fits her to become the voice of the soul. Another foreshadowing of the principal quaternities is thus established at Wuthering Heights for a year: Hindley and his wife Frances, Heathcliff and Catherine. But the two pairs are on the most hostile terms with each other, although the relations between the two individuals in each pair are deep and firm.

Interestingly enough it is Heathcliff himself who makes the suggestion which leads to so much trouble between Catherine and himself and eventually to Catherine's marriage with his rival. He and Catherine are banished to the cold back kitchen for some trifling fault, and he suggests that they run on the moors in the rain. It is this excursion which leads them to Thrushcross Grange. Until this time, except for seeing each other at Church, there has been no communication between the two houses. Catherine is badly bitten by a Linton dog and has to remain at the Grange for five weeks. Heathcliff reveals himself here for the first time as the principle of individuation; for, entirely against his own interest, he opens the way to the light opposite and to the first attempt at establishing a quaternity containing *both* opposites.

When I say that he reveals himself as the principle of individuation, I do not mean that Heathcliff is the *spiritus rector* of the entire process. On the contrary, I mean that the unknown center, which "acts like a magnet on the disparate materials and gradually captures them as in a crystal lattice," begins at this point to draw Heathcliff into the role of the principle of individuation, whether willingly or unwillingly we cannot tell. The alchemists often referred to the Devil as the principle of individuation in the same sense.

This second internal quaternity at Wuthering Heights is broken up by the death of Hindley's beloved wife, soon after the birth of the boy Hareton. Hindley, very much as Branwell did after the loss of Mrs. Robinson, goes straight to the devil. He degrades Heathcliff more and more and the house becomes a veritable hell, a state of affairs which lasts for several years. It is a very dark time, comparable to the later time when Mr. Lockwood pays his visit to the Heights. But there is one great difference: Catherine retains her friendship with the Lintons and behaves very differently with them than she does in her own rough, comfortless home. It does depict a time of animus possession, but less complete, and Hindley moreover represents a very different animus figure than does Heathcliff. The latter becomes completely demonic, archetypal and closely related to the devil of the collective unconscious; whereas Hindley, for all his destructive rages, drunken orgies and complete lack of self-control, more or less remains within human dimensions, in that he is swayed by personal vices and shows little or no connection with the figures of the collective unconscious. His personal ambition to see his sister married to the heir of the Grange keeps him from imprisoning her to anywhere near the extent that Heathcliff later imprisons her daughter.

Moreover, such imprisonment was impossible, for Catherine is never impressed by her brother and has always kept the upper hand as far as her own personal freedom is concerned. She was a wild tomboy as a child. Nelly Dean says of her: "From the hour she came downstairs till the hour she went to bed, we had not a minute's security that she wouldn't be in mischief. Her spirits were always at high-water mark, her tongue always going—singing, laughing and plaguing everybody who would not do the same. A wild wicked slip she was—but she had the bonniest eye, the est smile and lightest foot in the parish." Nelly goes on to say that in spite of everything she has a good heart, which she shows "when once she made you cry in good earnest. . . . She was much too fond of Heathcliff. The greatest punishment we could invent for her was to keep her separate from him. . . . They forgot everything the moment they were together again."

Even after her stay at the Grange and her friendship with the Lintons, Catherine remains Heathcliff's constant companion whenever he can get away from his work on the farm. But as Hindley abuses Heathcliff more and more, she gives up any idea of marrying him. "It would degrade me to marry Heathcliff now," she tells Nelly Dean. Yet she also confides, when she decides to marry Linton, that, "In my soul and in my heart, I'm convinced I'm wrong." And indeed, her soul is made of the same substance as Heathcliff's, while Linton's is as different "as a moonbeam from lightening, or frost from fire." She even declares later, "Nelly, I *am* Heathcliff."

Heathcliff overhears this conversation, but only to the point where Catherine says that she has decided to marry Linton and that it would now degrade her to marry Heathcliff. He then takes himself off into the unknown, disappearing for several years. This is a major catastrophe for Catherine; she reacts with a dangerous illness. She does recover, but from then on she begins to change, her illness being more psychic than physical, with the serious threat of a seizure when she falls into her almost insane rages.

This is the first unmistakable sign that the figure which represents Emily's feminine side in the first part of the book is unstable, much too emotional, and may turn out to be not sufficiently anchored on earth to be able to carry through to the end. Later we shall see the reasons for this more clearly; for the moment we need only note that Catherine no longer meets the situation with the warmheartedness she had always shown as a child, however "wild and wicked" she may have been. She is beginning to become self-centered, to choose the alternative of power rather than love. The doctor says that "she would not bear crossing much; she ought to have her own way; and it was nothing less than murder in her eyes for anyone to presume to stand up and contradict her."

But, as is always true when the fourth is absent, things seemingly settle down again and move along very tolerably for a few years. Catherine is engaged to Edgar Linton for about three years, during which time his parents die and he becomes the owner of Thrushcross Grange, living there with his sister Isabella, an arrangement that continues even after his marriage to Catherine. When the latter moves to the Grange, a triad of three main characters is therefore established. Nelly Dean is forced to leave her beloved nursling, Hareton, to accompany Catherine to the Grange. She says:

> "I got Miss Catherine and myself to Thrushcross Grange; and, to my agreeable disappointment, she behaved infinitely better than I dared to expect. She seemed almost over-fond of Mr. Linton; and even to his sister she showed plenty of affection. They were both very attentive to her comfort, certainly. It was not the thorn bending to the honeysuckles, but the honeysuckles embracing the thorn. There were no mutual concessions; one stood erect, and the others yielded: and who *can* be ill-natured and bad-tempered when they encounter neither opposition nor indifference?"

And later:

> "I believe I may assert that they were really in possession of deep and growing happiness." [15]

About six months later, however, this harmony is again shattered by the return of the fourth—Heathcliff. We have

[15] *Wuthering Heights*, pp. 107-08.

information about where he was in the meantime, but we hear that Nelly is astounded at "his transformation." He had left Wuthering Heights as a dirty, ignorant ploughboy, but he returns as a tall man with an upright carriage, well dressed, evidently educated, "plentifully supplied" with money and, moreover, he looks intelligent and retains "no marks of his former degradation."

His return makes a "jubilee" for Catherine, although naturally her husband hates it. Catherine handles the situation so brilliantly, however, that it looks at first as if she will succeed in maintaining her relationships with both men. Indeed were it to remain a triangle this might quite possibly have worked out, for it is again the intrusion of the fourth that leads to the final quarrel and to Catherine's death a few months later.

The triangle is not described in human terms, it reads rather like a page of Greek mythology. Catherine behaves much more as a goddess than as a human girl who, as we hear later, is expecting her first baby. She has such faith in her husband's love that she believes she "might kill him and he would not wish to retaliate." Moreover, from the first page to the last she knows that she is Heathcliff's "idol," "immeasurably superior . . . to everybody on earth," as Heathcliff himself describes her. In Jungian language, she is the anima of both men.

When a man is unconscious of his anima, as the majority of men still are, she usually projects herself onto a real woman in order to be noticed at all, as we have seen in Chapter II.[16] The woman then seems almost or quite a supernatural being to the man, full of all the fascination and mana of a goddess. This naturally gives a woman an intoxicating sense of power over the man, and it is a great temptation to her to identify with the anima. In fact, if she is that type, as Catherine was, it is exceedingly difficult for her not to do so. But such projections carry a compelling

[16] See above, p. 22ff; see also below, p. 274f.

force; the woman finds herself, consciously or unconsciously, obliged to play a role, often the role of a goddess *per se*. This naturally alienates her from her human qualities, and since no human being can identify with an archetype unpunished, sooner or later her humanity catches up with her and makes trouble.

Women who are especially liable to become anima types have usually already played the role of anima to their fathers. Mr. Brontë was a comparatively young man when he lost his wife and one must give him full credit for having recognized that he should marry again. But as his efforts failed—and certainly Aunt Branwell was no anima type!—it was inevitable that his anima should project herself onto one or more of his daughters. We have already noted that the wife aspect was projected onto Charlotte, particularly in the last years of her life. But a man like Patrick Brontë would have a far more elemental, archetypal aspect to his anima than either Charlotte or Anne could carry. Emily, on the contrary, from all we know of her, was eminently suitable to receive such a projection, daughter of the moors and nature as she was, "great granddaughter of the Titans," as Mrs. Gaskell expressed it. One may, therefore, assume that the first Catherine's anima quality owed a great deal to the projection of Mr. Brontë's archetypal anima on Emily, and that part of the latter's failure to become rooted in outer life was due to this secret and unconscious bond with her father. At all events, the voice of Emily's soul or psyche produces a marvelous image of a woman who is blessed or cursed with the faculty of receiving the projection of a man's anima. Both men, Edgar and Heathcliff, are so completely fascinated by Catherine that they are willing to endure almost anything—even each other—for her sake. She is well aware of her power over them and is very probably capable of maintaining a balance between the two. However, she is living too far above her roots, having left her human—her all-too-human—qualities unheeded. These qualities fit her sister-in-law, Isabella Linton, only too well. Isabella, who has been pushed into the background and neglected since Heathcliff's return, now appears with her just but blind claim to live as an equal part of the totality. She announces that she loves Heathcliff more than Catherine ever loved Edgar, and that he might love her if only Catherine would let him.

Catherine is horrified, for she now sees very clearly how the archetypal, "fierce, pitiless wolfish" Heathcliff would crush Isabella "like a sparrow's egg" and warns the girl against him in the strongest terms. But when her sister-in-law will not believe her, thinking that she speaks from "wicked selfishness," she replies: "Try for yourself, if that be your spirit, I have done and yield the argument to your saucy insolence." Naturally Emily could not realize that, in depicting such a superwoman as Catherine, she would be bound to cast a shadow, composed of all the trivial and banal qualities of which the human being also consists. Isabella fits the picture exactly. Nelly Dean describes her as "a charming young lady of eighteen; infantile in manners, though possessed of keen wit, keen feeling and a keen temper, too, if irritated." She invariably reveals quite human and personal reactions, and has no identification with, or even relation to, the archetypal anima. She also possesses some pitiful, less heroic qualities, such as cowardice, lying and deceit, all of which are missing in Catherine, who simply despises her from the heights of her own identification with the anima. The wide gulf between the two figures representing Emily's feminine side in the first part of the novel is really the principal reason for the failure of this quaternity to establish itself in a durable form. As Catherine sees no reason to take her sister-in-law's pretensions seriously, she punishes her insolence "by telling her secret to Heathcliff," although she has told Isabella that "he'd be quite capable of marrying your fortune and expectations: avarice is growing with him a besetting sin."

This is exactly what Heathcliff decides to do. It fits perfectly into his plan for revenge against Hindley Earnshaw and Edgar Linton. But he does not mean to hurt Catherine herself: "I seek no revenge on you. That's not the plan. The tyrant grinds down his slaves and they don't turn against him. You are welcome to torture me to death for your amusement, only allow me to amuse myself a little in the same style, and refrain from insult as much as you are able." A stormy scene follows. Afterwards Catherine tells Nelly: "Heathcliff's talk was outrageous, after you left us; but I could soon have diverted him from Isabella, and the rest meant nothing." This is probably the truth, for Heathcliff always gives in to Catherine. She might even have been able to make him treat Isabella decently, and she had told Nelly that she could make Edgar Linton consent if Heathcliff could convince her he liked Isabella. She might thus have established a quaternity in place of the triangle. I say "might," for Heathcliff's aversion to Isabella grows stronger and stronger, and while Catherine identifies so completely with an archetypal figure, and does not herself show any understanding for Isabella, the situation was too much up in the air for this quaternity to have any real chance to survive. Even the gods, as mythology has shown us again and again, must take some responsibility for their own shortcomings in order to continue. Catherine merely washes her hands in innocence, blames everyone else and says to Nelly: "You are aware I am in no way blamable in this matter." With such an attitude, she really signs her own death warrant.

Although Catherine is probably more to blame in "this matter" than anyone else, she has no opportunity to exert her full influence over Heathcliff or Edgar, on account of interference from an unexpected quarter: Nelly Dean. Although Nelly apparently intervenes *against* Heathcliff, she seems throughout the book to have a secret unconscious bond with him, so that she continually furthers his plans when she consciously wants to defeat them. Or we can look deeper and surmise that the unknown center uses Nelly as

Heathcliff's assistant, whenever it is a matter of the process of individuation. Now although Heathcliff's outer purpose in courting Isabella is certainly to gain power and money, if we look below the surface we can see that again, as in the matter of making contact with Thrushcross Grange, he is acting as, or for, the principle of individuation. By marrying Isabella he will establish a double marriage, connecting the Grange and Wuthering Heights indissolubly, whereas if he gives up this purpose at Catherine's command, he will have left the main characters forming a triangle. It is the only place in the novel where he does *not* obey Catherine, although even here, had Nelly Dean not interfered, she could probably, as she says, "have diverted him from Isabella."

Nelly interferes by telling Edgar that Heathcliff is courting Isabella and that Catherine is in the kitchen "sadly put out by Mr. Heathcliff's behavior." Unaware of this, Catherine accuses her husband of "listening at the door." A violent quarrel than takes place which drives them all apart. Nelly keeps Edgar in ignorance of the violent fit of frenzy into which Catherine has fallen and of the fact that she subsequently shuts herself into her room without food for three days. Nelly knows that Catherine is pregnant and that, after her former illness, the doctor has warned them very seriously of the danger in crossing Catherine.

Such behavior seems so foreign to Nelly Dean's loyal kindness and motherly nature that it and other similar lapses have often been commented on. It is frequently regarded as a conscious device of Emily's in order to keep the story moving forward! But Emily needed no such devices and she was far more aware of the opposites in human nature than were most of her critics. If we ask the simple question, "What is brought about by Nelly's behavior here?" we see at once that it is the success of Heathcliff's plan to elope with Isabella. This elopement takes place in those three days and would never have been allowed if Catherine had not been locked into her room. Nelly, like Heathcliff himself when he took Catherine to the Grange years before, is acting against her own interests, for she certainly does not consciously want Heathcliff to marry Isabella. Both are evidently moved by the pattern of the totality, the unknown center which underlies the whole book, to act in a way that furthers *its* purposes rather than their own.

Heathcliff and Isabella are absent for two months, and in these months Catherine encounters and conquers "the worst shock of what was denominated a brain fever." Nelly tells us that "no mother could have nursed an only child more devotedly than Edgar tended her" and that there were no limits to "his joy and gratitude when Catherine's life was declared out of danger," although the doctor had told Nelly "the threatening danger was not so much death, as permanent alienation of intellect." There is indeed a return to infantility and childhood in her delirium, following her declaration that she is "in no way blamable," during which she imagines she is still a girl at Wuthering Heights. As far as entering into human life is concerned, this representation of Emily's femininity is still in many ways an irresponsible child, just as infantile as Isabella herself, although in a different way. As I see it, it is above all the redemption of this childishness in both these aspects of Emily's feminine side that forms the leading theme of the story, as we saw in Mr. Lockwood's dream at the very beginning of the book.

Nelly's description of Catherine during her brief convalescence does not give any impression of an "alienation of intellect." It seems rather a description of a woman who has given up because she has found it impossible to live her complete identification with the archetypal figure of the anima under human conditions. She has changed, according to Nelly Dean, but there seems "an unearthly beauty in the change. The flash of her eyes had been succeeded by a dreamy and melancholy softness; they no longer gave the impression of looking at the objects around her: they appeared always to gaze beyond, and far beyond—you would have said out of this world." Surely this is exactly what she is doing, having as it were decided to escape the struggle by passing over into the archetypal world. On the morning of her death, during her last fatal interview with Heathcliff, she says: "The thing that irks me most is this shattered prison [her body] after all. I'm wearying to escape into the glorious world, and to be always there: not seeing it dimly through tears, and yearning for it through the walls of an aching heart: but really with it and in it. Nelly, you think you are better and more fortunate than I; in full health and strength; you are sorry for me—very soon that will be altered. I shall be sorry for *you*. I shall be incomparably beyond and above you all." It seems to me that these words are strong evidence that Catherine has identified so completely with her immortal anima aspect that she only now wants to escape into its "glorious world," and to be "incomparably beyond and above" the struggle of human life.

In the meantime, Isabella, the figure that carries the human feminine side, is faring very badly. Heathcliff soon shatters her illusions and treats her with almost incredible cruelty. When they return to Wuthering Heights, she contrives to send a letter to Nelly Dean begging her to call at the Heights, as she is unable to elude Heathcliff's vigilance in order to come to the Grange. Edgar allows Nelly to go but refuses to have anything more to do with his sister.

During Nelly's visit to the Heights, Heathcliff makes a statement that reveals his role in the drama much more clearly: "I have no pity! I have no pity! The more the worms writhe, the more I yearn to crush out their entrails! It is a moral teething; and I grind with greater energy in proportion to the increase in pain." Behind Heathcliff's inhuman cruelty, then, there is a purpose of which he is dimly conscious, a moral teething, the application of torture with an object: to remove the milk teeth, the infantile innocence of the figures in Emily's psyche, to enable them to overcome by accepting their suffering, the only way, as Jung said so much later, that women could overcome. As we shall see, once Heathcliff accomplishes this purpose, he loses the wish to torture or destroy.

It is probable that much of the torture which the animus inflicts on women has this same end in view. The quality, which is most fatal for anyone who is touched by the process of individuation, is childish irresponsibility. Yet it is unfortunately a very wide-spread quality these days, and is an almost irresistable temptation to those who are governed by a will to power. Dictator states could never come into being were it not for the prevalence of this quality. Heathcliff in his small world is a dictator type *par excellence*. At least there is a purpose behind his torture, however; whereas dictators clearly have no such goal, they even try to keep their subjects infantile, although it is quite possible that they themselves are the instruments of a higher power to bring about this same highly necessary "moral teething."

Be this as it may, Heathcliff then devotes himself to persuading Nelly Dean to arrange a meeting, without Edgar's knowledge, between Catherine and himself. This time at least she is conscious that she will be "playing a treacherous part in her employer's house." In the end she gives in, as she always does to Heathcliff. A few days later, when Edgar and the servants are at church, she leaves the front door open and tries to prepare Catherine for the visit of Heathcliff.

The interview between these two, which leads to Catherine's death the same evening, has frequently aroused comment by its strange quality. Although it has been called the most passionate love scene in English literature, everyone seems to agree that the element of *physical* passion is entirely missing. It seems, moreover, that *every* human element is lacking in this scene. When we consider its inhuman cruelty —the absence of the slightest human consideration for each other, although they both know and admit that Catherine is dying; their nevertheless undying and immortal love and the ultimate basic reality they both reach—the passage reads far more like a page of Greek mythology than a scene between two human lovers. But if we regard it as an interview between two spirits or archetypes, it then does seem to be one of the greatest love scenes in literature. Emily allows the archetypes to speak through her in an unsurpassed way, although her genius has eliminated their "bombastic style" entirely.

The raw emotion is too much for Catherine's weakened body. She never regains consciousness after Heathcliff leaves her, and at midnight that same night she gives birth to a seven months child, the younger Catherine, and dies as "quietly as a lamb," as Nelly tells us. "She drew a sigh and stretched herself, like a child reviving and sinking again to sleep. . . . No angel in heaven could have looked more beautiful than she appeared" after death.

With Catherine's death, however, the quaternity has again failed to produce a lasting symbol, for she alone, as the image of the ego, could have established it. It was a far more complete quaternity than either of its predecessors; it included the light Linton aspect, the tumultuous Earnshaw aspect, and the dark and doubtful fourth: Heathcliff. It sometimes came very near to establishing itself, but Catherine was altogether too archetypal and left too many of her human qualities to her shadow, Isabella, including the valuable quality of self-criticism. Isabella is able to criticize herself and to realize fully what a fool she has been to trust Heathcliff: "I think the concentrated essence of all the madness in the world took up its abode in my brain the day I linked my fate" with Heathcliff's. Isabella has certain qualities that are exceedingly valuable: she plucks up her courage to run away from Heathcliff, has sufficient insight to see if she can "contrive a clear escape"—Heathcliff would not chase her over England on account of his strong aversion to her—and then faces a new life in the South of England with the "delicate and ailing" son who is "born a few months subsequent to her escape."

The break-up of this quaternity in *Wuthering Heights* can be compared in some respects to the similar break-up in *Precious Bane*. Emily, however, had a far more tolerant attitude to the opposites than Mary Webb. There is no division of good and bad qualities in Emily's characters; practically all of them present that bewildering mixture which is the true substance of human nature. Emily was under no temptation to let one opposite triumph over the other and to escape, as Mary Webb did, into a one-sided solution. On the contrary, she picked up her broken pieces and made another attempt—or allowed another attempt to be made through her—to establish a more enduring image of totality.

In the beginning of the second attempt there is again a complete separation between the Grange and the Heights, the *separatio* of the alchemists. The younger Catherine is kept in a kind of retort, as if the utmost care were being taken to see that this new feminine seed in Emily is given every chance to become a healthy plant, more capable than her mother of rooting in the earth. And indeed from the beginning she is far more human and a better combination of the opposites than her mother ever was. Nelly Dean says of her:

> She was the most winning thing that ever brought sunshine into a desolate house: a real beauty in face, with the Earnshaw's handsome dark eyes, but the Lintons' fair skin and small features, and yellow curling hair. Her spirit was high, though not rough, and qualified by a heart sensitive and lively to excess in its affections. That capacity for intense attachments reminded me of her mother: still she did not resemble her: for she could be soft and mild as a dove, and she had a gentle voice and pensive expression: her anger was never furious; her love never fierce: it was deep and tender.

Fortunately she lacks the archetypal quality of her mother,

therefore it has often been thought, especially by men, that the second part of the novel is in no way equal to the first.[17] From a literary point of view this may be quite true, but psychologically it is fascinating to observe the way in which the weaknesses that led to the break-up of the quaternity in the first part have been eliminated and replaced by just those qualities that can lead to a more enduring result. Cathy, for instance, is a fortunate mixture of the best qualities of her mother *and* her aunt Isabella. How much of this happy result was due to Emily herself and how much was brought to her from the unconscious we cannot say, but the subtlety displayed is certainly more than consciousness alone could be expected to achieve.

While Cathy is growing up at the Grange, Heathcliff is in complete possession of the Heights. With diabolical cunning, he has won the farm, the land and all of the Earnshaw money at cards from the drunken and dissolute Hindley who dies penniless about six months after his sister. Hindley's son, Hareton, is left entirely dependent on Heathcliff, who degrades him to ploughboy level. Hareton, however, has a naturally fearless nature, he never thinks of "writhing like a worm." Heathcliff therefore has no incentive to torture him, so, beyond denying him education and culture, allowing him to swear unchecked and taking his heritage from him, Heathcliff treats Hareton better than anyone else in the book! He fully realizes his intrinsic value, he tells Nelly that he is deliberately revenging himself on Hareton for his own degradation by Hindley—that he has got him lower still for "he takes a pride in his brutishness" and scorns "everything extra-animal as silly and weak." But, he admits, Hareton "is gold put to the use of paving stones" and boasts to Nelly that should his father "rise from the grave to abuse me for his offspring's wrongs, I should have the fun of seeing the said offspring fight him back again," because he is "damnably fond of me." Like Cathy, Hareton develops exactly

[17] The film versions even omit the latter half altogether.

those qualities needed for durability. He is brought up in an entirely masculine environment by Heathcliff and old Joseph, just as Cathy was surrounded by feminine qualities, for even her father was always a very feminine man.

Things remain like this for twelve or thirteen years. Then there is a brief contact between the two houses when Cathy breaks bounds while her father is at Isabella's death bed. Edgar brings Isabella's son, Linton, back with him but he is claimed immediately by his father, and Cathy is kept in ignorance of the fact that he went only as far as Wuthering Heights. So things settle down peacefully again, with no communication between the two houses, for about four more years.

In contrast to the "gold" in Hareton, Heathcliff tells Nelly that his son is "tin polished to ape silver." He would quickly have perished in the rough comfortless house, had Heathcliff not had an interest in keeping him alive to inherit the Grange. In order to secure the Linton fortune as well, he decides to marry the cousins to each other as soon as they are sixteen. We need not go into the unscrupulous, not to say demonic, manner in which he furthers this plot, although one must admit that Cathy herself plays into his hands at every turn. She takes a very long time to recognize how worthless Linton Heathcliff is and she rejects Hareton on account of his illiteracy and his boorish appearance. She pours all the romantic ideas she has imbibed from her reading into her relationship with the peevish, sickly Linton, deceives Nelly Dean and even her beloved father, and rides over the moors to the Heights almost every evening after Nelly and her father are in bed while Nelly is ill for the only time in her life.

By this time Edgar Linton is a dying man, and when he discovers this escapade of his daughter he is sorely puzzled over what to do about it, for the Grange is entailed through Isabella on Linton. Yet he is rightly afraid that Linton is merely the tool of his hated father. He finally consents to allow Cathy to meet Linton once a week on the moors, half way between the houses, in the presence of Nelly Dean. By this time Cathy is so worried about her ill father that she becomes lukewarm towards her meetings with Linton. Nelly's secret bond with Heathcliff is never more clear than on the fatal day when the latter decides to wait no longer, for, should Linton die before his uncle, all of his plans to gain the Grange will come to nothing.

On the day in question, Cathy does not want to leave her father, but Nelly insists. When they meet on the moor, she allows Heathcliff to trick them into the house, although Edgar Linton has definitely forbidden Cathy to enter it again. They are immediately imprisoned there—as Nelly could have well forseen—and again she fails to call out when Edgar sends three men from the Grange to find out where they are. The next morning Cathy and Linton are obliged to marry, but Heathcliff keeps both Cathy and Nelly imprisoned for five nights and four days before allowing Nelly to go back to the Grange. He retains Cathy, however, out of sheer desire to torture and to keep her from her father's death bed. At last however she induces her wretched husband to let her out and arrives just in time to see her father still alive. Nelly Dean says:

> He died blissfully, Mr. Lockwood: he died so. Kissing her cheek, he murmured, "I am going to her; and you, darling child, shall come to us!" and never stirred or spoke again; but continued that rapt, radiant gaze, till his pulse imperceptibly stopped and his soul departed. None could have noticed the exact minute of his death, it was so entirely without a struggle.[18]

That Nelly again plays Heathcliff's game does not directly aid the process of individuation this time, as no quaternity is immediately established. Indirectly, however, it leads to

[18] *Wuthering Heights*, p. 334.

the same result, for it enables Heathcliff to continue his "moral teething" until the childishness and selfishness are ground out of Cathy through sheer suffering. The elder Catherine's influence has by no means ceased with death; we not only hear later that she has haunted Heathcliff unceasingly (as indeed he prayed she should after her death: "Take any form—drive me mad! only *do* not leave me in this abyss where I cannot find you!") but also that Edgar Linton's passionate longing to refind her has certainly contributed to his early death, making him forget to do what he could at the end to insure some independance for Cathy. His ecstasy at rejoining his wife causes him to leave his daughter entirely dependent on Heathcliff.

There has been a real separation between the divine feminine and the human feminine elements, as is indeed a necessity in any process of individuation, a point we shall consider further in the final chapter. In our story, the elder Catherine has taken her anima, goddess qualities into the Beyond, where they still have a compelling effect on the two men whose anima she had been. Cathy is left on earth with her beauty and her human qualities, but with no trace of the superhuman attraction that emanated from her mother on every page.

Cathy is now confronted with the loss of everything she cares for, her home, her books, her beloved father. Heathcliff even deprives her of the care of Nelly Dean. She is allowed to remain at the Grange until after her father's funeral, but that same evening Heathcliff comes to fetch her. From then on she is his prisoner at Wuthering Heights. But even he has to admit that she is "no weakling," and although she has no power to avoid submitting, she answers his ultimatum that she return to her husband at Wuthering Heights by saying:

"I shall. . . . Linton is all I have to love in the world, and though you have done what you could to make him hateful to me, and me to him, you *cannot* make us hate each other. And I defy you to hurt him when I am by, and I defy you to frighten me!"

And later:

"I know he has a bad nature . . . he's your son. But I'm glad I've a better, to forgive it; and I know he loves me, and for that reason I love him. Mr. Heathcliff *you* have *nobody* to love you; and however miserable you make us, we shall still have the revenge of thinking that your cruelty arises from your greater misery. You *are* miserable, are you not? Lonely, like the devil, and envious like him? *Nobody* loves you—*nobody* will cry for you when you die! I wouldn't be you!" [19]

Catherine speaks with a kind of dreary triumph; she seems to have made up her mind to enter into the spirit of her future family, and draw pleasure from the griefs of her enemies.

Cathy very intelligently decides to assume some of the negative spirit of her tormentor, instead of merely retiring into her own undoubted virtues. This is exceedingly sound psychologically for one can overcome nothing with a one-sided attitude, but only by discovering the same qualities in oneself, where one can do something about it. By "entering into the spirit of her future family" she places herself in the strongest position she can in her well-nigh intolerable situation.

Heathcliff continues to torment her with his "moral teething." When she gets to Wuthering Heights she finds Linton mortally ill and asks his father to send for a doctor. Heathcliff replies that "his life is not worth a farthing, and I won't spend a farthing on it. . . . Walk out of the room . . . and let me never hear a word more about him! None here care what

[19] *Ibid.*, p. 338.

becomes of him; if you do, act the nurse; if you do not, lock him up and leave him." And he actually leaves the girl of seventeen, the spoiled darling of the Grange, completely alone to struggle with death. Only when she sends word to him that she is sure his son is dying does Heathcliff enter the chamber to find Linton already dead. Then again Heathcliff, inhuman devil that he is, reveals that he is acting, or is obliged to act, with a purpose, for he asks Cathy twice: "How do you feel?" She replies: "He's safe, and I'm free. . . . I should feel well—but," she continues with a bitterness she cannot conceal, "you have left me so long to struggle against death alone, that I feel and see only death! I feel like death!"

Heathcliff finally seems to feel that it is enough. For once he does not go on grinding but allows her to stay in bed and alone for a fortnight. He visits her only once during that time, to show her Linton's will, leaving everything to his father. (Emily's complete lack of knowledge of worldly affairs shows clearly here, for of course no minor can make a valid will. She realized this was the case regarding land but not that it also applied to money and "moveable property." However, the point is unimportant, for Nelly is herself doubtful of Heathcliff's legal standing in the matter. She does not see how his possession can be disturbed, as Cathy is "destitute of cash and friends.")

What the girl suffers during that fortnight can hardly be exaggerated. She has really loved her father from the bottom of her heart, in spite of her frequent deceptions, even her disobedience in the matter of seeing Linton. She must have added to her grief for him a fear that she had herself harmed him by her obstinacy in the matter and the galling knowledge of how entirely wrong she had been. Then—though it was difficult to love such a "nought" as Linton, once his character was recognized—the really tender-hearted girl must have suffered agonies watching his struggle with death, unable to relieve his sufferings in any way. The housekeeper had refused any help, and she believed the same was true of Hareton, although much later she learns that not only had Hareton begged Heathcliff to let him relieve her with Linton at night but had also made Heathcliff angry a hundred times by taking her part. But at the time she regarded them both as enemies and explained to them that, though she was eventually driven downstairs by the cold, it was not from any wish for their society. She thus drives herself into complete solitude. The dark time then sets in which is still reigning when Mr. Lockwood pays his visit some months later. The latter is very much attracted by Cathy's beauty and by all that Nelly Dean has told him about her during his long illness. It would be easy for Cathy to escape from her unendurable life by marrying him, as her mother had done before in accepting another rich man. But Cathy's reaction to her troubles is infinitely more human than was her mother's, indicating much more heart and a greater acceptance of reality. She does not love Mr. Lockwood and makes no attempt whatever to further his evident admiration of her. She even almost incredulously asks him: "Does Ellen like you?" (Cathy usually called Nelly Dean, Ellen.)

This part of the novel indeed is almost entirely preoccupied with Cathy's attitude to her tormentor, Heathcliff, while Mr. Lockwood, the stranger from the South of England, makes no real impression on the principal characters. Catherine does slowly achieve an attitude that brings about the right solution: an acceptance of her suffering, combined with an absolute refusal to writhe like a worm. It is very evident, of course, that we are dealing here with a projected image of the process of individuation, not with the same process in a conscious individual. Every necessary ingredient is present and clearly visible, but in reality it would take much longer, even more pain, to arrive at the same place. Furthermore, Cathy is much younger than most women are when faced with the same problems consciously and is therefore permitted a certain license that a conscious individual would probably find herself denied.

Nevertheless, as far as is possible in a projected process, Cathy achieves the right attitude to Heathcliff. We learn later that this produces an effect in the unconscious itself. Her mother, the elder Catherine, never absent from Heathcliff's thoughts, begins to engross his attention more and more and thus to divert him from torturing Cathy. This is also usually the case in an individuation process that is being realized consciously. The ego alone is very limited in what it can achieve, but when it finds the right attitude and the limits of its endurance, help always comes from the far more powerful figures of the unconscious.

It is at this point that Heathcliff begins to relent in his mistreatment of Cathy, not indeed from any magnanimous motive but because her lack of writhing robs him of the *wish* to destroy. The first sign comes a fortnight after Mr. Lockwood leaves for a long visit to London, when Heathcliff sends for Nelly Dean to come live once again at Wuthering Heights, telling her that he is tired of seeing Cathy and that Nelly must keep her in the little parlor out of his sight, except at meals. This is, of course, a great improvement for Cathy, for Heathcliff never enters the little parlor. Nelly can therefore "smuggle over a great number of books and other articles that had formed her amusement at the Grange," whereas formerly Heathcliff had burned any book of hers he saw.

At first she is contented, but there is a serious mistake she must still realize and repair. Although on the occasion when she broke bounds and visited Wuthering Heights when she was about twelve, she had liked Hareton at first, she was furiously resentful when she learned he was her cousin. At that time she only wanted cultivated "gentlemen" cousins, like the worthless Linton, and burst into tears at the idea of being related to the uneducated, rough Hareton. When, four years later, she again went to Wuthering Heights, she never let an opportunity slip of mocking Hareton with her worthless "gentleman" cousin. When Hareton, from the beginning full of admiration for Cathy, made a tremendous effort to learn to read to please her, she only mocked the more at his pronunciation; in fact nothing he could do pleased her and she treated him abominably.

Now Hareton is pure gold, and though when she first goes to live at Wuthering Heights Cathy treats him even worse, for a long time he still remains loyal to his feeling for her and is helpful as far as he can be. But at last her taunts succeed in arousing his pride and resentment. Then he avoids her and gives up his attempts not to swear in her presence. Her scorn even rouses him to burn the books he has begun to love. But just after Nelly returns to the Heights, Cathy begins to realize her mistake and to seek for ways to reconcile Hareton. She does not find it easy, for Hareton has had enough of her "mucky pride" and "damned mocking tricks," and "if it made him a king" he will no longer be "scorned for seeking her good will." At last she convinces him that she is sorry for the past and wants now to be friends and to help him with his efforts to educate himself.

When Heathcliff realizes that the former enemies are now sworn allies, he informs Hareton that if he listens to Cathy he will be sent to seek his bread where he can get it, and tells her: "Your love will make him an outcast and a beggar." Cathy, on her side, tries to enlighten Hareton regarding Heathcliff's devilish behavior. He replies that he wouldn't "suffer a word to be uttered in his disparagement: if he were the devil it didn't signify; he would stand by him and he'd rather she would abuse himself, as she used to do, than begin on Mr. Heathcliff." He finds "means to make her hold her tongue, by asking how she would like *him* to speak ill of her father?" When Cathy realizes that Hareton is attached to Heathcliff "by ties stronger than reason could break—chains forged by habit that it would be cruel to attempt to loosen," she gives up. Nelly Dean says, "I don't believe she has ever breathed a syllable" in Hareton's hearing "against her oppressor since."

This is the ultimate sacrifice for Cathy, and means that

she has cast out a strong power motive from her love for Hareton, for to leave him free to love Heathcliff is the most difficult thing she can do. She thus also makes her own supreme submission, for in freeing Hareton she accepts Heathcliff herself. From now on, we hear no word of Heathcliff trying to divide the two: he even accepts their love for each other.

Heathcliff finally begins to explain his conduct to Nelly Dean. After watching the two together—both have inherited the eyes of the elder Catherine, but with Hareton the resemblance to her is "singular at all times, *then* it was particularly striking"—he tells Nelly that now that he is able to revenge himself on his old enemies in the persons of their descendants, he has lost the desire to do so. "I don't care for striking: I can't take the trouble to raise my hand. . . . I have lost the faculty of enjoying their destruction, and I am too idle to destroy for nothing. Nelly, there is a strange change approaching; I'm in its shadow at present. I take so little interest in my daily life that I hardly remember to eat and drink." Then he explains that just now Hareton seems "a personification of my youth, not a human being." His startling likeness to Catherine is the least potent factor, for Heathcliff sees her everywhere, the "entire world is a dreadful collection of memoranda that she did exist, and that I have lost her. Well, Hareton's aspect was the ghost of my immortal love; of my wild endeavours to hold my right; my degradation, my pride, my happiness, and my anguish."

Nelly asks him what he means by "change." He replies: "I shall not know till it comes, I'm only half conscious of it now. . . . I have neither fear, nor a presentiment, nor a hope of death . . . yet I cannot continue in this condition! I have to remind myself to breathe—almost to remind my heart to beat! . . . I have a single wish and my whole being and faculties are yearning to attain it." The single wish is, of course, to refind Catherine. On Catherine's side, she had expressed, when she was dying, the utmost surprise that

Heathcliff should wish to survive her: "I wonder he won't be near me. . . . I thought he wished it." As a ghost she seems never to have changed her attitude: "I only wish never to be parted." From beyond the grave, she draws him increasingly and unrelentingly towards her and, now that his work on earth is done, he is free to rejoin her. From his own point of view, he has stayed to revenge himself on his enemies and to possess himself of everything that they had. But from the point of view of the totality, he has stayed to complete the "moral teething," to drive out the childishness and superfluous trivialities from the last representatives of the Earnshaws and the Lintons. Actually the "change," which Heathcliff foresaw but could not identify, turns out to be death, for, as Catherine appears more and more clearly before his eyes, he becomes incapable of eating and at last evidently his attention is *only* on her. He must have forgotten to remind himself to breathe or his heart to beat, for Nelly Dean finds him dead one morning on the bed he had shared with Catherine in their early childhood.

Heathcliff never made a will for he could not decide how to leave his property and wished he could "annihilate it from the face of the earth." Therefore it returns to its rightful owners, Hareton and Cathy, who are to be married on New Year's Day, thus finally uniting Thrushcross Grange and Wuthering Heights and the two ancient families of Linton and Earnshaw.

In "The Psychology of Transference" Jung compares the process of individuation with an old alchemistic text and describes how the process can proceed in a modern analysis. (Only a small percentage of those who try analysis go on, or have the vocation to go on, to become conscious of this process.) The alchemist usually had a *soror mystica*, a woman who helped him with his work, and together they realized the two main figures of the unconscious whom they found symbolized as King and Queen, or sun and moon. In a deep analysis, Jung points out, the vital point is also to distinguish the human pair, analyst and analysant, from their inner counterparts, the anima and animus, who are also a divine or royal pair. He adds that one cannot overrate the importance of these inner figures; but they must never be used to escape a difficulty or problem between the human pair whose relationship is also indispensable to the process.

It is this vital phase in the process of individuation that comes out most clearly in its projection onto the end of Emily's great novel. The first pair, Heathcliff and Catherine, was a bewildering mixture of the outer and inner, of the human and divine. As children they were still very human, but as they grew up, Catherine became more and more identical with the archetypal anima and Heathcliff even identified with the Devil himself. They both at bottom despised the more human but rather weak pair, Edgar and Isabella Linton, although they each married one of the despised couple. Indeed they had to do so, from the point of view of the totality, or all of the human qualities would have been lost. But when Catherine died, she took her immortal, archetypal qualities into the Beyond, into the unconscious, where they were, however, not buried and lost but continued to work on the living, particularly on Edgar and Heathcliff, who never forgot her for a moment.

When Catherine died the unknown center had evidently not finished with Heathcliff on earth, and he was thus separated from her for about twenty years. In that time, although what personal life he had was lived for his revenge, he nevertheless was used as the principle of individuation itself, a fact he even dimly realized himself when he said that he tortured as a kind of "moral teething." The human pair in the last quaternity compensate in the most amazing way for the faults of their predecessors and remain entirely human. There is no trace of any identification with the archetypal in either. Hareton remained himself. No degradation touched his basic good nature, and he took the action that is necessary for a man in the way he continually made Heathcliff furious by taking Cathy's part and by the great efforts he had to make to overcome his ignorance and lack of any culture. Cathy, as we have seen, overcame in a wholly feminine manner by accepting her suffering. The human pair, therefore, after much tribulation and effort, symbolically reached an attitude that promised an enduring relationship and a meaningful life on earth.

The archetypal pair were also united in their "immortal love," and, like Catherine while she was by herself in the Beyond, they did not disappear into the unconscious, they still appeared on earth. Joseph asserted that he had seen them together looking out of the window every rainy day since Heathcliff's death at Wuthering Heights, and Nelly, though it went sadly against her beliefs, admitted to Mr. Lockwood that a little boy with a "sheep and two lambs," whom she met on the moors, refused to pass along a path, about which the boy had sobbed out: "There's Heathcliff and a woman yonder, under t'nab un' I darnut pass 'em."

We can see here how indispensable the conscious individual is to the process of individuation. In this projected form, although the separation between human and immortal is perfectly carried out and the human pair have undergone all the essential preparation, there is still no abiding connection between the two pairs. Heathcliff and Catherine are only seen, as far as we know, by minor characters. There is nothing to indicate that Hareton and Cathy were aware of the presence of their immortal counterparts. Hareton had indeed mourned Heathcliff with the utmost sincerity; Nelly Dean says:

> Poor Hareton, the most wronged, was the only one who really suffered much. He sat by the corpse all night, weeping in bitter earnest. He pressed its hand, and kissed the sarcastic, savage face that every one else shrank from con-

> templating; and bemoaned him with that strong grief which springs naturally from a generous heart, though it be tough as tempered steel.[20]

And Mr. Lockwood declared that neither he nor Cathy would fear any ghost: "Together, they would brave Satan and all his legions." But what is lacking, and must indeed be missing from all *projected* forms, is the conscious individual who will connect and reconcile the two parts, human and immortal, of the whole psyche. In the final chapter we will consider how this can actually be done.

We hear no more from the Beyond of either Edgar or Isabella. Edgar's part in the final resolution of the story seems to lie in his fatherhood of Cathy. In that indeed he lived on, for many of the qualities that enabled her to endure where her mother had failed were inherited from him. Moreover he was an excellent father to her, and her good and cultivated mind owed its foundation to him. Isabella's descendant was much more transitory. The peevish, sickly Linton played indeed an important part in Cathy's life for, without her marriage to him, she would never have fallen into Heathcliff's hands to receive her "moral teething." But Linton had no sooner played this role than he too vanished without a trace into the Beyond. Only the members of the last quaternity were made of strong enough material to survive; the others were, so to speak, absorbed by the four. Cathy had a good many of the qualities of her aunt Isabella, and the personal Edgar disappeared into Catherine in his ecstatic death, forgetting everything earthly in the hope of rejoining her, but presumably without enough dynamism to exist separately beside her, as Heathcliff undoubtedly did.

The establishment of a quaternity which, from having undergone the *separatio* between the human and immortal parts of the psyche, has a very good chance of survival,

[20] *Wuthering Heights,* p. 398.

naturally also entails a considerable reconciliation between the opposites. The opposites of good and evil indeed are not torn far apart as they are in *Precious Bane* or in Charlotte's or Anne's novels. Emily seems to have been singularly little moved by traditional Christian morality, with its deep abyss between good and evil, but to have been much more impressed by their relativity. Heathcliff was indeed "a fierce, pitiless, wolfish man" and very frequently identical with a demon or with Satan himself. He has shocked many people, including Charlotte who said in her preface to the 1850 edition: "Whether it is right or advisable to create beings like Heathcliff, I do not know: I scarcely think it is." But Emily had no such scruples, she was no more afraid to depict Heathcliff's full darkness than Rembrandt was afraid to paint his chiaroscuro. And, it is very clear, the positive end of the book could never have been realized had Heathcliff been one iota less dark and infernal.

Emily's opposites are indeed separated at the beginning of the book, where there is no communication between the two houses and families, no knowledge whatever of each other. At the end the two are reconciled, even married to each other, and the two estates have become one. Emily, however, treated the opposites very differently than Mary Webb and her own sisters. One may almost say she did not treat them, they were no problem to her, she let this part of her story flow to her from the unconscious. Good and evil are after all human abstractions, they naturally pervade the book as light and dark pervade Rembrandt's canvases, but each finds the place it belongs, where it ultimately helps the other opposite instead of losing all of its energy in ceaseless struggle.

When it comes to venturing a hypothesis regarding where Emily was on her way back to Eden when she died, we find ourselves in a situation totally different from that of any of our foregoing examples. To start with she was a genius, so that her first responsibility was to that genius. This responsibility she took on her shoulders as few have done, she lived for it and gave it full expression. She did more. She worked unceasingly to receive its inspiration in the best possible soil, facing even exile in Brussels to increase her range. In this sense, as we can clearly see in *Wuthering Heights*, by performing "the arduous duties every year, of a mysterious nature," she not only averted the doom foretold in Charlotte's vision but in her great novel provided a lasting place *on earth* for an image of the process of individuation.

This novel could never have been written had Emily not reached the fourth gate, at least in her writing, and come to terms with the old serpent that guards it. As far as her work is concerned, we can say that she circumambulated the walls of paradise very closely and died with a clear view of the re-entry to paradise and the lost wholeness of man before her. But this re-entrance evidently took place in death, as her early return to the Beyond bears witness.

Emily certainly belonged to those creative people who are unable to tear themselves away from Eden. She was thrown out, in common human fate, when she was sent to Roe Head at the age of seventeen, but she at once sickened and had to return to Haworth, where for the rest of her life, with the two already mentioned exceptions, she could camp very close to the walls of Eden. At first she probably looked longingly outwards, towards the world, for we hear from a poem[21] that "Wealth and Power . . . Glory's wreath and Pleasure's flower" had once seemed "Beings divine." Apparently they soon lost their fascination, either because she was forced to recognize that it was not her way to reach them during her life, or because she found the very idea of them a disappointment and disillusionment. At all events she certainly turned her gaze inwards, towards Eden, while she was still very young. The above quoted poem is dated

[21] See above, p. 198.

1844, when she was twenty-six, but it sounds as if she had long turned her back on the world. *Wuthering Heights* and some of her poems bear eloquent witness to her single-minded concentration on the inner world where the most basic pattern, which lies at the bottom of every human life, revealed itself to her.

As mentioned before, Emily Brontë made too few roots in outer life to have the strength, even if she had had the knowledge which was not then available, to take back her projected process of individuation into herself. Jung thought that it could be done without analysis if there was a sufficiently strong relationship to a partner of the other sex. Emily had no such relationship, as far as we know, no outer Hareton, as her own Cathy had, which gave the latter the roots to overcome her bitter suffering and even, at the very last, to accept the demonic Heathcliff.

We can only be intensely grateful to Emily Brontë for her complete surrender to the creative spirit and for thus giving us a unique formulation and representation of the process of individuation. If I have sometimes pointed out how it would be possible for the creator of *Wuthering Heights* to view the novel as an image of her own psyche and thus, very slowly, with our present opportunities and infinite labor, to withdraw the projection, I did so only in the service of our own *search for wholeness*. I am aware that many admirers of *Wuthering Heights* will feel this to be a sacrilege, and I can understand this point of view. But the book is not only a literary masterpiece. It can also help us, as no other woman's book that I know, to see our lost wholeness. The whole individual, as Jung often said, is the only hope of our culture surviving these catastrophic days. Charlotte's vision of the "one mighty globe, which will roll in solitary grandeur through the vast wilderness of space" if "certain arduous duties" are not performed, has an ominously prophetic sound as an only too probable result of atomic war on a large scale. Nevil Shute depicted such a development in his novel and film *On The Beach*. If enough individuals undertake these "arduous duties," we may yet avert the doom foretold in Charlotte's vision. With this aim in view, and in no sense as a criticism of Emily, I undertook to speak of *Wuthering Heights* in these terms.

# 11 THE PRESENT OPPORTUNITIES

NOT ONLY IN *Wuthering Heights* but in all of the examples that we have considered, the reader may have felt that I have allowed myself too critical an attitude. I have emphasized that we have only seen the process of individuation in a *projected* form and have frequently pointed out that this or that pattern was not realized or the appropriate conclusion drawn. This was not done in order to criticize the authors involved; on the contrary, I regard them all as pioneers in that most difficult country round the fourth gate of Eden and feel a great debt of gratitude towards them. But the discoveries of C. G. Jung have given us both a new *point de départ*, regarding the process of individuation, which he brought back, as it were, out of projection, and a standpoint from which we *can experience it directly*.

As projection is one of the most misunderstood of Jungian terms, I should like to repeat that we do not *make* projections but discover elements in the outer world that are afterwards recognized as belonging to the inner psyche. One almost has the feeling that these elements themselves felt unseen and ignored as subjective contents and projected themselves into the outer world in order to be seen at all!

Be that as it may, in the foregoing examples we have dealt with people who came under the influence of the process of individuation but who had only the deep urge of every living creature towards its own wholeness to guide them back to Eden. Not that this deep instinct is an unreliable guide. Far from it. But in our rational days (which may be said to have been inaugurated by the crowning of the Goddess of Reason in Notre Dame during the French Revolution) this instinct is so deeply buried beneath our one-sided conscious outlook that it could only be followed blindly and unconsciously.

Of our examples Stevenson came the nearest to realizing that his deep preoccupation with the duality of man was primarily his individual concern. This may have been to some extent a matter of the time. The archetype of individuation, though present from the beginning, seems for several centuries to have been once more gradually approaching the level of consciousness till it was recognized and brought up into consciousness by C. G. Jung, and Jung was grown-up when Stevenson died. Like every other archetype, it is far beyond our comprehension, but Jung has given us a working hypothesis with which it is possible to recognize the fourfold structure of the central core of our psyche. This enables us to take back many projections and to see the process, which we have already seen projected into several of the books we have considered, as *primarily our own concern.* We cannot tell what further realizations may be made by coming generations. Jung himself once said to me that he thought coming generations—perhaps several hundreds, even thousands of years in the future, for these elements only rise to consciousness very slowly—would discover his books and those of his followers and think what a queer lot of old people they must have been; they were on the right track, but how little they discovered compared to what became known later; why couldn't they have carried on and seen this or that self-evident fact?

Whenever we try to work with these basic but incomprehensible elements, we should maintain a historical perspective and view anything we are fortunate enough to discover as a truth of today that at any time may be corrected or amplified by a truth of tomorrow. Jung learned this historical perspective through his studies of the Gnostics and of alchemy through the ages, in both East and West, to mention only two of his numerous fields of research. The basic foundation is always and everywhere the same, an eternal truth, traces of which can be found in every sincere attempt to unite man's developing consciousness with its eternal basic roots. The eternal root itself does not change, but developing consciousness does. Therefore attempts to unite the two naturally go out of date, so to speak, and earlier attempts can seem decidedly queer and archaic, simply because the state of *consciousness* has changed. Anyone who takes the trouble to read the old alchemists, for instance, can see this at once for himself, and particularly clearly, for in no field has consciousness developed and changed so rapidly as in chemistry and physics. Naturally there were a lot of alchemists who were literally trying to make ordinary gold, for like the materialists of today, they were not at all concerned with the eternal basic roots of man but were absorbed by a hope of material gain from the work in their retorts. But there were also many infinitely more serious-minded alchemists who constantly declared: "*Aurum nostrum non est aurum vulgi*" ("Our gold is *not* the ordinary gold"). They were deeply concerned with the process of individuation which they projected into their retorts. Even a few particularly gifted old alchemists saw that this process primarily concerned themselves. For example, a very early alchemist, Morienus (7th-8th century A. D.), says of the philosopher's stone: "This thing is extracted from thee, for thou art its ore; in thee they find it, and, to speak more plainly, from thee they take it; and when thou hast experienced this, the love and desire for it will be increased in thee." [1] And Rosinus: "This stone is some thing which is fixed more in thee [than elsewhere] created of God, and thou art its ore, and it is extracted from thee, and wheresoever thou art it remains inseparably with thee . . . to express it otherwise, fixed in thee: namely in the Mercurius of the

[1] Quoted from Jung, *Aion*, par. 256.

wise."[2] (Expressed psychologically, in the Self, not the ego.) Morienus continues: "Thou art its *prima materia*, and thou guardest it in secret and out of thee will it be extracted, since it will be redeemed and reduced to its essence by thee. While without thee it cannot be completed, and without it thou canst not live."[3] We could not ask for a clearer description of how the process of individuation works in us. Morienus refers also to its fourfold structure when he says: "And as man is made up of four elements, so also is the stone."[4]

Another alchemist who emphasized the crucial importance of self-knowledge was Gerhard Dorn (16th century), a pupil of Paracelsus. He exclaims, for instance: "Transmute yourselves from dead stones into living philosophical stones." This statement clearly indicates, as Jung points out in *Aion*, that "he recognized the identity of the stone with the transformed man."[5] The reader who is interested will find many additional examples in *Aion*.

There is a strong modern prejudice against any analytical work on oneself. It is regarded as auto-erotic, egotistical, overvaluing one's own importance, and what not. This is due to a misunderstanding concerning what "work on oneself" really is. Were it concerned with the often already overvalued ego, the criticism would be justified, for it would indeed be introspective nonsense and taking oneself too seriously. What I mean by "work on oneself" is work on the *unknown part of the psyche*. As Anne Brontë recognized intuitively, over a hundred years ago:

*How little know we what we are,*
*How less what we may be.*

[2] *Ibid.*, par. 258.
[3] Quoted from von Franz, "The Idea of the Macro- and Microcosmos in the Light of Jungian Psychology," p. 28.
[4] *Aion*, par. 258.
[5] *Ibid.*, par. 264.

Anne probably had no idea what a world-shaking idea she had glimpsed for a moment here, for this is a truth that, were it generally known and the consequences drawn, could alone stop the catastrophic trend of world events. In 1937, just after Hitler had marched into Austria, a woman had the following dream: "*I saw a superior sort of woman approach Hitler, half angry, half pleading, and say to him: 'I told you not to touch Austria, and now you will have to take the consequences.' I was not quite sure what the consequences were, I only heard something about sleepless nights. But the woman said to Hitler: 'If you touch Czechoslovakia it will be worse, and if Poland, then it will be the end'.*" This dream was dreamed before anyone could have known the order in which the two latter countries would be attacked, and I quote it as an illustration of how different the course of history might have been had Hitler been a man who realized the value of self-knowledge which is primarily to be gained by attending to dreams. The superior woman is obviously an aspect of his anima which had, at least according to this dream, a genuine wish to prevent Hitler from carrying out his wholesale destruction and thus also from completely destroying himself. The opposite of the conscious point of view is *always* present in the unconscious; this is Stevenson's "dual nature of man."

We may say then that the first step in working on oneself is to look for the *opposite of one's conscious point of view in the unconscious*. The unconscious supplies the missing ingredients, either in the form of dreams or surprising waking thoughts or sometimes as outer events. Analysis with an analyst who has gone through the process himself can be very helpful, but it is not absolutely indispensable *if* there is a deep enough relationship with another person who can sympathize with such efforts. It is dangerous, however, to undertake the process entirely alone, particularly in an unrelated state, for a journey into the unconscious almost always leads to such cold, unknown archetypal depths that the warmth of human companionship is a *conditio sine qua non* in order not to be swept away. It was not chance but sound instinct that led the Brontës as children to face the unconscious *together*, as four at first, later in couples. When Branwell fell out, Charlotte rejoined her sisters in their evening reading and discussion of what they had written during the day. This was very wise indeed, for they might easily have lost themselves had they faced the unconscious *alone*.

Encountering the opposite of one's conscious ego usually begins with the personal shadow. We have seen the ego-shadow pair projected into most of our examples. I hope it is clear how much wider and more comprehensive the figure which represented the ego would have become had it been able to assimilate the qualities personified in the figure that represented the personal shadow—more comprehensive, but in many cases also much more unpleasant. Unfortunately it is no longer possible to cherish the illusion that the human being can be *only* pleasant. To take one example: Archie Weir was determined to be only the introverted, gentlemanly laird and thus left his anima, the younger Kirstie, unprotected against his very different, unscrupulous but also more natural shadow. In an enantiodromia from Archie's gentlemanly restraint and caution, his shadow aspect seduced her and left her to face her pregnancy alone. Yet it was this crime on the part of his shadow that at last produced enough courage and manliness in Archie to stand by Kirstie. However, as is so often true when the ego is *unconscious* of the acts of the shadow, the enantiodromia leads the ego too far, in this case to murder and subsequent imprisonment. This is the great danger of repressing the shadow. The more one tries to live only one's good qualities, the worse do their repressed opposites become. Sooner or later, moreover, they will break their bounds and the individual will either be completely smothered under an empty persona or an enantiodromia into the buried opposite will occur.

This can be dramatically demonstrated. There was once, for instance, a well-known philanthropist who after years of well-doing woke up one night and said to his wife, "I know what I really am, I am a scoundrel." The very next day he began a life of unbridled dissipation, and within a very short time he had gambled and otherwise squandered his large fortune. With all of the disadvantages of having to live in a world where such an enantiodromia has taken place on a world-wide scale, there is one tremendous advantage for the individual today: *he is able to work on the opposites in himself more consciously than ever before*. Instead of being condemned to a one-sided life, with the constant danger of enantiodromia, or of being forced to swing between the opposites, he can make up his mind to face the problem of the opposites *within himself*, which is obviously the only place where he can do anything about them. Once when Jung was asked during a discussion at the Psychological Club in Zurich if he thought that the atom bomb would be used on a large scale, he replied: "I think it depends on how many people can stand the tension of the opposites in themselves; if enough can, I think we may just crawl round the worst danger, but if not and atom warfare breaks out our civilization is doomed as so many have been on a smaller scale in the past."

We find this same idea very frequently in the East. When the German Sinologist, Richard Wilhelm, was living in China, he was once in a village which was suffering from such a persistent drought that everything was critically dangerous. The village authorities had tried everything of a practical and religious nature they could think of and at last declared, to Wilhelm's astonishment, that they must send for a rainmaker. He was so interested that he made a point of being present when the rainmaker arrived. A wizened little old man got out of a covered cart, sniffed the air in a disapproving way and then asked for a cottage on the edge of the village where he could be entirely alone. His food was to be put down outside the door and he was not to be disturbed till he appeared again.

His wishes were carried out. After three days the rain not only poured down, it even snowed, which was unknown at that time of year. Wilhelm, amazed and impressed, sought out the old man and asked wonderingly, "So you can really make rain?" "What nonsense," replied the old man, "how could I make rain?" "But," insisted Wilhelm, "you came, and it rained for the first time for many months?" "O, well," replied the man, "that was not rain-making, it was something quite different. I come from a province where everything is in order, the people are in Tao, it rains when it should and the crops are sown and reaped at the right season. But the people here are not in Tao, they are quite out of themselves. I felt that at once when I arrived. I was naturally infected by it and came out of myself as well. It took me three days solitude to find the Tao again. Then naturally it rained."

We find the same idea in the West, though it belongs to the wholeness of man and is therefore buried in the unconscious today. It seems very strange to us in these rational times. Yet such experiences are really the foundation of the widely separated, opposite fields of prayer and witchcraft. Insofar as prayer is *experience*, and not empty words, its effect depends on establishing contact with the creative, constructive forces we call God. St. Gertrude of Magdeburg, for instance, was said to be able to influence the weather by prayer, and similar phenomena were attributed to many western saints and wise men of the past. The witch aims in exactly the opposite direction. By coming *out* of himself, he tries to get in touch with destructive, disorderly powers, which we associate with the Devil.

That our state of mind can have a great influence on our surroundings is clear enough in daily life. If we "get out of bed on the wrong side," proverbially everything goes wrong: we are out of ourselves, rub everyone the wrong way, get into and cause trouble wherever we go. On other days everything seems to go of itself, we are welcome everywhere, and instead of spreading disharmony we spread a harmony which is welcome to everyone. But this will also inevitably follow the law of enantiodromia, and one opposite will continue to follow the other until at last we are able to see both opposites clearly, to stand the tension between them, and thus to reach our own individual equivalent of Tao, or "the middle way."

After this digression to offer some hints that the aim and purpose of gaining self-knowledge is by no means an egotistical affair but has a collective side as well and may even have a small contribution to make towards averting the worst dangers that threaten our world today, we must return to the first task of the work: to recognize and realize the personal shadow. This is often very painful, as when an Englishwoman, who was particularly fond of animals, dreamed that she was torturing some small kittens and was enjoying the pastime. After her first understandable rejection of the possibility that her genuine love of animals could also be expressed in such an opposite form, she began to remember certain thoughts that had flitted through her mind as a child: a longing to punish a favorite animal unreasonably, a sneaking feeling of pleasure when her dog was given a well-deserved beating, and so on. Such thoughts had been immediately buried and if possible forgotten, but the unconscious, which never forgets anything, reproduced them as her first exceedingly painful intimation that no love is secure that has not faced its own opposite.

Some years later this realization had to be faced again on a practical level. For a long while she had not been able to have a dog, but at last she was given one which had spontaneously fixed its affections on her while she was visiting friends. It imprinted itself, as Konrad Lorenz would have called it. It was love at first sight with both, and she decided to face the difficulties of fitting a dog into her present life. Apparently she succeeded and felt it as a great enrichment in every way. She was therefore horrified one day to catch herself thinking, "Now I could get rid of the little beast," when it was trotting before her on a high bridge over a ravine. Forgetting her early dream and the remembrance of her childhood thoughts (for these things seldom make an indelible impression until they are met in life itself) she immediately repressed her thought with horror and refused to draw the consequences. But somehow she could do nothing right for the dog. In spite of her most conscientious attempts, it no longer flourished. This went on until, some weeks later, she was crossing the same bridge and the same thought came to her. This time she drew the consequences and realized that, although she really loved the dog, it had disturbed her life in a way she deeply resented. She had to get up early to take it for a walk before work, rush back at lunch time, give up many things she had enjoyed, to walk the country-bred dog in the woods. Therefore, she said to herself, "There is no doubt that I love and enjoy this dog, but I also hate it and resent it having disturbed my life." This realization was exceedingly painful to her. At first she felt torn by these opposites and was in an unbearable tension over every silly little decision that had to be made between the dog's claims and her own. Then she noticed that the dog was flourishing again, had got back all of its earlier love of existence, and that although its new life was very inferior to the country paradise of its youth it was undoubtedly happier than ever before. The tension in her relaxed and they settled down to a thoroughly satisfactory ten years together, somehow fitting into each other's pattern with no further strain or difficulty.

This may seem a very trivial example, and of course it was only the first of a long series of experiences of the opposites for this woman. But she never forgot it and it often helped her in far more painful situations, for example, in a difficult but rewarding relationship with the man she afterwards loved. Nowhere are the opposites so painful to a woman as in the realm of relationship, and it is particularly difficult for a loving woman to admit: "Unless I realize that somewhere I also hate this man and resent my dependence on him, sooner or later I shall court the inexorable law of enantiodromia."

In the early experience with the dog, this woman was already in the position of Dr. Jekyll when he first saw Edward Hyde in the mirror, for she was forced to say, "This too is myself." This took place only in one corner of her psyche, however. Gradually she had to recognize that she was so indulgent in refusing to see herself that she had built up a one-sided personality. This had in its turn given rise to a personified autonomous shadow, or other woman in herself, embodying all the qualities she had refused to see in herself. The shadow figure did not consist only of negative qualities —like hating the dog and latent cruelty—there were also many positive traits that had been repressed because of the effort or responsibility they would have entailed.

This work is different in every case, but it always follows more or less the same general lines. It can take a very long time, stretching into many years, or in some cases it goes surprisingly quickly. The more thoroughly it is done the better chance there is of being able to face the more difficult further exploration of the psyche. The personal shadow is often very elusive and new aspects have a disconcerting habit of appearing even in a much later stage of the work. It is wiser, therefore, never to feel sure that one knows one's personal shadow completely and always to be ready to face further disagreeable, or more rarely agreeable, discoveries. Moreover, other figures often appear in dreams before the work on the personal shadow is completed. In this first stage of the work one keeps the spotlight as far as possible on the personal shadow, for a considerable knowledge of it is really a *conditio sine qua non* of further work on the unknown part of the psyche. The *personal* shadow is really a part of the knowledge of the ego and, until we know this, it will project itself and distort our view.

The personal shadow is composed of material that can all, at any rate theoretically, be assimilated by the ego. One of the great difficulties in this assimilation, however, is the fact that the personal shadow is frequently contaminated with the collective shadow. Very often when people begin to learn that they are not so harmless and well-meaning as they have always naively assumed, they go much too far in attributing negative qualities to themselves, even to the extent of identifying with the Devil himself. This can be very dangerous, for it leads to an inflation—"All good to God and all evil to man"—which would naturally, if one considers it logically, give a terrific sense of power into finite human hands. Man stands there as the opponent and equal of God! And the balance between the opposites is fatally disturbed.

Perhaps the most important part then of the work on the shadow is separating personal from collective qualities, or, as one might put it, accepting the limitations of the ego. One sees the difficulty very well in the elder Catherine in *Wuthering Heights*. She had no wish or tendency to identify with the light side and could easily have seen her shadow had it been archetypal in character, evil on a grand scale. But it was entirely beyond her to accept it on the petty everyday level represented by Isabella Linton. For example, when Nelly Dean warned her not to ram Heathcliff and her joy at his return down her husband's throat, she replied, "But does it not show great weakness? I'm not envious." Yet envy and jealousy are human qualities, we can only *know* them in ourselves, never entirely eradicate them. As *The Secret of the Golden Flower* says: "Indolence of which a man is conscious, and indolence of which he is unconscious, are a thousand miles apart." [6] It is unnecessary to add that this applies to all human weaknesses.

We saw that Stevenson had the same difficulty in *Jekyll and Hyde*. Hyde is equivalent to the Devil himself and no human could accept him as his personal shadow without be-

[6] Quoted by Jung in *Alchemical Studies*, par. 17.

coming insane. Stevenson must have dimly sensed this, for the shadow figure in *The Master of Ballantrae* is much more human, and Frank Innes in *Weir of Hermiston* is composed entirely of human qualities that belong in the personal realm and are capable of being integrated.

The shadow figure is always of the same sex as the ego, so that the tension between the opposites is primarily a moral conflict. This stage would necessarily end in a deadlock if the anima did not intervene, as we saw, for example, in the tragic end of *Jekyll and Hyde*. But as the personal shadow is more and more recognized, as the ego becomes more complete by slowly seeing and integrating its lost qualities, the anima or the animus invariably appears on the scene. Its effects have indeed been visible in the environment long before, but are usually invisible to the person involved. It is often as if anima or animus were hidden behind the unseen shadow, or as if the ego were too one-sided to attract it. But as this situation improves the anima or animus becomes increasingly visible. Moreover, the ego, for the first time, is now in a position to face it.

If Stevenson's Archie Weir, as we have seen, had known that many of the qualities he found so maddening in Frank Innes were really his own, it is clear that he would have been in a much stronger position to deal with the next figure in his psyche, his anima. But since all of his independence, all of his belief in his own attraction for women were projected onto Frank, he could only feel helpless before the "ambiguous face of woman as she is" and blindly allow fate to take control of his destiny. If we take these two as ego and shadow figures in Stevenson himself—he said of Archie that "he was the same kind of fool" as himself—we might perhaps venture to say that if Stevenson had also seen that Frank Innes too was himself, he *might* have been able to meet the terrific demand his new book put on him. For some unknown reason, he was forced to look at "the ambiguous face of woman as she is"—in Jungian language, to meet his anima. As Archie alone this was too much for him; he was struck down in the middle of his task by this "wilful convulsion of brute nature." Yet I suggest very tentatively that if he had been conscious as well of the qualities of Frank in himself, he might have had the *breadth* of character and knowledge necessary to complete his task.

In Emily Brontë's *Wuthering Heights,* on the contrary, we observe the successful integration of the representation of the personal shadow in the story. As noted above, it was the inability of the elder Catherine to recognize her personal shadow at all that led it, in the autonomous form of Isabella Linton, to defeat all of Catherine's wishes and even to bring about her death indirectly. There is no description in the story of a reconciliation between ego and shadow, but since *Wuthering Heights* is primarily a projection of the *whole* process of individuation this stage takes place in the unconscious, offstage as it were, and in the second half of the book a figure appears in which Catherine and Isabella are reconciled: the former's daughter and the latter's niece. The qualities of both appear very clearly in the younger Catherine and, largely because there is no autonomous and unrecognized shadow figure playing against her, she succeeds, where her mother failed, in completing the second stage: having it out with the animus.

The projected character of the process is indeed very clear in this transition. A more or less completely integrated personal shadow is achieved in real life only by hard, unremitting work, accompanied by a considerable amount of suffering, over a long period of time; whereas, in the second part of *Wuthering Heights,* such a figure simply appears. Emily Brontë certainly had no idea that her book had anything to do with her own psychology, so she could reproduce an image of the process of individuation quite naively. If my hypothesis is correct, the process itself was much nearer the surface of consciousness with Stevenson, and this prevented him from ever producing the clear image of individuation that the more unconscious Emily could represent with untroubled objectivity.

In *Jekyll and Hyde,* although the two main figures are almost archetypal in character, the problem is that of ego and shadow. In *Weir of Hermiston,* although the ego and shadow are unfortunately still unreconciled, the limelight is already on the problem of the anima, the first figure in the completely unknown realm of the psyche. Speaking once of self-knowledge in a lecture at the Eidgenössische Technische Hochschule in Zürich, Jung said:

> As to this self-knowledge, this real penetrating knowledge of our own being, do not make the mistake of thinking that it means seeing through the ego. To understand the ego is child's play, but to see through the Self is something totally different. The real difficulty lies in recognizing the unknown. No one need remain ignorant of the fact that he is striving for power, that he wants to become very rich, that he would be a tyrant if he had the chance, that he is pleasure-seeking, envious of other people, and so on. Everyone *can* know such things of him or herself, because they are mere ego knowledge. But Self knowledge is something completely different, it is learning to know of the things which are unknown.[7]

We get an idea here of what a terrific task lay before Stevenson, and we cannot possibly be surprised that it proved too much for him. This last scene, the last he ever wrote, describes a man meeting the unknown, the unconscious, represented by the figure of his anima. Such an encounter, as Stevenson describes it, is still a shattering experience which almost transcends human endurance and ability. Louis, however, was an early pioneer in a completely unknown country, with nothing to guide him except what must have been an unusually strong urge towards wholeness; while we, thanks

[7] E.T.H. Lectures, Vol. 5, p. 72, (p. 83, old edition).

to C. G. Jung, have a great deal more knowledge, even as it were a rough map of the country involved, to guide us now in our search and experience. But as every case is individually different, it still demands the utmost we can give.

This is equally true for women, but this first step, the recognizing of unknown inner figures, particularly the anima, within themselves, is undoubtedly more difficult for men.

I remember that when I first analyzed a man who was very anima possessed, I asked Jung's advice as to how to handle the case. He warned me very strongly against saying too much about the anima at first and told me to advance very slowly—much more cautiously than with women and the animus—and for the following reason: Since the earliest days man has always been responsible for the safety of his family and tribe. He was forced to stand outside the camp, even on the earliest embankments, to watch the surrounding country with an eagle eye for any movement that might betray the advance of an enemy. Woman, on the other hand, was comparatively protected within the camp, and while she was tending the household fire and watching the children, for instance, she had leisure to dream and to allow strange thoughts to come in to her mind in a way that makes her, from the hereditary point of view, much more able to face the unconscious and to welcome the inner unknown. From the same hereditary point of view, it is more difficult and can even be dangerous for man to turn his attention within, and most men have far more resistance to it, a fact which Jung advised me to treat with the greatest respect.

Usually the first indication of the anima manifesting herself in a man's psychology is a certain moodiness. He gets up in a bad mood perhaps, or feeling below par for no physical or outer cause, and is unable to reason this mood away. Or he is hyper-sensitive, easily offended, a molehill is made into a mountain, or he altogether behaves—if he could stop to analyze it—in a womanish way. But the great difficulty is that, although these moods are very visible to his environment, the man himself usually blames them on outside causes, with no idea that they are originating in himself. If he can take this, to him nonsensical, step, he will be able to see further that his anima is causing the trouble in order that he should at last see and recognize her existence. It is usually very easy to point out the manifestations of the anima to a man's wife (the husband is equally able to recognize his wife's animus) because they are part of everyday life for her, and she has generally puzzled over these irrational moods which often seem to be entirely foreign to his usual character. But it is very difficult for her to point them out to her husband; she comes up against all of the hereditary resistance of men to the very idea of an enemy (or friend) *within.*

When a man finally decides to risk this hypothesis, the objectivity he has accorded to the outside world is exceedingly valuable to him. Once he has seen that there is a *real* inside world, he is usually able to look at it in a more impersonal way than most women. Then his hereditary tendency to watch for any disturbance—a hindrance at the beginning—becomes an asset, for he will deal with *inside* facts in the same efficient way that he has dealt with *outside* facts for countless generations.

It is generally in dreams that a man begins to recognize his anima figure, which is normally the first figure he encounters when he turns to the fully unknown part of his psyche. In her right place, the anima is the bridge, as it were, between conscious and unconscious. She has an individual side which is different, even unique, in every human being, and yet she reaches deep down into the collective unconscious, even into the realm of the pre-Christian goddesses who have been terribly forgotten in the 2,000 years that we have worshipped an exclusively masculine God-image. When the anima is not recognized and realized, she can turn very negative and invade a man's conscious world most destructively; but she can also be very positive, particularly if she feels that she is being allowed her part in his life.

While not seen, she has the tendency to project herself into outer women and, as she is at bottom a goddess, she rarely stops short at one woman. A man's leading principle is *logos*, discrimination, which serves him well in his studies and work. But he is inclined to be very blind when it comes to relationship, *eros*, which is the feminine principle *par excellence*. So naturally the anima, as a kind of inferior woman in himself, is inclined to mix herself into his relationships until he is able to recognize her "fine Italian hand" and come to terms with her. We can observe the animus doing much the same with women, particularly in the realm of the mind.

There is an early paper of Jung's,[8] originally written when he was himself in the throes of his first encounter with the unconscious,[9] that describes such difficulties particularly clearly. He emphasizes that a man should on no account take these manifestations of his anima as "springing from his own weakness" but should try to investigate what it is that lives behind them. He will, if not too much blinded by understandable prejudice, thus slowly realize his own feminine side, and he will have the best chance of relating to this feminine side and of eventually coming to terms with it if he personifies the anima. His dreams will surely give him every chance to do this, for as a dream figure she almost always appears personified, either as some real woman of the dreamer's acquaintance or as an unknown woman who often fascinates the dreamer by her unusual quality.

I remember a man of 58 who was having great difficulty in realizing the anima as an inner figure at all. Yet in his case it was particularly important for him to do so, as she had projected herself onto a girl, and he could only have followed this fascination, which almost possessed him, by breaking up her life and his own. He was naturally unwilling

[8] "The Relation of the Ego to the Unconscious," in *Two Essays*, pars. 202-507.
[9] *Memories, Dreams, Reflections*, pp. 170ff.

to do this, and yet he was quite unable to overcome his feeling for her. Then he had the following dream:

*At a party of his relatives he met a woman whom he realized at once was the woman he had always been looking for but had never met in outer life. She was beautiful and very attractive physically, but there was more than that. He felt at once that she was the essence of relationship, completely self-contained and independent of him and yet fully related. Wherever she went, she held out her hand to him and evidently enjoyed his company. There was no touch of constraint; he felt completely free and natural with her. They went to a store downtown together and every moment was a joy.*

The dreamer experienced the anima figure in the dream as the most wholly satisfying woman he could possibly imagine. She was not only more beautiful than the girl he was in love with; he was even more struck by her complete understanding and her qualities as the ideal, related companion. He found a picture in a magazine which reminded him of her and for some weeks carried it about in his pocket. For the time being the actual girl lost all her importance. The fact that he met her among his relatives underlines the fact that she was an inner figure, belonging to him. He saw this theoretically, but as an extravert he kept hoping that the dream was a prophecy of an outer woman he was about to meet. There were unfortunately other reasons which made it especially difficult for this man to realize the reality of his inner figures,[10] but I mention the dream as a good example of how the unconscious introduces a man to his anima. One could quote countless other examples.

To return to Jung's paper, he strongly recommends this personification of the anima but admits freely that "to any one accustomed to proceed along purely intellectual and rationalistic lines, this may seem altogether too ridiculous."

[10] This case is reported in some detail in Hannah, "Regression oder Erneuerung im Alter."

Nevertheless "a modern European living in the contemporary world" has sooner or later to realize that he is still "the child of paleolithic man" in that unknown side of his nature which was known to our ancestors as the "land of spirits." If he is to explore this unknown realm, he will be obliged to "submit to living in a kind of pre-historic kindergarten until he has got the right idea of the powers and factors which rule that other world. Hence he is quite right to treat the anima as an autonomous personality and to address direct personal questions to her. I mean this as an actual technique." [11]

By putting "direct personal questions to her," Jung means holding conversations with her as if she were a woman of the man's acquaintance. It certainly requires "the greatest objectivity and absence of prejudice," as Jung points out, to play "such an apparently absurd game with oneself." This "absurd game" afterwards developed into the method of active imagination.[12] It is an admirable technique for having it out with and coming to terms with these inner figures, as it opens direct negotiations with them. It requires, however, a very open mind, freedom from prejudice, undeviating honesty in recording what is seen and heard, and sufficiently strong roots in the outer world not to be swept away by the unconscious. Moreover, even more than that, it requires an understanding human companion,[13] more so than does watching one's own dreams. It is by no means a method for everybody. Jung only encouraged a comparatively small percentage of his patients to use it; for most

[11] *Two Essays*, par. 322, 323.

[12] See above, p. 27.

[13] Preferably someone who has done a good deal of active imagination himself. It is also very important that active imagination should be used only in the service of the process of individuation and on no account for egotistical purposes. In a seminar Jung once defined the witch as someone who uses the powers of the unconscious for his or her own private ends. This may work for a time but the unconscious always resents being exploited and revenges itself in the long run. The history of witchcraft is very enlightening in this respect.

of those it proved to be a royal road to independence. He once said to me: "Active imagination is the touchstone of whether my patients want to become independent or whether they just want me to carry their problems for them." It is, however, definitely dangerous if used in the wrong way, or by a too lonely, unrooted person.[14]

Before speaking of the later stages of the work on the anima, let us turn now to women and the animus. The latter, like the anima in man, is usually the first figure after the personal shadow to represent the unconscious after the woman has begun to explore the unknown realm within or, in our simile, the country round the fourth gate. But he is very different in character from the anima. A woman indeed has quite as many or more moods than a man but she can usually, if she is honest, account for them, they do not come to her from an unknown realm as they do to a man, and unless she is really animus possessed she can deal more easily with her personal relationships. But the animus is first manifested in her in a lot of ready-made opinions which form an unknown, unseen foundation for her mind and are never questioned by the woman herself. An extreme but very typical example was provided by an aunt of mine who was in the middle of an emotional argument with my father. He said reflectively, "Well, I think. . . ." She interrupted: "And I don't agree with you!"

Just as men have the greatest difficulty in recognizing their moods, their hypersensitivity and the like as springing from their own psychology, so women are incredibly blind to the unreality of their ready-made opinions. They are indeed much more open to the idea that they have an animus, than are men to the idea of the anima; Emma Jung used to say that the idea was very welcome to them in our

[14] Cf. C. G. Jung, "The Transcendent Function," in *Structure and Dynamics*, par. 131-193; Introduction to "The Secret of the Golden Flower," in *Alchemical Studies*; "The Relation between the Ego and the Unconscious," *Two Essays*, pars. 323-340; *Psychology & Alchemy*, pars. 390-400; *Mysterium Coniunctionis*, pars. 705ff, 752f.

man-organized society, where, in spite of all recent manifestations to the contrary, we are all convinced somewhere that man is a superior creature to woman! At any rate, it is very striking that in the great majority of cases women at once take to the idea of having a "man within"; they sometimes even seem to feel rather flattered that they do; whereas men almost invariably feel "a woman within" as humiliating.

It is not as a rule, therefore, the fact of an inner animus that disturbs women. It is rather that he is so ingrained that they are totally unable to see his manifestations. Nothing could have induced my aunt, for example, to wait and hear what my father thought; she *knew* it would be wrong whatever it was, that was an indisputable fact, it just was so. The blindness can go even further, as in the case of the wife of an uncle of Jung who always denied the utterances of her animus after they were made. Her husband was able to record one example of them on an old version of a tape recorder and played it back to her. She exclaimed in all good faith: "I never, never said that, it is faked!" These deeply ingrained opinions, which the woman herself takes for granted or never even notices, is *the* greatest difficulty for her, particularly where her mind comes into play.

To illustrate the manner in which the animus forms a woman's mind, Jung once related an experience of his own at a dinner party when he sat next to a woman he had not met before. She talked to him unceasingly, airing her views on philosophy, expressing a great deal of knowledge of her subject and mentioning exceedingly abstruse ideas. Then she suddenly stopped and asked him, "How do my ideas strike you?" He asked in reply if she really wanted to know. When she assented eagerly, he said, "You do not think." "Not think!" she exclaimed. "Why, I have been speaking of some really profound ideas." "Quite so," he replied, "but I could have read it all in an encyclopedia." "But that is how my mind works, it all comes into my mind like that, ready-made as it were." "But I should like to hear what *you* think about it all yourself." Deflated, she murmured, "But then I should have to *think* about it!"

It is very hard work for most women (there are, of course, exceptions) to find out what they really think, just as it is difficult for a man to find out what he really feels, because the animus automatically thinks for the woman and the anima automatically feels for the man. Therefore the first task for a woman—after the personal shadow has been faced—is to deal with her animus opinions. The two tasks overlap even more than they do with men, because the opinions of the animus obscure the real facts about the shadow. One technique, recommended by Jung, is for the woman to listen carefully to what she says and to attend to the thoughts that pass through her mind, then to ask herself afterwards whether she really agrees with the opinions she has expressed or thought. Surprisingly often, if she is honest with herself, she will find that she does not! So she quite naturally begins to ask herself: Then *who* said (or thought) that?

The main source of information concerning her animus is to be found in a woman's dreams. The animus, like the anima, appears there personified, sometimes as a man the woman knows in real life, sometimes as a stranger, very often as a group of men. The tendency of the animus to appear as a plurality is connected with the collective character of his opinions; he always wants "to settle every question for the 11,000 virgins for the next 10,000 years," as Jung once said in a seminar. He never sees, and seems to try never to let the woman see, the individual aspect and the importance of the here and now, of the unique moment in time and what belongs to it.

Another reason for the "plurality of the animus, in contrast to the unity of the anima," is that "this remarkable fact seems to me to be a correlate of the conscious attitude. The conscious attitude of woman is in general far more exclusively personal than that of man." The man's world is much more collective in its preoccupations, "the nation, the state, business concerns, etc.," whereas the woman's natural interests are more centered on "fathers and mothers, brothers and sisters, husbands and children." [15] Moreover it suits a woman's nature if she finds a man who means enough to her for her to be faithful to him for life, whereas man is much more polygamous by nature. Modern life and the constellation of animus and anima have modified this picture since Jung's essay was written, and, interestingly enough, the plurality of the animus in dreams also seems to me to have become less frequent. When I first came to Zurich in the 1920s dreams with this theme abounded, but in the last two decades they have become comparatively rare. Not that they have by any means ceased, for the basic fact remains, and will probably always remain, that woman is far more personally oriented than man, and, while it remains, the plurality of the animus will endure.

When the completely collective opinions and plurality of the animus are sufficiently overcome, he begins to reveal himself as a more individual figure; but he always has a dual nature. I remember a woman who had been working on her animus problem for years and who had also succeeded in establishing a relationship with a very positive inner figure who was helpful to her in many ways. One day she suddenly had a waking dream of a crowned figure crying for help in the middle of the lake of Zurich. She had read a good deal of alchemy and was reminded of the King's son who calls from the deep: "Whosoever will free me from the waters and lead me to dry land, him will I prosper with everlasting riches." [16] Jung points out that "the connection with the *rex marinus* of the 'Visio Arislei' is obvious." [17] The woman thought naively of the King of the Sea and hurried out in active imagination to his rescue. She found he had a tail, like a merman, which was entangled in the

[15] *Two Essays*, pars. 338-339.
[16] Maier, *Symbola aureae mensae*, p. 380.
[17] *Psychology and Alchemy*, par. 435.

rocks and she helped him to free it. He darted off without a word of thanks and she was left staring rather doubtfully after him.

At that moment the positive animus figure appeared and informed her that she had acted too impulsively, which was dangerous. "That is a very destructive figure," he said, "closely related to the Devil. Be very careful for the *three days* he will be loose. Then he will be caught again by positive forces and once more held in his place."

At that time the woman had only theoretical ideas concerning the reality of these images and was unaware that they could manifest themselves so concretely in outer life. On the third day following she had the first serious motor accident she had had in over thirty years of driving, and indeed her accident occurred on Neptune Street! (No one was hurt although both cars were seriously damaged.) To make matters still more uncanny, while she was recounting her adventure at home, the doorbell rang; it was a man trying to sell a vacuum cleaner named Proteus!

This may sound incredible to present-day rationalists, but it happened exactly as related. It was a so-called synchronistic event,[18] in which an inner event and, in this case, two outer events coincide in a meaningful way. It would lead us too far to go into the question of synchronicity itself, but I mention the experience for two reasons: (1) to illustrate the positive and the negative aspects of the animus, for the King of the Sea and her helpful figure were evidently very closely connected and well-informed about each other, if not actually identical; (2) to illustrate the kind of experience that really convinces us beyond doubt of the reality of these inner figures. Although this woman had been working for years, it took the shock of her first serious accident to wake her up to the fact that inner explorations are *really* as dangerous as outer voyages of discovery, and that a mistake

[18] Cf. Jung, "Synchronicity: An Acausal Connecting Principle," in *Structure and Dynamics of the Psyche,* pars. 816-968.

might even cost her her life. It follows the same principle as Wilhelm's Chinese rainmaker, only here in reverse, so to speak: if the woman had realized the vital necessity of remaining in herself, in Tao, during those three days, no such accident would have been necessary.

As a general rule, unless he is unusually anima-possessed, man is not molested by the anima in his own masculine field. At first she seems to content herself with interfering with his feelings and with the whole realm of relationship. But in these days, the animus by no means stops short at the woman's mind; he weaves his opinions most disastrously into her own field of relationship. There is certainly a connection here with the fact that women have succeeded in establishing their own economic independence of man and have entered so many professional fields that have heretofore been reserved for men. This, in itself, is a great achievement and a necessary step on woman's way back to her own wholeness, but it has undoubtedly, one hopes only temporarily, complicated her relationship to man. There are far fewer women than there were formerly who find their whole interest in life only through men.

Emma Jung once commented on this situation in a seminar, stressing the fact that women who are completely submissive to their husbands have become very rare. She asked the question: "But where is this complete submission? It is a typical feminine quality." She came to the conclusion that it is now, in very many cases, turned towards the animus. The woman secretly, and usually quite unconsciously, submits to the ruling of her animus, just as she used in days gone by to allow her decisions to be made by her husband. This, of course, has strengthened the power of the animus over her to a most undesirable extent and has made it imperative that she learn to know of his empirical existence.

The results of this development are probably most apparent in professional women or in those who are in some other way leading lives that call their more masculine characteristics into play. Such women often have great difficulty with their relationships with men, particularly if they do not marry. I have mentioned an example[19] of a conversation between a woman and her animus in which the latter informed the woman that he was forced to flow in wherever she left a vacuum, i.e., did not function herself in some situation or other. Therefore it is wiser for woman not to be too sure that the fault lies entirely with the animus, but to ask herself if she is taking enough trouble in her relationships with men.

Moreover, when the animus flows into the sphere of relationship, he naturally constellates the man's anima. Then only too often what should be a conversation between two human beings turns into an exchange between animus and anima. Naturally they both say inhuman things and then both feel that *the other* has no human understanding whatever, or at all events certain remarks rankle which, if only the partner could stop to think, were not really meant by him or her at all. In no field could a knowledge of the anima and animus help more than in precisely that of human relationships.

This has been very obvious in several of our examples. Helen Huntingdon in *The Tenant of Wildfell Hall*, for instance, begins very early in her marriage to allow her animus to talk and preach at her husband, and shows less and less human feeling for him. Jung often points out how inhuman we become if we identify with an autonomous complex, yet that is what Helen does consistently throughout her marriage. We can see the same mechanism at work, though on a different level, in *Wuthering Heights*, particularly in the ruthlessly cruel statements that Heathcliff and the elder Catherine make to each other in their last interview. Nothing is more urgently needed than that men and women

[19] See above, p. 28ff.

should become aware of their own autonomous complexes, particularly the animus and anima.

It is obvious to everybody that man has never been in such urgent need as he is today of understanding another's point of view. At bottom all of the complexities of the Iron Curtain phenomenon are the result of the inability of human beings to see themselves or to understand another point of view. As Jung pointed out again and again, we can only begin with the individual. For example, in "The Relations between the Ego and the Unconscious" he writes: "There is no cure and no means of improving the world that does not begin with the individual himself. To put the matter drastically, the man who is either a pauper or a parasite will never solve the social problem." [20] The failure of the well-meaning League of Nations and its impotent successors should have taught us beyond all doubt that problems such as beset the world today can never be settled on a collective basis. Even in politics, nothing decisive has ever been achieved except by an individual, such as Churchill, to mention the last shining example. The usual assumption, that such geniuses are a gift from heaven about which we can do nothing, is only partially true, for if one examines the life of such men they are usually seen to be individuals who have done a lot about themselves and who owe their ability to stand like a rock in the worst storms, at least as much to their own efforts as to innate gifts. Of course Churchill, as a very extraverted man, would never have worked directly on his inner life, as the introverted Jung learned to do. But in his own way, learning from outer events, Churchill certainly became unusually whole and knew very well how much depended on his own attitude to his problems. The fact that he always found time to pursue his painting, an activity that brought a completely opposite side of him into play from his usual work, is the most

[20] *Two Essays*, par. 373.

evident sign that the urge for wholeness was very strong in Churchill.

The process of individuation takes a very different course in the extravert and in the introvert. The former does the work on external things, the latter on internal things. Both are naturally mixed with the other and the solution, the revelation of wholeness, comes as a rule from within to the extravert and from without to the introvert. Although the way of learning to know one's inner figures is in itself more congenial to the introvert than to the extravert, a great many extraverts come into analysis. Although they have been much more interested in the outer world than the introvert and are usually a great deal cleverer in dealing with it, they tend, because their whole attention has been engaged with it so long, to find their interest in it wearing thin with advancing years and feel the need of their lost wholeness quite as acutely as the introvert who, being clumsy in dealing with the outer world, secretly longs for it more than the extravert does. That is why the solution comes to each from his neglected side.

The initial difficulty, for any man, of jumping the hurdle, of realizing there is a woman in himself, does not seem to be very much more difficult for the extravert than the introvert, because the anima's habit of projecting herself into outer woman has often led the former into more trouble than the shyer, less enterprising latter. It can even be a relief to an extravert to discover that it was not just disloyalty that led him into so many involvements. But, whereas the introvert finds it a relief to work directly on his inner figure and to get to know her once he has admitted her existence, the extravert usually sees his anima first outside in Miss Y or Mrs. X, and it is in these actual relationships that he will become acquainted with the projecting factor.

We can see this already in the Brontës. Charlotte made her great step forward after meeting M. Héger. Her inner animus figures are portrayed very clearly in her early writings, but it was not until she met her animus projected onto M. Héger that she was shaken out of her identity with him and was able to write as a woman and allow her genius to develop. Her early work is very difficult to read and, in spite of her fame, has never become popular or even familiar except to a small circle of admirers. I think the reason is because it was written almost entirely by the animus; it is therefore not *humanly* interesting; whereas after her experience of loving M. Héger the inhuman element almost completely disappeared. We know, however, of no such experience in Emily's life, and, as a true introvert, it would indeed not have been necessary to her, as it was to the more extraverted Charlotte, for Emily could find her sphere of work entirely within. Had she lived longer she would undoubtedly have had to take the outer world more into account.

I do not wish to devote much space here to the problem of either attitude or function types, although it is very important in the practical work; in order to make it clear to the reader, I should have to go into too much detail. Moreover, there is no pure type. Each is always an individual mixture, although the one or the other type usually predominates, sometimes to a very marked extent, as with Emily Brontë.

It must be understood that although I am representing the task of self-knowledge in its necessary stages, in actual fact these stages are by no means so clearly defined. There are many anima and animus dreams in the stage of realizing the personal shadow, and indeed there are often anticipatory dreams of the Self which appear at the beginning of the work. One of the clearest I recall actually explained its purpose in so many words, which is rather rare in dreams whose language is always symbolic. A woman of 37, only about six weeks after starting analysis and in the midst of some most unpleasant realizations about her shadow, dreamed that *she saw a marvellous vision in the sky: two pairs of suns or stars were dancing with each other in sublime harmony, in a quaternary rhythm, emanating a "peace beyond all understanding."* As *she stood transfixed, a voice said to her: "This is what you will become, and is shown you to demonstrate that it is worth while looking behind every corner, however dirty, unpleasant or banal it may be."* The very next night her dreams resumed their pitiless searchlight into all she had tried to ignore and forget.

The stage of *Auseinandersetzung* between the man and his anima or the woman and her animus is above all directed towards banishing them from the outside world where, as the Siamese twin example has shown,[21] they are totally out of place and only get us into difficulties. It must be emphasized that this desirable result is not only achieved by work on the inside figures but also, as *conditio sine qua non,* by a readaptation in outer life in which the conscious ego must take responsibility for many things it has neglected or ignored. This, to an introvert, is the most uncongenial aspect of the whole work but also the most necessary. Jung says: "Such a way is possible and successful *only* when the particular worldly tasks, undertaken by these same individuals, are also *carried out effectively in reality.*" He adds: "The shirker experiences nothing but his own morbid fear, and this brings him no meaning" and "the fruits of the mind" fall to him "who pays *his tribute to life.*" [22]

Until one gives one's whole mind to it, it is very difficult to realize how much we have always left to be done by our unconscious. We leave an astonishing number of vacuums, into which the anima or animus must flow, in our daily lives. For example, the woman sitting next to Jung at that dinner party allowed the animus to provide her whole conversation; it sounded well, full of profound ideas, and she never stopped to consider whether she agreed with what she said or not! When man pours out a lot of sentimental banalities without

[21] See above, p. 28.

[22] *Two essays,* par. 369; italics added.

ever stopping to compare them with the actual facts before him, he is letting the anima feel for him, just as the animus thought for Jung's dinner companion.

However impressed one may be with his dreams, however fascinated by the perspectives opened up by active imagination, it means nothing if there is no result in daily life. Not that these results should be looked for too soon, or expected to be dramatic, but it must always be kept in mind that the work is aiming at a change of personality, a widening of consciousness and that, if there is any neglect of outer tasks or relationships, the inner work will suffer, just as much as vice versa.

The paramount importance of the practical side of the work on anima and animus becomes clear when we consider how many effeminate men and masculine women there are today, a state of affairs which, when we look at the extravagances of present-day youth, seems to be getting worse rather than better. This is perhaps most visible in the regrettable number of young girls who rush into sexual experiments at a very early age. They have adopted this pattern ready-made, as it were, from young men to whom such escapades are natural enough. Jung says in "Women in Europe": "A man thinks he possesses a woman if he has her sexually. He never has her less, for to a woman the Eros relationship is the real and decisive one." [23] But too many women seem to have lost sight completely of their own principle and of their own strength, which amounts sometimes to genius, in Eros relationship. Instead they allow the animus and his masculine principle to govern their actions and thoughts, whereas the sphere of relationship (where woman should be able to help man, as he can help her in the things of the mind and in many of the difficulties of the outer world) is thus allowed to disappear into the unconscious.

The individual who tries to throw some light on all of this contemporary confusion—which naturally he will also

[23] In *Civilization in Transition,* par. 255.

find in his own unconscious—will soon discover that it serves no purpose to work only inwardly on his or her personified masculine or feminine side, without checking it out with life itself, in spite of the great importance, even the necessity, of the inner work. We should ask ourselves, for instance: Are we succeeding in seeing and then separating the sexes in ourselves? Are we taking the responsibility for this or that *consciously*, particularly in the realm of our own principle or are we still allowing something unknown to look after it for us? Are we understanding other people better? How much have we succeeded in banishing anima moods (or animus opinions) from our daily life? And can we relate to these figures as a kind of function, messenger or bridge between our conscious personality and the unconscious? All of these questions can only be answered through our *actual experience in daily life*.

The ego alone can never bring this stage of the work to a satisfactory conclusion, however. Their infinite subtlety and their roots deep down in the unknown make the anima and animus too much for our more limited conscious personalities. But if we are sincere in our own efforts, help comes from the unconscious itself. We saw this projected into *Wuthering Heights*. When the younger Catherine had done all she could to accept her suffering, to come to terms with the formerly despised Hareton and, through love for him, even to accept her persecutor, Heathcliff, the elder Catherine in the Beyond came to her daughter's rescue and drew the whole of Heathcliff's attention to herself. In other words, she drew him back into the unconscious, leaving her daughter and nephew free to live their own lives and the lands to revert to their rightful owners.

In the direct, non-projected form, we also find a figure from the Beyond (the unconscious) intervening when consciousness has done or is doing its best. There are figures in the collective unconscious that are far more powerful than the animus and anima, for the latter derive their autonomous power mainly from the inefficiency of the conscious personality. The first that appears as a rule in the psychology of the male is the Wise Old Man, or some other very powerful aspect of eternal masculinity; and in woman this role is taken by the Great Mother or some other aspect of the "eternal feminine."

This should be made clearer by an example. A woman in analysis in Zurich was at the stage in which she was trying to see and catch the whole network of animus opinions that were always cropping up again and again and preventing her from experiencing *reality as it is*. But these opinions seemed to her like the ground elder that had flourished in her garden as a child; she kept pulling it up but some roots always remained and led to another crop of the same weed. When she was near despair, she had the following dream:

*She had to pass through the customs of her native land in order to arrive in Switzerland. She had a great deal of luggage and she knew that it contained many things the customs officials would not allow to leave the country, yet it was essential that she should bring them all with her. She was near panic, felt terrified of being caught smuggling and had no idea how to manage the situation. At that moment, a beautiful, very elegantly dressed lady appeared. The dreamer knew she was "the Queen of Night" and looked at her with awe. The lady said to the officials, pointing to the dreamer: "This woman is traveling with me." All of her boxes were chalked without further comment, for evidently the officials were anxious to please such an imposing and attractive woman. Then the dreamer discovered they were really traveling together. She could hardly believe her good fortune and yet she felt full of apprehension for she realized there could be no further shirking and that this Queen of Night would demand things of her that would go dead against all of her traditional ideas of morality. She woke up as she was following her onto a ship.*

The dreamer had lived too much on the light side and was a slave to traditional morality, therefore in this early manifestation the Self appears as the "Queen of Night," as the dark side of her complete being. The dreamer then realized that, in order to accompany her, she must give up living by the letter of the law and reach down to a real ethos on a far deeper level, and that this would involve her in many things she had always avoided, not out of real morality but because she was afraid.

The animal psychologist, Konrad Lorenz, tells some stories [24] that illustrate very well an important aspect of this deep instinctive morality. When he was a young zoologist at the Vienna Zoo, Lorenz was in charge of the reptile house and had to feed some of his snakes a diet of mice or baby rats. Baby rats were economically preferable, for they could be used shortly after birth, whereas mice had to be fed until they were almost full-grown. Nevertheless, Lorenz had a deep resistance to using the baby rats. They are quite charming when very young and extraordinarily like human babies, so for a long time he used only mice. Then he told himself not to be sentimental, hardened his heart and fed the snakes one day on baby rats. To his surprise his whole nature reacted against his action; he had terrible dreams about baby rats turning into human babies and protesting most touchingly against their fate. He had the wisdom to realize that if he went on doing something so contrary to his deep instinctive conscience it would lead to a neurosis and resolved, however economically sound and traditionally right an action was, never to do it if it conflicted with his own deep ethos.

He found the same deep ethos in animals and tells a story of his own French bulldog to illustrate this. This animal had been his only, very devoted dog for some years, when circumstances forced him to bring home a second dog. The

[24] In *Man Meets Dog*, in the chapter entitled "The Animal with a Conscience."

French bulldog was jealous beyond measure and at last, driven by his fury and despair, had a desperate fight with the intruder in his master's study. Lorenz tried to separate the combatants and the bulldog, entirely by mistake, bit his hand badly, upon which the fight was finished and the bulldog retired heartbroken, refusing to eat or to be consoled. He had broken his own deep ethos, he had bitten his master, and the fact that the bite had been intended for the other dog and that, in human judgment, it was therefore not his fault, simply did not register with him. It was a week before he would resume his normal way of life.

From this and other examples, Lorenz draws the conclusion that an animal has no conscience, in the human sense at all, but that it has this deep instinct of what may and may not be done and is bound by it. The same instinct exists in every human being but, together with the idea of wholeness, it has fallen into the unconscious and seems no longer available to most people. It appears quite often indeed in simple people, and then we speak, for instance, of "nature's gentlemen."

As far as one can see, this deep ethos is the morality of the Self, and it often brings one into conflict with the legal code and traditional morality. I do not mean to disparage either; they are absolutely essential in any society; but it is in the conflict of duties that this deep instinctive ethos comes to light. There is such a conflict of duties in our dream: the dreamer had either to follow the law of her country and *not* export certain forbidden articles or fail to act as the unconscious was demanding of her in her analysis. She was at the end of her conscious resources, as she was in her fight against animus opinions (represented in the dream by the customs officials) in her analysis, and very near the point of panic, which is always the only real danger in working with the unconscious. Then the matter was decided for her: the articles were brought through customs by a higher authority.

The animus always gives way to the Self, for like the ego he is contained in the totality and really derives most of his excessive power over a woman by the fact that at first he stands between and thus obscures the woman's view of the Self. But just as the animus often seems to delight in thwarting the ego—the customs officials would certainly have thwarted the woman's need to export the things she needed if they had found them—so he seems glad to be put in his right place by the Self, just as the officials in the dream were glad, even honored, to oblige the superior woman.

The Self is always an *unio oppositorum* and, although such interventions as we see in this dream are by no means rare, we cannot really live with the Self, live as a harmonious part of our totality, until we have accepted *both* opposites. Therefore the woman in the dream, although she was thankful beyond all measure to have her problem solved, nevertheless felt very apprehensive when she learned that they were to continue their journey together. She knew that she had not yet accepted the dark opposite sufficiently to be able to live up to the demands likely to be made on her from this side.

The Moses of the Koran had exactly the same difficulties with El-Khidr, who is a clear symbol of the Self. They too went on a journey together and, although Moses was completely fascinated by El-Khidr, just as our dreamer was by the Queen of Night, yet he was horrified at his actions, which appeared to him to be directly criminal. But when they parted, El-Khidr explained their constructive background and once again one gets a glimpse of this deep ethos which is almost beyond our comprehension, for most of us have been trained since earliest youth in traditional conceptions of morality, so well depicted in the Moses of the Koran.[25] El-Khidr, on the other hand, acts from a morality that is ultimately based on the "absolute knowledge." By this term Jung[26] understands a form of consciousness and

[25] The details of the story of Moses and El-Khidr can be found in Sura 18 of *The Koran*.

[26] Cf. *Structure and Dynamics*, pars. 923, 931, 948.

even of intelligence which exists in the collective unconscious, entirely independently of ego consciousness. It consists of images which we have not imagined ourselves but which manifest spontaneously in the meaningful arrangements of nature. In religious language, this same phenomenon has often been called "Providence" or "supernatural guidance." In the Old Testament, we sometimes hear that this guidance awoke reactions very similar in character to those of our dreamer and of Moses of the Koran—Balaam's ass is a classic example.[27]

The great difficulty in this stage of the work is that we are obliged to face the terrifying problem of evil. It was clear in Mary Webb's *Precious Bane* that the quaternity (wholeness) simply dissolved when evil was not allowed its place in it. Accepting the opposites is no empty phrase, it really means according each opposite its full rights and doing one's best to endure the tension between them, until at last, at least relatively, we are able to find a middle way between them. Of course we meet the problem of evil in the first stage of the work, in the personal shadow, but unless there is an inextricable contamination with the collective shadow it still has human dimensions. As we have seen, Jung called it child's play in comparison with what comes later. We have some help from our education in this stage, for we are seldom encouraged to think that we have no faults. But on that stage of the journey where we travel with the Self—the Queen of Night, to use the language of our dream—sooner or later we shall probably have to look at the face of pure evil. The doctrine of the *privatio boni*, or the desire to deny the power of evil, is very strong in most of us, but we live in a time when we can no longer afford to indulge in such optimism. Jung says:

> Light is followed by shadow, the other side of the Creator. This development reached its peak in the twentieth century.

[27] Numbers 22.

> The Christian world is now truly confronted by the principle of evil, by naked injustice, tyranny, lies, slavery, and coercion of conscience. This manifestation of naked evil has assumed apparently permanent form in the Russian nation; but its first violent eruption came in Germany. That outpouring of evil revealed to what extent Christianity has been undermined in the twentieth century. In the face of that, evil can no longer be minimized by the euphemism of the *privatio boni*. Evil has become a determinant reality. It can no longer be dismissed from the world by a circumlocution. We must learn how to handle it, since it is here to stay. How we can live with it without terrible consequences cannot for the present be conceived.[28]

Evil is most dangerous when allowed to work in the dark, in the unconscious, whereas the light of consciousness hinders its growth. The further the light is from darkness, the deeper and more obscure the latter will be, and the less we shall know of what is being prepared in its depths. The more we avoid the burning problem of evil, the greater the risk of terrible things, even atomic war, being hatched within it.

To give an example from our material, Gideon, in *Precious Bane*, could only murder his mother because Prue did *not* turn the light of consciousness on his intention. He took several weeks, even months, to carry out his plan. Her mother warned Prue at the beginning: "Dunna let my son Sarn come. . . . He'd lief I was dead and sodded." Yet Prue did let him come every evening and she faithfully recorded his words, pressing his old mother to say that she would as soon or rather be dead. But the face of pure evil (such as is represented here as matricide) was too terrifying, and Prue looked away from the possibility, just as we are all tempted to do in the world of today. It is true we are all very willing to see it in our enemies and to proclaim our shock and horror, exactly as Prue would certainly have done had

[28] *Memories, Dreams, Reflections*, p. 328f.

Sexton's Tivvy or Beguildy, instead of Gideon, been preparing the deed. But to look for it nearer home, the only place we can do anything about it, needs great courage and willingness to suffer. Yet we shall never really experience good, or have any hope of standing the tension between the opposites, until we have looked evil in the face, have recognized it in ourselves and *not* behind the Iron Curtain.

A dream may make this point clearer. A woman dreamed that *she stood at the gate of a garden. It was unbelievably beautiful and all the people she loved and respected most were there. Shyly she entered and found that she herself was one of these people, related to them in a harmony beyond anything she had ever known. She could hardly believe she had any right to be there and remained near the entrance, expecting every moment to be asked to leave. Then a voice said, "Yes, you may enter freely but only because you have promised to spend half of your time in this place."* *At that moment the beautiful garden vanished and its place was taken by its polar opposite: a neglected, hideous garden, filled with the people she disliked most and with whom she had the least in common. All of her worst problems were waiting for her and she had no idea how to relate to her companions. The voice continued: "While you spend half your time here, you have the right to spend the other half in the beautiful garden; but if you try to cheat, even by a minute, the doors of the desired one will close forever against you."*

The dream reveals the opposites still widely separated, but it was a tremendous encouragement to the dreamer who had felt lost in the discouraging garden. Indeed, as her work on herself continued, it often seemed to her that she still had to spend most of her time there. It was, however, the same in alchemy. Michael Meier points out: "There is in our chemistry a certain noble substance . . . in the beginning whereof is wretchedness with vinegar, but in its ending joy with gladness. And so I supposed it would fare with me, that at first I should taste, endure and experience many hard, bitter, sad, and wearisome things, but at length would see that everything became pleasanter and easier."[29] Although dream time seldom coincides with clock time and cannot as a rule therefore be taken literally, yet this dream of the opposites presents the situation exactly: the return to paradise is impossible without the sojourn in the opposite, which we find situated round the fourth gate. Although most of us unceasingly pursue the light opposite and the happiness represented by the beautiful garden, it is the last way we shall ever find it; whereas it unbelievably opens of itself, as it did in the dream, if we face the horrors of its opposite.

This dream illustrates a very necessary stage in the work during which the opposites are fully discriminated and seen as each other's polar opposite. The old alchemists also laid great stress on the stage of the *separatio*, when they completely separated the four elements from each other. There can be no union until this stage is completed, and in our dream such a condition is depicted. It is brought about by conscious work—nothing at all would happen without that—but on the other hand it also needs the cooperation of nature. The dreamer again had done what she could but the actual separation had taken place in the unconscious and was announced in the dream. It was a great encouragement to the dreamer, but by no means the end of the work on this stage.

Nor, if this separation could be completed in a human life, would the subsequent uniting of the opposites be possible to consciousness without the cooperation of the unconscious. It reaches far beyond human comprehension, as indeed everything pertaining to the Self always does. The alchemist, Michael Maier, expressed it in the following way:

> Nature, I say, when she turned about the golden circle, by that movement made its four qualities equal, that is to say,

[29] *Symbola aureae mensae*, p. 568.

> she squared that homogeneous simplicity turning back on itself, or brought it into an equilateral rectangle, in such a way that contraries are bound together by contraries, and enemies by enemies, as if with everlasting bonds, and are held in mutual embrace.[30]

This is a particularly clear description of the way the opposites, hostile as they are at the beginning, are yet in the end brought into harmony with each other and also how this stage is beyond human power to complete. We can only find the opposites in ourselves and grant them equal rights, however much against the grain it goes to do so. And particularly when it comes to good and evil, all of our training and indeed Christianity itself are dead against us. Christ himself, however, evidently did realize the necessity for the opposites. The parable of the unjust steward is one illustration and there are many more to be found in the non-canonical books.[31] But the Church, beginning as early as its Fathers, stressed the good more and more and held it up as the only desideratum. This was absolutely necessary at that time. Evil will flourish in and for itself, but it seems to belong to the nature of good—in human nature at all events—that it needs to be cultivated and supported. The opposites were hopelessly entangled at the beginning of our era. In fact, as Jung says, Christianity "was accepted as a means of escape from the brutality and unconsciousness of the ancient world." [32] At that time good had to be striven for and evil discouraged as much as possible, or no discrimination could ever have been achieved. But our present age has taught us beyond doubt that we can no longer afford to ignore evil, for if we do it is only too likely that it will revenge itself by destroying our planet. It must now be given

[30] *De circulo physico quadrato*, p. 17. Cf. Jung, *Mysterium Coniunctionis*, par. 1, note 3.
[31] Cf. James, *The Apocryphal New Testament*.
[32] *Symbols of Transformation*, par. 341.

equal rights with good, in order that the contraries should be "bound together by contraries and enemies by enemies," and should hold each other in "mutual embrace."

In this mutual embrace the opposites become relative to each other and are completely transformed. They no longer try every possible trick in order to prevail over each other, but each assumes something of the nature of the other, so that the law of enantiodromia is at last overcome. I have pointed out that we cannot really love until we have realized that the greatest love may only too easily turn into hate, and that somewhere we always resent the loss of freedom that love involves. But a love that has bound its contrary to itself and is held in a mutual embrace with hate can really be relied upon, for it is total, there is nothing left outside to thwart its expression and development.

No one who reads James' *Apocryphal New Testament* carefully will have much doubt that the compilers of the official New Testament omitted the most paradoxical of Christ's sayings, particularly those regarding evil, although a few remain such as "Be ye wise as serpents, and harmless as doves."[33] But there is another very difficult facet of Christ's teaching of which we hear very little, namely his statement reported in St. John's gospel 10:34: "Ye are gods." Jung says of this:

> We have always been taught that the Incarnation was a unique historical event. No repetition of it was to be expected, any more than one could expect a further revelation of the Logos, for this too was included in the uniqueness of God's appearance on earth, in human form, nearly two thousand years ago. The sole source of revelation, and hence the final authority, is the Bible. God is an authority only in so far as he authorized the writings in the New Testament, and with the conclusion of the New Testament the authentic communications of God cease. Thus far the Protestant

[33] St. Matthew 10:16.

> standpoint. The Catholic Church, the direct heir and continuator of historical Christianity, proves to be somewhat more cautious in this regard, believing that with the assistance of the Holy Ghost the dogma can progressively develop and unfold. This view is in entire agreement with Christ's own teachings about the Holy Ghost and hence with the further continuance of the Incarnation. Christ is of the opinion that whoever believes in him—believes, that is to say, that he is the son of God—can "do the works that I do, and greater works than these." (John XIV, 12) He reminds his disciples that he had told them they were gods. (John X, 34) The believers or chosen ones are children of God and "fellow heirs with Christ." (Romans VIII, 17) When Christ leaves the earthly stage, he will ask his father to send his flock a Counselor (the "Paraclete"), who will abide with them and in them for ever. (John XIV, 16f.) The Counselor is the Holy Ghost, who will be sent from the father. This "Spirit of truth" will teach the believers "all things" and guide them "into all truth." (John XIV, 26 and XVI, 12) According to this, Christ envisages a continuing realization of God in his children, and consequently in his (Christ's) brothers and sisters in the spirit, so that his own works need not necessarily be considered the greatest ones.[34]

In the last stage of the work—the realization of the Self and the abdication of the ego in its favor—we come right up against this too much neglected statement: "Ye are gods." We are back at what Jung calls "the thorny problem of the relationship" between "eternal man and earthly man," the problem with which Charlotte Brontë's paper "Strange Events" was concerned.[35] The reader will recall the figures, hundreds of feet high, beings that looked exactly alike and had the same voices as their earthly counterparts; and the

[34] *Psychology and Religion*, par. 655.
[35] See above, p. 112ff.

yogin in Jung's dream who had Jung's own face.[36] It will be clear at once that if "earthly man" should identify with "eternal man," "hundreds of feet high," the result would be an appalling inflation of the former, which must end, if persisted in, with the latter's destruction. It was this great figure, "eternal man," which is yet ourselves, that Christ meant when he said: "Ye are gods"—"us," not "we," in Charlotte's language. St. Paul understood this distinction when he wrote, "I live, yet not I, Christ liveth in me,"[37] but the danger of this remark being misunderstood led the Church to emphasize Christ as "a unique historical event" and more and more to insist on an *objective* God, *outside* man.

The Self, "eternal man," is an archetypal fact, however, which did not quite fit into the Church's teaching in this respect. Jung has often pointed out that such ideas still functioned, but underground, as it were, in such movements as Gnosticism and alchemy. Moreover the idea, "Ye are gods," has always burst out unpleasantly, from time to time, in people who, confusing the ego with the Self, behaved as if they were convinced *they* were gods. Perhaps Hitler is the most obvious example, and the most flagrant. But there have never been so many examples of people who have made this error as in our time.

It is indeed the most difficult of all tasks to comprehend the truth of Christ's saying without falling into this mistake. Everything depends on our ability to distinguish between the eternal man and the earthly man within us, and to realize that the former needs the latter quite as much as vice versa. For instance, Jung says (in interpreting his dream of the yogi with his face): "My Self retires into meditation and meditates my earthly form. To put it another way: it assumes human shape in order to enter three-dimensional existence, as if someone were putting on a diver's suit in

[36] See above, p. 114.
[37] Galatians 2:20.

order to dive into the sea . . . In earthly form it can pass through the experiences of the three dimensional world, and by greater awareness take a further step toward realization." [38] As I see it, the whole meaning of life consists in discovering what this further step is and fulfilling it to the best of our ability. For this to be possible, it is absolutely necessary to be able to distinguish between the eternal man who asks the question, as it were, and the earthly man who has the task of doing everything he can to answer this question during his life in the flesh.

It is clearly impossible for earthly man, enclosed in his body and bound by all the limitations of space and time, to be able even approximately to comprehend or grasp eternal man in his boundless and unlimited existence. Obviously the more we can understand and experience this eternal being, the more possible it is for us to "take this further step" that is being asked of us. Spontaneous experiences are the most convincing and the greatest help here, but these happen to us or they do not, and we cannot provoke them. When we consciously set about the task of learning to know more of this Anthropos, or eternal man, we find our best opportunity to do so in his fourfold structure,[39] because we also find this fourfoldness in our conscious personalities, in the shape of the four functions. The alchemist Morienus (7th-8th century) knew and expressed this when he said: "And as man is composed of the four elements, so also is the stone." All four functions are necessary if we are to be in a position to fulfill the Self's demand for a "further step towards realization." Yet, as we have already seen in our simile of leaving Eden, at least one gate, river or function is left behind and forgotten on our journey out into the world, i.e., it is left in the unconscious. An example will make clear how this works out in practical reality.

The case I have in mind was that of an intelligent woman

[38] *Memories, Dreams, Reflections*, p. 324.

[39] See above, p. 2.

who had been married for many years to a man who meant a great deal to her. In spite of this mutual love and esteem, the early years of their marriage had been stormy, mainly because the husband, having suffered from a tyrannical mother, was allergic to the slightest display of power and even to the mildest scene. His wife was much too fond of having her own way and came from a family where scenes had been a part of daily life. This combination naturally led to a lot of trouble. Both of them slowly realized, particularly after the children were grown and had left the house, that they could only solve their problem by learning to know *themselves* better. So both went into Jungian analysis.

The wife was an intuitive type, and it took her no time at all to grasp the situation intuitively; in fact she had really recognized it long before she began analysis, but she felt powerless to change. Her dreams soon acquainted her with her feeling reaction, revealing to her how even more valuable her husband was than she had realized. At the same time they also pointed out her resistances to him, how distressed she was that she was treating him in what she well knew was the wrong way. Things improved quite a bit with this realization, but scenes still occurred from time to time, and now more than ever they gave her a dangerous feeling of inferiority. At this point she decided to study Jungian psychology more deeply and to read all of Jung's books. Her previous analysis had been concerned primarily with the personal shadow and the surface of her daily life; now the animus problem emerged and was dealt with very honestly to the best of her ability. As her work progressed, her dreams began more and more to introduce her to symbols, such as mandalas and divine figures, symbols of the "eternal man" in her—in psychological language, the Self. This led to a development of her third function, thinking, for which the way had already been paved by the reading she had done.

Her dreams of the Self caused her to ponder a great deal, with her newly found thinking, about the meaning of her marital situation. She came to the conclusion that part, at any rate, of the "further step towards realization" that the Self was demanding of her [40] was to give up her ego-will in her marriage and to learn what real love was after it had been cleansed of ego demands. She said to me, "If the Buddhists should be right about reincarnation, I am sure that I must have had many incarnations as a hen-pecking wife and now this horrible karma must be brought to an end." Her husband was a man of sterling character and she knew very well that her interferences were a hindrance to him.

To return to our simile of Eden, this woman had now fully explored the country to the right and left of the river which she had followed out into the world. She had circumambulated more than half the walls of her lost paradise and established the position of three of its gates. Or, to put it in other words, she now saw her life and the "eternal man" from three aspects, and this was sufficient to change her a great deal. She no longer made scenes, and this had an excellent effect on her relationship with her husband. She had found a meaning to her own life in trying to fulfill the "further step" the eternal Self wanted her to take. This satisfactory state of affairs lasted for several years. Then a new and unexpected difficulty arose. Her husband became seriously ill and, because his mother had used his illnesses to gain power over him as a child, he proved to be an exceedingly bad patient. Therefore for a time she was forced to interfere in order to prevent him foolishly ruining his health. Insidiously, however, this situation revived her power, and, after he had recovered, to her dismay the scenes began again. She did her best to stop them, recalling all of her previously successful realizations. But to her horror they no longer seemed to help. She was near despair and terrified that her previous work had been a fake. While things were at this impasse, she was threatened by a fatal disease.

[40] See above, p. 115.

She now entered a period of black despair, in which everything she had gained seemed lost and she thought she would have to die with her life's problem unsolved. It was a time comparable to the misery of the younger Catherine in *Wuthering Heights* when everything was in the hands of Heathcliff. This woman had her own inner Heathcliff, in a network of animus opinions which, although she had believed them to be overcome, reasserted themselves and made everything a thousand times worse. The idea that her previous work had been a fake was a master stroke of the autonomous animus trying to re-establish his lost power over the woman. Yet, negative as everything now seemed, she had in her misery entered the untracked country round the fourth gate, and it became very clear to me and soon also to her that her future depended on accepting her suffering.

It is a fact that amazes me again and again that *accepted* suffering always changes and sometimes even removes its cause. We saw this phenomenon projected into *Wuthering Heights* when Heathcliff lost his wish to destroy after the younger Catherine had accepted her suffering. Soon after, this woman accepted *her* suffering, in "dying uncompleted," as she expressed it, or, when she used Indian language, with her "hen-pecking karma unresolved." Then to everyone's amazement her fatal disease turned out to be a wrong diagnosis.

The evening they learned that it was a false alarm, she made a serious mistake which caused her even greater suffering, but which at last pointed very painfully towards a solution. Her husband, as a thinking type, was naturally very inarticulate in any situation calling for the feeling function, and it suddenly struck her that, although he seemed pleased, he had not *told* her how glad he was that she was not going to die. So she very foolishly asked him, "Are you pleased that I am going to stay with you?" He replied truthfully, "Very pleased, if you mean to leave me free and not make scenes." She asked, "Well, you know I try. But if I don't succeed?" "Then I am not so pleased." This sensation statement completely shattered her for a time. She had long known that he must have his freedom, she had given it to him for years with the best results, she knew that it was most meaningful for her herself to do so, but, she told me, it was not until she realized that he would rather she died than that he lose that freedom that the situation became inexorably real. She had at long last seen the problem from the point of view of the fourth function, as a sensation reality which pinned her right down. Unknown to herself, her intuition had always prevented her from feeling the full pain by luring her away from the *facts* into enticing but quite unreal other possibilities, in fact away from the country round the fourth gate. Now she had to make a complete sacrifice of such retreats and evasions, she could no longer indulge in secret flights of fancy, but must deal with the basic truths of her daily life, one by one, however painful that might be.

The dangerous period for this woman, as for all of us, whatever our functions may be, was the time when it became necessary to include the fourth function. (We have already seen this psychological fact projected into *Wuthering Heights* where it was always the appearance of the fourth that led to trouble.) The temptation to regress into the previously effective three functions is very strong, and unfortunately too often yielded to. Jung used to say it was much wiser not to try to live his psychology than it was to do so and not to go through with it. Indeed, if this woman had not been able to accept the pain of her first *total* realization of her husband's reality ("women overcome by accepting their suffering") she would have been in a far worse state than before. When the time comes to take a step forward, earlier realizations no longer work *by themselves*, although, as this woman found, they all take their place in a meaningful whole when the building, as it were, is secured by the fourth cornerstone.

Although she had long been searching for her wholeness in an intuitive way, aided by feeling and thinking, this woman had now for the first time *experienced* the state of wholeness as a sensation reality and a condition of her daily life, and was no longer satisfied by anything less. It still took a long time for her to learn to live with her inferior function, for the ego never gains control over the latter. But in the course of a lifetime the more controlled superior function wears thin, and the inferior function, which is and always remains in the control of the Self, gains far more substance. Certain parts of it indeed can be worked on, but the essential part cannot and is usually experienced at first as a series of shocks. As the ego slowly learns to work with the Self, it usually discovers that the solution of the most essential problems comes through the mediation of the originally despised inferior function.

The *Auseinandersetzung* with the inferior function is usually a difficult and long phase of the work and entails remaining very faithfully in the neighborhood of the fourth gate. I have mentioned several times that paradise can only be re-entered through this fourth gate, and now we can see the reason why. As the angel with the flaming sword in the Genesis story so aptly symbolizes, man can never re-enter paradise by his own efforts alone. However much we accustom ourselves to the country round the fourth gate, learn to endure the shocks by which it is experienced, withdraw projections and learn to include this difficult area in our whole life, we still can never re-enter paradise at will. The fourth gate is and always remains in the hands of the Self, who is superior to any angel or flaming sword, and any experience of re-entrance, which may be vouchsafed to us during our lifetime, is something which *happens to us* by the will of the Self—or by the grace of God, to use Christian language. Nevertheless the life of anyone who has penetrated to and not retreated from the fourth gate has changed out of all recognition. That individual has escaped from the one-sided, rational, limited goals that are the blight of our age and is in constant refreshing contact with the lost wholeness, with Eden, in our own simile.

Christianity has placed the actual re-entry into paradise in the Beyond, which is almost certainly where it really belongs as an *enduring condition.* Nevertheless there have been people who have undoubtedly had temporary experiences of it in their lifetime and have left us convincing testimony. There is one common factor in all of this testimony, insofar as I am acquainted with it, namely that paradise is a place where the opposites are completely reconciled. It is therefore usually symbolized by the *hieros gamos* or sacred marriage.

The latest of these testimonies is to be found in the chapter on "Visions" in Jung's *Memories, Dreams, Reflections.*[41] He experienced these visions when he was at the point of death in 1944, and although it was seventeen years before his actual death, his testimony confirms yet again that this blissful condition of completely reconciled opposites is a condition that really belongs to the Beyond and can only be experienced very relatively and fleetingly while we still belong to the three-dimensional world. Moreover, many of the most vivid descriptions of the *hieros gamos* which have come down to us from the past are connected with death. There is, for example, the description in the Zohar of the death of Rabbi Simeon ben Yochai, when his disciples heard a voice saying: "Up and come to the marriage of Rabbi Simeon! Let there be peace and let them rest upon their couches." St. Augustine even interpreted the crucifixion as a marriage.[42]

No doubt the reason that we are able to have only transitory glimpses of the re-entry into the reconciled opposites of paradise during our lifetime is that the tension between the opposites is a *conditio sine qua non* of life in this world. It is only through this terrestrial condition that the eternal figure in us can experience the definiteness of this world and

[41] *Memories,* pp. 289-98.
[42] von Franz, *Aurora Consurgens,* p. 428.

thus take a "further step toward realization." [43] Even as regards the most fleeting experiences of paradise, the condition for the Self allowing a living human being through the fourth gate seems to be expressed best by Meister Eckhart's *sich lassen,* i.e., as complete a sacrifice as possible of all ego will. This sacrifice and complete acceptance of the will of the Self should not be confused with a passive fatalism or with the Inshallah of Islam which is really a somewhat primitive, one-sided and even irresponsible attitude. Accepting the will of the Self always entails accepting *both* opposites, never deciding for this or that, but accepting the uncertainty of not knowing which, sometimes for a long and painful period. It must also be pointed out that this sacrifice of ego will is by no means reserved for dramatic moments in fate, nor is it often rewarded by *direct* experience of paradise. It is rather a constant acceptance of the Self in the apparently trivial events of everyday life which may even outwardly seem banal. I will try to make this clearer by an example.

An overworked Jungian analyst was very set on buying a certain piece of land in the depths of the country, a property which seemed to him a paradise on earth. He wanted to build himself a small cottage there as a refuge from his too busy town life. At the last moment, however, the farmer to whom the land belonged played him a dirty trick. Misled by fantastic illusions as to the value of the land *in the future,* he refused to sell, after all the formalities except the actual signing had been completed.

This was a terrible blow to our doctor for he had already planned his building as an expression of bringing into reality his process of individuation.[44] But in the midst of his bitter disappointment and just indignation, he realized that such a

[43] *Memories,* p. 324. Cf. also. p. 114 above.

[44] Cf. Jung's description of his own urge to do this in the chapter on "The Tower," in *Memories, Dreams, Reflections,* pp. 223-237.

manifestation of his individuation process, although it seemed essential to him, might not belong to the pattern the Self was weaving [45] and that, if this turned out to be the case, he must renounce his burning wish for such a refuge. He did not feel fatalistic about the catastrophe. He went on looking for property, but gradually he completely accepted the possibility of failure, i.e., he became willing to find or fail to find his passionately desired bit of land. When he had really accepted both possibilities for quite some time, another piece of land, even better than the first, quite unexpectedly fell into his hands and he was able to realize his longed-for plan. Moreover in a few more years a highway was built that rendered the first piece of land untenable. (Incidentally, it also hopelessly devalued the faithless farmer's land.)

I offer this example in order to illustrate the way the Self's will crosses our own. Our doctor was fortunate in that his cherished plan really belonged to the pattern of his individuation, for of course this is by no means always the case. He had also learned how superior the will of the Self is to that of the ego, for apparently the former could see into the future: it saw the construction of the highway, although it was not even planned at the time, and it saw that the place where the man's individuation belonged would only come onto the market and be found much later. However, even when one has experienced this superiority, it seldom or never seems that way at the time our wills are crossed. On the contrary, we have the impression that some rather perverse fate is robbing us of what we most want and should really have. Yet slowly it becomes clear that even such things must be accepted, and one learns the value of such sacrifices, although this way is admittedly so difficult that, as mentioned before, Meister Eckhart said of it: "Very few can stand it who know what it really means." [46] Yet this difficult but highly

[45] See above, pp. 78ff.
[46] *Works*, Vol. 2, p. 6. Cf. above, p. 217.

rewarding effort is apparently the *conditio sine qua non* for that completely objective realization of the Self which, as Jung says, seems to be the "central secret" of a "completed process of individuation." [47]

[47] *Memories, Dreams, Reflections*, p. 296f.

# BIBLIOGRAPHY


ADDISON, Hilda. *Mary Webb*. London: Cecil Palmer, 1931.
*Apocryphal New Testament*. See JAMES.
*Apocrypha and Pseudoepigrapha of the Old Testament*. See CHARLES.
APULIEUS. *Metamorphoses or The Golden Ass*.
AUSTEN, Jane. *Mansfield Park*. New York: Random House (The Modern Library).

BALFOUR, Graham. *The Life of Robert Louis Stevenson*. London: Methuen & Co., 1901.
BENOIT, Pierre. *L'Atlantide*.
BRONTË, Anne. *Agnes Grey*. London: Everyman's Library.
———. *The Tenant of Wildfell Hall*. London: Everyman's Library.
BRONTË, Charlotte. "Biographical Notice of Ellis and Acton Bell." In Modern Library edition of *Wuthering Heights*.
———. *The Foundling*.
———. *Jane Eyre*. New York: Random House (The Modern Library).
———. *The Professor*. Oxford University Press (The World's Classics).
———. *Shirley*. Oxford University Press (The World's Classics).
———. "Strange Events." In RATCHFORD.
———. *Villette*. Oxford University Press (The World's Classics).
BRONTË, Emily. *The Complete Poems*, edited by C. W. Hatfield. New York: Columbia University Press, 1941.
BROWNING, D. P. Introduction to the 1960 edition of STEVENSON, *A Child's Garden of Verse*.

CHARLES, R. H. *The Apocrypha and Pseudoepigrapha of the Old Testament*. Oxford: at the Clarendon Press, 1913.

DANTE ALIGHIERI. *The Divine Comedy*.

ECKHART, Meister. *The Works of Meister Eckhart,* translated by P. de B. Evans. London: John M. Watkins, 1931.
EVANS, P. de B. *See* ECKHART.

FRANZ, Marie-Louise von. *Aurora Consurgens.* Princeton University Press (Bollingen Series LXXVII), 1966.
———. "The Idea of The Macro- and Microcosms in the Light of Jungian Psychology." In *Ambix,* Vol. XIII, Feb. 1965, p. 28ff.
———. *Die Visionen des Niklaus von Flüe.* Zurich: Rascher Verlag, 1959.
FURNAS, J. C. *Voyage to Windward.* London: Faber & Faber, Ltd.

GASKELL, Elizabeth C. *The Life of Charlotte Brontë,* Oxford University Press (The World's Classics).
GÉRIN, Winifred, *Anne Brontë.* London: Thomas Nelson & Sons, Ltd., 1959.
GOETHE, Johann Wolfgang von. *Faust.*

HANNAH, Barbara. "The Animus in Charlotte Brontë's 'Strange Events.'" *Harvest,* Vol. 10, 1964.
———. "Regression oder Erneuerung im Alter." In *Psychotherapeutische Probleme.* Zurich: Rascher Verlag (Studien aus dem Jung-Institut, XVII), 1964.
HARRISON, Ada and STANFORD, Derek. *Anne Brontë: Her Life and Work.* London: Methuen & Co., Ltd., 1951.
*Harvest,* Vol. 10. London: Analytical Psychology Club, 1964.
HATFIELD, P. W. (ed.). *The Complete Poems of Emily Jane Brontë.* New York: Columbia University Press, 1941.
HOPKINS, Annette B. *The Father of The Brontës.* Baltimore: Johns Hopkins Press, 1958.
HUXLEY, Aldous. *Ape and Essence.* New York: Harper & Row.

JANET, Pierre. *L'Automatisme psychologique.* Paris, 1889.
JUNG, C. G. "After the Catastrophe." In Vol. 10 of *Collected Works.*
———. "Answer to Job." In Vol. 11 of *Collected Works.*
———. *Collected Works of C. G. Jung.* Princeton University Press (Bollingen Series XX), especially the following:
Vol. 5: *Symbols of Transformation,* 1967.
Vol. 6: *Psychological Types,* 1971.

Vol. 7: *Two Essays on Analytical Psychology*, 1966.
Vol. 8: *Structure and Dynamics of the Psyche*, 1969.
Vol. 9(2): *Aion*, 1968.
Vol. 10: *Civilization in Transition*, 1964.
Vol. 11: *Psychology and Religion: West and East*, 1969.
Vol. 12: *Psychology and Alchemy*, 1968.
Vol. 13: *Alchemical Studies*, 1968.
Vol. 14: *Mysterium Coniunctionis*, 1970.
Vol. 15: *Spirit in Man, Art, and Literature*, 1966.
Vol. 16: *The Practice of Psychotherapy*, 1966.

———. E. T. H. (Eidgenössische Technische Hochschule) Lectures. *Modern Psychology*, Vols. III and IV. Zurich: privately printed.

———. *Memories, Dreams, Reflections*, edited by Aniela JAFFÉ. New York: Pantheon Books, 1961.

———. "A Psychological Approach to the Dogma of the Trinity." In Vol. 11 of *The Collected Works*.

———. "Psychology and Literature." In Vol. 15 of *The Collected Works*.

———. "Psychology of the Transference." In Vol. 16 of *The Collected Works*.

———. "The Relation between the Ego and the Unconscious." In Vol. 7 of *The Collected Works*.

———. Commentary on *The Secret of the Golden Flower*. In Vol. 13 of *The Collected Works*.

———. "Synchronicity: An Acausal Connecting Principle." In Vol. 8 of *The Collected Works*.

———. "The Transcendent Function." In Vol. 8 of *The Collected Works*.

———. "Woman in Europe." In Vol. 10 of *The Collected Works*.

JUNG, Emma. *Animus and Anima*. New York: Analytical Psychology Club, 1957.

LAYARD, John. "The Incest Taboo and the Virgin Archetype." In Eranos Jahrbuch XII: *Studies on The Problem of the Archetypal* (For C. G. Jung on His Seventieth Birthday, July 26, 1945), 1945.

LOCK, John and DIXON, W. T. Canon. *A Man of Sorrows*. London: Thomas Nelson and Sons, 1965.

LORENZ, Konrad. *Man Meets Dog*. Boston: Houghton Mifflin, 1955.

MAIER, Michael. *De circulo physico quadrato*. Oppenheim, 1616.
———. *Symbola aurae mensae*. Frankfurt am Mein, 1617.
MAURIER, Daphne du. *The Infernal World of Branwell Brontë*. London: Victor Gollancz, Ltd., 1960.
MOULT, Thomas. *Mary Webb, Her Life and Work*. London: Jonathan Cape, 1932.

RATCHFORD, Fannie E. *The Brontë's Web of Childhood*. New York: Columbia University Press, 1941.
RHINE, J. B. *Extra-Sensory Perception*. Boston: Boston Society for Psychic Research, 1934.
———. *New Frontiers of the Mind*. New York: Farrar, 1937.
*Rosarium Philosophorum*. Frankfurt, 1550.

*Sacred Books of the East*, Vol. 49. Edited by Max Müller. Oxford University Press.
SHORTER, Clement. *The Brontës, Life and Letters*. London: Hodder and Stoughton, Ltd., 1908.
SHUTE, Nevil. *On the Beach*. London: Heinemann, 1957.
SINCLAIR, May. *The Three Brontës*. London: Hutchinson & Co., Ltd., 1912.
STEVENSON, Robert Louis. *A Child's Garden of Verse*. London: Dent & Son, Ltd., 1960.
———. *Across the Plains*. London: Thomas Nelson & Sons, Ltd.
———. *The Letters of Robert Louis Stevenson*, edited by Sidney Colvin. New York: Charles Scribner's Sons, 1900.
———. *The Master of Ballantrae*. London: Thomas Nelson & Sons, Ltd.
———. *The Strange Case of Dr. Jekyll and Mr. Hyde*. London: The Medallion edition.
———. *Weir of Hermiston*. London: Thomas Nelson & Sons, Ltd.

*Tantric Texts*, Vol. 7. Edited by Arthur Avalon. London: Susa & Co.

WEBB, Mary. *Armour Wherein He Trusted*. London: Jonathan Cape (Sarn Edition), 1928.
———. *Precious Bane*. London: Jonathan Cape (Sarn edition), 1924.